Student Writing and Genre

Student Writing and Genre

Reconfiguring Academic Knowledge

Fiona English

continuum

Continuum International Publishing Group

The Tower Building	80 Maiden Lane
11 York Road	Suite 704
London	New York
SE1 7NX	NY 10038

www.continuumbooks.com

British Library Cataloguing-in-Publication Data
A catalogue record for this book is available from the British Library.

ISBN: 978-1-44117-1610 (hardback)

Library of Congress Cataloging-in-Publication Data
A catalog record for this book is available from the Library of Congress

Typeset by Fakenham Prepress Solutions, Fakenham, Norfolk NR21 8NN
Printed and bound in Great Britain

To my students

Contents

Acknowledgements

I have been very lucky, in working towards this book, in having the help and advice of many people along the way. Among them is Gunther Kress, who supervised me so patiently through the research that led to this work. His confidence in what I was trying to achieve kept me going and enabled me to ultimately come to this point. I'd also like to thank Jan Blommaert and Cathy Wallace, whose encouraging and useful feedback earlier in this process was invaluable. Next I'd like to thank my many colleagues over the last few years who have in their different ways helped me reach this point of completion, in particular Mary Scott and Theresa Lillis, whose advice and support have been more encouraging than I can say. And I must also express my great appreciation to my work colleagues at London Metropolitan University for helping me to find writing spaces in our hectic working environment. Thanks also to my former colleagues at SOAS who took the time to respond to all my questions whether online or face to face, and perhaps particularly to David Taylor, who gave me the chance to develop the module from which this study grew in the first place.

Of course, crucial to my work and my ideas have been the students that I have met during my years of university teaching. They have been and continue to be a great source of inspiration whether they know it or not. However, my biggest thanks must go to the students involved in this study. When we started out on our new course together none of us had much idea of where it would lead, but one thing is sure: without them and the work they produced, this book would never have come into being. Their enthusiasm and creativity ensured that I could not let things lie and it was this that inspired me to dig beneath the surface of the work they produced.

Last, but certainly not least, is my family, Mark and Stanley, who lived with this book alongside me, and who at times, I know, have found themselves walking on eggshells. For Mark it was a case of him 'feeding me up' both literally and metaphorically. For Stanley, this work has been a presence for almost half of his life. He made his way in and out of it, helping me reflect on the experiences of learning as he moved through his own schooling, until now he himself is a student writing at university. Thank you both for helping me through.

Introduction

Over the last few years I have been exploring the relationship between genres, academic knowledge and representation, particularly in relation to student writing. I have been interested in the genres students use in working with their course material and how those genres shape the ways they understand and interact with their disciplines. In other words, I have been interested in the affordances of genres in much the same way that Kress and Van Leeuwen (2001) and Kress (2010) have been interested in the affordances of modes.

My interest in this first emerged when I was working on an interdisciplinary first year module on critical language awareness and academic literacies that I had been asked to develop in connection with the university's new learning and teaching agenda. One of the themes that I had been keen to explore with the students was that of genre, particularly in relation to academic work, and for one of the module assignments I invited the students to experiment with writing. This involved them reworking an essay from a different module using a genre of their own choice, a process I now call *regenring*. The work they produced, which included a play in eight acts, a simulated radio phone-in and a children's expository article, was so exciting and so fundamentally different in terms of disciplinary engagement in comparison to the original essays that it led me to embark on the research on which this book is based.

Initially, I had simply wanted to be able to explain my own reactions to the work and justify it as academically rigorous, anticipating institutional challenges to its obviously a-typical approach. I also felt that it merited more than a simple grade and a few sentences of feedback. However, as my investigations proceeded and I started comparing both versions of the work, it soon became clear that there had been a profound shift, not only in terms of what I might once have thought of as generic 'shape', but in the materiality of the work itself. In fact, these different genres had brought about a transformation that enabled the students to introduce new perspectives, debate new issues and show a greater sense of ownership over the topics than was apparent in their original essays.

This book, then, is about the relationship between knowledge, writing and genre. It problematizes the dominance of the essay in relation to disciplinary learning and teaching and shows that when students are given the chance to write differently new learning opportunities and experiences emerge. The book offers a different way of thinking about genre and genre pedagogy in that it takes it out of the 'ghetto' (Swales, 1990) of remedial work into the mainstream of disciplinary activity. Instead of focusing on genre as a pedagogical goal, it focuses on genre as a pedagogical resource.

The Focus of the Book

The book is organized around several interlinking themes, which can be presented as a series of questions. What is the relationship between genre and disciplinary knowledge? What role does writing play in student learning? What opportunities do the genres available to university students offer for their learning? What is the effect of using non-academic genres when writing about academic things? In dealing with these questions, I offer a new theorization of genre which shifts the focus from *appropriacy*, that is learning which genres are allowed, to *affordance*, which considers what genres allow. This shift brings about a change in how we can think about genre and how we can use it in learning and teaching; not as a linguistic form, as in structural approaches, or as a pedagogical goal, as in functional approaches, but as a semiotic resource (Kress, e.g. 2010) with pedagogical implications.

The discussion, which is interwoven with interview contributions from the students themselves, includes extracts from their work to exemplify the different effects arising from the genres they used. The methodology I developed to analyse the student texts offers a social semiotic approach to 'doing' literacy research. It provides a usable framework for analysis, drawing on multimodal terms of reference (Kress and Van Leeuwen, 2001), where instead of being a pedagogical goal, genre becomes a clear, articulated tool for discussing the relationship between texts, knowledge and identity.

The approach presented here offers a dual perspective on the effects of genre choice using the concept of 'orientation': *contextual* and *discursive orientation*, which are associated with social aspects of production such as identity and agency, and *thematic* and *semiotic orientation*, which are associated with material aspects of production such as choice of mode or textual resources. In this way, I was able to identify key differences between the productions and to articulate important ways in which genre choice affected both the producers and their different productions using the framework outlined above. Four areas of interest emerged: (1) agency and discursive identity; (2) (re)configuration of information – in other words, the effects of the materials used and the meanings produced; (3) the activity of disciplines – 'lived' experience rather than 'read' experience; (4) reflections on being a student. These four themes provide insights not only into the nature of academic knowledge and the close association between the genres used and the knowledge produced – something akin to Bernstein's (2000) vertical and horizontal discourses – but also into the experiences of students in their attempts to interact with the disciplines they have chosen. (See also Barnett, 2009.)

This new perspective provides pedagogical solutions to contentions around 'genres', 'disciplines', 'academic discourses' and their relation to student learning, identity and power. It not only proposes a new way of thinking about genre but also a new way of thinking about student writing and its role in disciplinary learning. It argues, like Andrews (2003), that although essayist writing fulfils a useful function within the academic writing repertoire, it limits students to expressing what they understand to particular ways of 'knowing'. By juxtaposing these different ways, students can get a clearer idea of how academic knowledge fits with the everyday and in so doing can develop a more flexible approach to what knowledge and learning entails.

Genre and Writing Pedagogy

Student writing at university has a long tradition, particularly in the USA, where writing programmes, emerging from a tradition in rhetoric and composition, have been part and parcel of undergraduate degree programmes for all students (see Davidson and Tomic, 1999) for a considerable amount of time. A substantial literature in this field has emerged out of that context, from Bartholomae's 1985 article 'Inventing the University' through Bizzel & Herzberg (1990) to Elbow (1995) and Prior (1998). However, writing at university came to be recognized as an issue in the UK only relatively recently, resulting from both the rapid increase in international students with their different languages and their different educational experiences and the widening participation agenda during the 1990s. Two main strands of activity emerged: English for Academic Purposes, which largely developed out of an applied linguistic background (e.g. Jordan, 1997, Hyland, 2006), and Academic Literacies (e.g. Lea and Street, 1998; Ivanic, 1998; Jones et al., 1999; Lillis, 2001), which owes as much to social anthropology as it does to social linguistics in its concerns with literacy as practices (see also Lillis and Scott, 2007). Unlike in the USA, where writing programmes were aimed at developing the 'person' from a liberal arts perspective, in the UK the approach was much more pragmatic. Academic writing courses were established to 'fix' the problem of student writing, which was treated 'as a kind of pathology' (Lea and Street, 1998, p. 159).

Discussion of genre in particular, in relation to student writing, also has different traditions, which have led to different approaches. Miller's (1984) discussion, which challenged notions of genre simply as a form, proposed an alternative view which connected it to social and rhetorical practices. Others, such as Bazerman (1988), explored genre as mutually and socially enacted practice in knowledge making in his book *Shaping Written Knowledge*. The genre studies from Australia (e.g. Cope and Kalantzis, 1993) bring together pedagogical debates on genre as both social and linguistic practice, including Martin (1993), whose work, focusing on the structures and functions of written genres in schooling, promoted the idea of access through genre awareness. Others who have adopted this linguistic focus have investigated the linguistic choices that typify disciplinary fields and disciplinary domains (Swales, 1990; Hyland, 2000), and others (Hunston, 2000; Charles, 2006) have explored discoursal strategies in evaluation. Devitt (2004), in her comprehensive study of genre, has foregrounded genre awareness as key to developing students' writing while Russell (1997) and Russell and Yañez (2003), viewing genre through an 'activity theory' lens, promote the idea that genres as complexes rather than singular entities can be used as a tool in the development of writing to explore why people write the things they write in the ways they write them.

These last questions are similar to the ones which concern my approach. But instead of working within an activity theory frame of reference, I use a social semiotic perspective, which enables me to explore both the social and the material impacts of genre choice. Like Russell, this enables me to shift the focus from genre as pedagogical *goal*, typical of much genre teaching, towards genre as a pedagogical *resource*.

The Methodology Used

As I have already explained, this book arose out of the normal practice of my own teaching and the material which forms the core data for analysis was the outcome of a normal end-of-unit assignment. In other words, it is the result of my investigation of a phenomenon that arose as a result of my practice and which led to the development of a theory-generating analysis. As such, it provides an example of the usefulness of practice-derived research in the development of new ideas and innovative approaches to pedagogy.

The data comprises three main elements: the work produced by the students in response to an end-of-module assignment, follow-up interviews with the students, and later on interviews with some of their lecturers. The student productions comprise the main data while the interviews provide additional insights that I would not have considered had I focused solely on the texts.

This approach typifies much research in academic literacies (e.g. Lillis, 2001; Thesen, 2001; Crème, 2005), which is not surprising since academic literacies as a field is, itself, a practice-oriented epistemology (see Lillis and Scott, 2007) and most academic literacies researchers are teachers working directly with students. Research undertaken in the field is inevitably oriented towards practice, though not without a theoretical perspective. The combination of these two elements ensures that this kind of research is accessible and usable for teachers and researchers alike, not to mention students themselves. In the case of my study, the research is both theory generating (the affordances of genres) and pedagogically motivated (new practices in disciplinary writing).

The analysis of the texts in conjunction with the student interviews reveals that when these student writers were given the opportunity to use alternative genres it affected what they paid attention to, how they articulated their ideas and how they positioned themselves as 'knowers'.

A Different Experience – 'Regenring'

I now want to offer an example from my research both to illustrate what I mean by regenring and to show how a shift in genre can enable a student to relocate academic knowledge and, in so doing, reconnect with it. I will not go into any detailed discussion of the work, as this will be done thoroughly in later chapters. My aim here is simply to show the kind of things that happened. The example comes from the work of Sonia (not her real name) who was taking a degree in African Studies and had completed the first term of the course. The extracts below come from an essay written in response to the following instruction and represent different phases in the essay: *Give an account of the origin and present-day function of one African lingua franca.*

Example 1

> The word 'Swahili' is Arabic in origin and means 'coast'. Swahili is spoken on the East coast of Africa by many as a first language and has spread into the interior as far as the Congo as a lingua franca. Though Swahili uses words adopted from Arabic, English and Portuguese, it has the definite structure of a Bantu language and is written in the Latin script.
>
> Swahili is presumed to have started its life in the region of the Tana River estuary and to have spread further when Arabs and Persians settled in the area due to trading, thus spreading the language along their trading routes. In 975 Ali Ben Sultan al Hassan Ben Ali bought the island of Kilwa in exchange for a few bails of textiles and it became an important trading centre encouraging the use of Swahili along the coast south of the Zambezi River …
>
> There are a very large number of Swahili dialects that have derived from specific social situations, some of which are dying out because of a change in social circumstances. Due to the function of some of these dialects, such as the mode of common communication in the army and work force, the dialect has undergone considerable simplification and lost much of its structure until it can only be called a pidgin …

The first thing that strikes us about this extract is that Sonia has adopted a literal approach to the task and has followed the instructions exactly. The extracts typify the whole essay in their encyclopaedic exposition of the topic. There is no commentary on the information presented, nor is any indication given of its sources. In fact, although it is obvious that Sonia has been able to identify relevant information and use certain linguistic terms of reference, it is not clear whether she has 'mastered' the relevant body of knowledge or whether she has simply located it. Sonia herself was unhappy with the essay, as indeed she was with her disciplinary studies in general. She subsequently dropped out of the degree programme but returned a year and a half later to study for a different degree, which she successfully completed.

In contrast to the essay, the regenred work offers a very different take on the topic. Her alternative title – *Culturally Confused* – indicates a different kind of understanding of the topic compared to the original essay. It problematizes the idea of a 'lingua franca' by locating it in the context of culture and identity, which in turn implies a connection between language, multilingualism and identity, something that is not even touched on in the essay. In the new version Sonia has claimed the topic, using the original essay information, as required by the regenring task instructions, to produce a *view* on the topic rather than a display of 'facts' as in the essay.

The new version is produced as a dialogue, essentially a short play, with the aim of making the content of the essay accessible for a younger audience. Sonia felt that the topic lent itself to be 'told' rather than 'written', thereby reflecting what she considered to be the 'orality' of African languages. It is an enactment of a parent telling a bedtime 'story' to his two children aged eight or nine and so the information becomes grounded in a 'real world' context where things need to be explained rather than presented.

Example 2

> **Parent**: *[At this point seated in the armchair addressing the children.]* Can you remember what our bedtime story was about yesterday?
>
> **Child 1**: Yesssssssssss! It was about … *[six more exchanges]*
>
> **Parent**: OK, anyway, today I thought I could tell you the story about how Swahili came to be such an important language in East Africa. People always talk about the importance of English as a world language but they rarely consider that there exist many other important non-European languages all over the world. People need to learn one of these important languages so they can talk to people who have different first languages to themselves.
>
> **Child 1**: Umm … Why would they be speaking to people with a different language?

> **Parent**: That's a good question, you bright little spark! Now, in the situation of Africa there are two hundred thousand different languages spoken. It's not like in England. In Africa if you go from one village to the next you are likely to find a different language ...

The demands of dramatic genre, characterization and setting and the to-ing and fro-ing of dialogue between the children and the parent force Sonia to shape the information differently. The 'facts' of the essay are now mediated by the participants in the drama and are discussed and argued over and, despite the exaggeration regarding the number of languages spoken in Africa, this version introduces new dimensions to the work, not least of which is 'critical perspective', that most elusive, but desired, aspect of student academic performance. The somewhat earnest, didactic approach of the parent and the children's reaction to it offer additional opportunities for reflection, as will be seen in Chapter 7. A more detailed analysis of Sonia's work is found in Chapter 5.

What these two extracts show is how the shift from one genre to another revealed disciplinary understanding and engagement that may well have remained hidden, or, even worse, never developed at all had the student not been given the chance to write differently. Sonia's essay offers a *display* of disciplinary materials whereas her play offers a *recontextualization* of that material in a non-academic (though nevertheless didactic) frame. In this way she manages to blend experienced, everyday knowledge with the disciplinary in such a way that each contributes to the other.

All the students who feature in the book produced not only equally remarkable work but also gave extraordinary insights into the experience of engaging in the regenring activity. As already mentioned, I have incorporated their comments throughout the book, partly because they are so helpful in understanding the circumstances in which students write but partly because I wanted them to have a clear and visible presence.

Overview of the Book

Chapter 1 introduces the study from which the book emerged. It introduces the module that I taught, the students who participated and the institutional and wider political context in which it all took place. It also provides summaries of the students' work.

Chapter 2, in exploring the circumstances in which students and their lecturers interact around written assignments, problematizes the dual role of the coursework essay in serving both as summative and formative assessment. These issues are considered against a backdrop of discourses of 'apprenticeship', of 'skills' and of the 'marketization' of higher education with ever-increasing demands for 'transparency' in assessment criteria. Drawing on interviews with students and lecturers, I consider how the practices of essay setting and essay writing positions both tutors and students in what is often a frustrating and painful exchange. This results from a gap between the desires and expectations of students and tutors resulting from their different perceptions of the process itself and it is in this gap, I suggest, where learning takes place.

In Chapter 3 I take a closer look at genre as a category and offer a brief overview of different ways in which it is understood. I explain the particular approach to genre that arose out of the research that I use in this book and clarify the concept of 'affordance', which is central to my thinking. I also separate out the overlapping and sometimes confused concepts of genre, discourse and text in an attempt to reach a sense of terminological clarity. I draw particularly on the work of Kress and Van Leeuwen (2001) and of the so-called 'Russian School' of Bakhtin, Volosinov and Medvedev in developing my analytical perspective.

Chapter 4 explains the analytical framework that I use to describe the effects of genre in later chapters. It clarifies my terms of reference, introduces the tools that I use in analysing the student work and offers an example to illustrate the methodology.

With the tools established in the previous chapters, the next three chapters provide detailed analyses of the students' work. They examine the different ways in which genre choice impacted on both the material and social aspects of both the original essays and the regenred versions. Chapter 5 examines the concept of 'agency' and shows how the process of 'recontextualizing' (Bernstein, 2000) through regenring the original essay afforded a shift in what I am calling discursive identity.

Chapter 6 focuses on how regenring forces a reconfiguration of information as the result of the different semiotic resources available to each of the genres used. Chapter 7 looks at how regenring afforded students the opportunity to make visible the processes and practices through which academic knowledge is made, the process of 'doing the work', and to incorporate reflections on 'being a student', something that rarely has a place in conventional disciplinary work.

The final chapter discusses the implications of this approach to genre and genre pedagogy and considers how it might inform the learning and assessment frameworks in higher education and elsewhere. It reviews the kind of learning that the students discussed in this book experienced and argues that 'writing differently' should be included in the repertoire of student writing. In this chapter I show how I myself incorporate 'writing differently' into my own current disciplinary teaching and offer extracts from this new work to illustrate the effect. I do not propose abandoning essays, but instead argue that they may not be the only way for students to develop their learning. Even if the essay remains the pre-eminent assessment product, I suggest that different genres and even regenring itself can be used as a means to enrich students' disciplinary learning.

About the Data

It has been difficult to do full justice to the data that I have used in this book, the students' work and the highly insightful comments that both they and the lecturers I spoke to offered. I have tried to ensure that their voices are strongly represented throughout the book, including by framing each chapter with one of their comments so as to reflect the way their thoughts helped me to unpack the many layers involved in the analysis of the work. Whenever I have quoted from the students or the lecturers I interviewed, I have used italics to indicate this.

One big problem was how to present the students' work. To include the complete texts would involve well over a hundred pages, which would have meant that this would turn out to be a very long book indeed! Instead, at the end of Chapter 1, I offer summaries of each of the paired productions, the original essay and the regenred work, so that readers will have a fair idea of the content of the work. In subsequent chapters I use extracts from the work, so there is the opportunity to gain a flavour of their writing and their ideas.

Ultimately, this book aims to share the experiences I had whilst working as an academic literacies specialist with a group of students whose exceptional work led me to rethink the genres that we traditionally use for developing and assessing student learning. I have tried to make the account as relevant and accessible as possible to university teachers involved in either or both disciplinary and literacies work and hope that what I discuss here will open up new possibilities for disciplinary learning and representation.

Chapter 1

From Shadow Writing to Writing Differently

I do feel I'm kind of – what's it called – shadow writing. (Anya)

1.1 Introduction

In most disciplines students are expected to demonstrate what they understand about their subject with writing. Even where alternative modes
are common, such as in performance arts or design, a written accompa-
niment is required to validate the work within the conventional norms of
assessment. In fact, the tasks assigned to students appear to shadow those in
which disciplinary knowledge is produced and disseminated in the professional academic domain. However, there is a marked difference in the
circumstances in which the professionals produce and those in which their
students produce and these differences are represented in their names. For
example, a professional academic writes an *article* whereas a student writes
an *essay*; the professional gives a *lecture* while the student gives a *presentation*.
The different naming of these communicative practices reflects how differently they are situated, and this in turn effects in the way in which the text is
produced by the 'writer' and experienced by the 'reader'. For Anya above,
doing an essay felt like writing on behalf of someone else rather than on
her own behalf, using someone else's ideas rather than her own. She felt
that her work involved little more than, as she said, '*a regurgitation*' of
what she had been reading, doing it '*in the way they want you to*', as another
student said, enacting 'the mechanical reiteration of ideas presumed dear
to his professor' (Bourdieu and Passeron, 1994, p. 14).

As has been noted by others (Ivanic, 1998; Lillis, 2001), a student is not
expected to write as a 'writer' in the sense that the lecturer who reads the
essay might write: that is for a 'real' 'public' 'peer' readership. Instead,
student writing exists within a constrained, closed-off context, which can
lead not only to the kinds of frustration that the undergraduate students

referred to above, but to a sense of futility, as the following e-mail comment from a Master's student demonstrates very clearly.

> *A fear then comes up from deep inside of me: am I risking my 'life' in the sense I am just doing a 'dissertation' that leads to a degree, a 'simulated' work of little practical value? Is my effort worthwhile?* (John)

The feelings expressed by these students are not unusual, as many discussions on student writing have shown (e.g. Ivanic, 1998; Jones et al., 1999; Lea and Stierer, 2000; Lillis, 2001; Thesen and van Pletzen, 2006). Yet despite this and the plethora of dissemination options available today, the essay has retained its position as the gold standard, which is 'eminently assessable' (Andrews, 2003, p. 119) as well as the 'default genre' (Womack, 1993, p. 42).

This chapter introduces the research discussed in this book and contextualizes it in the debates around student learning. It problematizes the 'skills' agendas that have dominated much of the official discourse of recent years, focusing particularly on student writing, and explores the student essay as a particular and highly regulated genre. It introduces the first year module from which this book emerged and provides summaries of the students' work in preparation for the discussions that follow.

1.2 Student Essays

> The essay represents the state of a student's understanding and is assessed accordingly. The submission and the response ... have a formative function, but their principal function is to gain a mark or grade on the way to a degree.
>
> (Andrews, 2003, p. 117)

The student essay is a genre which sits firmly within a pedagogic, disciplinary and institutional frame. In the pedagogic frame is the obligation for students to write essays and the attendant penalties if they do not, the assessment involved in the interactions between lecturer and student, both formative and summative, the proving that learning has taken place (or not) and what kind of learning and so on. In the disciplinary frame is the adopting of disciplinary preoccupations and discourses whether one wants to or not and the identifying of what sorts of things are valued in the given community. In the institutional frame are issues of procedures, the aims and outcomes, how things are done round there, how the hierar-chies work. On top of this are all the other frames in which the students write, their personal goals and desires, their histories and experiences or even world events. These and countless other more immediate factors (Do they have a full-time job? Have they got children to care for? Have they got a headache? Are they happy?) in which a particular student writes and in which a particular tutor reads all contribute to the meaning potential of the work. However, although all these different frames co-exist, only certain ones, the pedagogic, disciplinary and institutional, are expected to be visible in the work.

Even without all the above dimensions, writing is a difficult thing to do, but it becomes even more so when what is being written is going to be read and evaluated by someone else. It not only involves activity such as using rhetorical 'techniques' or 'gathering' content but also emotions such as anxiety, frustration, satisfaction and even enjoyment, as has been discussed by writers such as Sharples (1999), who considers different stages and processes in becoming a writer, or Elbow (1999) in his discussion about private versus public writing. However, difficult though it is, writing is important because it affords reflexivity, a theme I develop further in Chapter 7.

In recent years, writing at university in the UK has become foregrounded as a particular institutional issue, as mentioned in my introduction. However, how writing is viewed at university depends on who is doing the viewing. Its current visibility is not, unfortunately, the result of a widespread recognition of the relationship between writing and disciplinary learning, but rather the result of it being seen as a problem. This has come about partly as the result of the rapid expansion in higher education that occurred during the 1990s, with a major increase in international students on mainly postgraduate programmes and a growing intake of students from 'non-traditional backgrounds' (see Lillis, 2001) on to undergraduate programmes. They are a much more diverse group than they were when I myself was an undergraduate; socially and culturally more varied, and from a wider age range. Moreover, there are many more of them. These changes have meant that traditional 'methods' where students could either sink or swim are no longer viable. This is even more pertinent because student success is now closely associated with university state funding, and even where it is not, the financial link is even more crucial, since it is the students themselves (or their families) who are paying.

1.3 Teaching in Higher Education

The changes in the university population that I have mentioned above along with more widely experienced changes in the economy, the workplace, communication and globalization (see e.g. Castells, 1996; Lea and Nicholl, 2002) have led to substantial changes in how a university education is conceived. Following the state-commissioned Dearing report (1997), attention became focused on teaching and learning, something that had not generally been prioritized at university. This in itself may appear strange, but traditionally emphasis has been on research activity. Even today, the status of teaching still lags far behind the status of research, and the relationship between these two practices is a contentious and hotly debated issue (e.g. Hattie and Marsh, 2004; Elton, 2000) particularly since funding is involved. Nevertheless, teaching in higher education, despite the many criticisms that can be made about the ways in which it is being promoted, is now firmly on the agenda, although linked closely to the contentious question of what a university is for.

Universities in the UK are, with one exception, state institutions but not state run. In fact, independence and autonomy are enshrined in their constitutions and governments have no official part to play. However, as the costs associated with university education have risen in connection with an ideological goal to achieve a far larger university-educated population, the government, of whatever hue, has become increasingly concerned that the money invested leads to what it considers tangible outcomes. This has led to the promotion of a discourse of skills, particularly what are known as transferable skills, transferable to the workplace, something that is clearly reflected in the change in name of the UK government department responsible for universities, which at the time of writing is known as the Department for Business, Innovation and Skills.

Bernstein (2000) and Barnett (2000, 2009), among many others (e.g. Parker, 2003, Haggis, 2004), have written extensively on this subject, analysing and challenging competency and performance ideologies which, they point out, misunderstand academic knowledge and the learning that a university education provides. For Bernstein, such ideologies have emerged because 'the principles of the market and its managers are more and more the managers of the policy and practices of education' (p. 86). He suggests that this has led to a market orientation to knowledge which stresses the notion of 'measurable skills' and which separates 'the knower and what is known'. In other words, knowledge is viewed as a product which can be moved around, exchanged for other products and which facilitates the ideologies of 'flexibility' and 'flexible workforce' and 'choice', which are so dominant today. Barnett's approach is more pragmatic, though no less critical (2000), and proposes the concept of 'supercomplexity' where the old certainties of what constituted academic knowledge (disciplines, bodies of knowledge) are being challenged by a 'capability' agenda. This he describes as 'the performative slide' (p. 260) where 'what counts is less what individuals know and more what individuals can do (as represented in their demonstrable skills)' (p. 255).

Such a skills-oriented ideology, with its inventories of skills and micro skills (NCIHE, 1997) to be ticked off as measurable learning 'outcomes' oriented to the 'marketplace', fails, as Parker (2003) argues, to recognize the complexities of learning at the disciplinary and epistemological level. It leads to thinking associated with the performative slide that Barnett, above, refers to, so that writing becomes 'doing' as distinct from knowing and the problem is simplified as poor grammar or bad spelling. As Turner (1999) points out, such views lead to a flawed and over-simplistic understanding of what is involved in the process of writing as a student in a university. She argues that the way in which universities tend to deal with what are seen as writing problems is to marginalize writing by separating it from the main event, the study of disciplines, and farm the 'problem' out to 'support tutors' who are themselves institutionally marginalized. In her discussion on student writing in the context of 'widening participation', Lillis (2001, p. 33) offers a critical evaluation of the different camps in this debate. She argues that:

> official discourse on the 'problem' of student academic writing in higher education ignores much recent thinking on language and literacy generally and research on student writing more specifically. In broad terms, the dominant official approach is to frame student writing as a skill, drawing implicitly on notions of language as transparent and of both language and user as independent of each other, and of context.

Her work proposes 'an alternative perspective [which] can be described as that of writing as social practice' (Lillis, 2001, p. 33).

A strong contribution to the 'recent thinking' that Lillis refers to is Lea and Street's (1998) proposal for an 'academic literacies'. Their work considers student writing (and reading) from a practices approach, which 'takes account of the cultural and contextual component of writing and reading practices' (p. 158). This thinking, which emerges from 'New Literacy Studies' (e.g. Street, 1984; Barton, 1994; Gee, 1996), considers three models of student writing which they have identified through discussion with students, tutors and analysis of student work. These are: a study skills model which takes a student deficit perspective and focuses on atomized surface features of student performance; an 'academic socialization' model where students are inducted into the new (academic) culture through a process of orientation to the different tasks that they will encounter; and an academic literacies model which incorporates the other two into 'a more encompassing understanding of the nature of student writing within institutional practices, power relations and identities' (Street, 1998, p. 158). In other words, student writing takes place within a dynamic social context which is far from homogeneous, as implied by an academic socialization approach.

Lea (1999) further argues that university learning should involve *negotiating* academic knowledge rather than receiving it, 'interweaving prior knowledge and ways of writing and reading texts with course requirements' (p. 105). She suggests that rather than viewing personal knowledge as totally distinct from academic knowledge (or second-order knowledge, e.g. Laudrillard, 1993) 'we need to blur the distinctions' (p. 105) to enable better opportunities for students to engage with their learning. However, in order for students to feel confident enough to do this, they need to be confident that the person marking the essay is willing to accept it. Read et al. (2001) point out that students are, on the whole, understandably unwilling to take chances with their assignments. As their study shows, 'Rather than risk receiving a lower grade, [students] will pragmatically determine which views will be favoured by each marker and present these views as their own voice' (p. 397).

My own view is that academic success is about understanding not only the information, but also the ways in which academic knowledge is produced and presented, as has been shown by Foucault (1972) or Bazerman (1988). It is about epistemologies, about the ways in which the different partici- pants are both positioned and position themselves. It is about the textual choices made and how those choices interface between the information, the informant and the informee, not in a unidirectional way but rather as a dynamic cycle (see Chapter 3 for further discussion).

1.4 Making Good Students?

So 'making good students' means inviting them to be more explicitly aware of the processes involved in the design, production and distribution (Kress and Van Leeuwen, 2001) of texts so that they become more familiar with how the texts they read and write in their various disciplinary fields work on textual, ideational and interpersonal (Halliday, 1985) levels. This, of course, does not happen in a vacuum, but within the context of other learning experiences across the institution including the subject specialism of my own module, that is, language in its widest interpretation. The critical evaluative perspective I refer to can serve to enhance students' interactions with their own disciplinary and other interests.

Whether this work should be undertaken outside or within the disciplines is a relevant question. After all, disciplinary knowledge, its discourses and its practices are 'produced' by the disciplinary practitioners themselves within their own disciplinary communities. Therefore it could be argued that learning how to write in a discipline is best done in that discipline itself. However, it does not have to be an either–or situation. Students need also to learn that there is something to learn apart from 'the body of knowledge' of the discipline. In this sense, then, my course did deal in transferability, but the kind of transferability that occurs whenever we get new knowledge and new ways of looking at things. All academic learning is transferable. In the case of my module, it was learning about how language works, thinking about the social, political and cultural contexts in which communications occur and considering the relevance of this in the students' own situations, both academic and otherwise.

The work that I consider in this book was produced by a group of first year undergraduate students at a specialist institution, which is part of a federal university in the UK. They had chosen to take a new module, 'Language Power and Ideologies', that I had been given the opportunity to develop in juxtaposition with the other courses I was responsible for: English for Academic Purposes, 'study skills' and other learning 'support' activity. Unlike the other courses in my remit, this one was incorporated into the mainstream first year undergraduate scheme and offered as a non-designate module that any student from any discipline could choose. The module was formally validated in the normal way, albeit rather late in the academic year, and was somewhat belatedly added to the list of first year options during the opening week of the academic year in which it was to run.

Institutionally, the module was located in the realm of 'academic skills development' with the hope that it would improve students' understanding of 'how to write essays' and 'how to read critically'. In other words, the institutional space was 'given' to me on the understanding that this course would make 'better' students of those who participated. The module, then, stood outside the usual business of the institution, both because it focused on academic practice rather than academic product, as represented as 'body of knowledge', and because it did not have anything specific to do with the specialisms that comprised the activities of the institution. It was marginal, even though it had the authority of being a fully fledged module with the attendant requirements that students pass it, as indeed was my own institutional position, or better, 'liminal', as both the module and I operated *between* the institutional boundaries of disciplines, of status and of activity.

For my part, I seized the opportunity with relish as I felt it could help in the battle to improve the status for the work and workers in the academic support unit I headed, all of whom were 'classified' as academic-*related* employees and not *academic*, which, in the UK, means that the terms of employment are less favourable in terms of teaching load and research time allocation than those of 'academic' employees. Swales (1990), arguing for a shift in attitudes, problematizes the status of workers in what are institutionally considered 'remedial' activities in which 'we have nothing to teach but that which should have been learnt before' (p. 2). And Turner argues for 'making [academic literacy] a more powerful force within the institutional discourse of academe ... in order to redress its marginalisation' (1999, p. 151). One way out of my 'ivory ghetto' (Swales, 1990, p. 11) was through designing a 'real' undergraduate unit which had visible 'currency' in the collection of undergraduate credits and, despite its 'liminal' position, the course was an opportunity to reclassify the work institutionally so that it would no longer be viewed as servicing the 'real work' that took place in the academic departments, but as 'real work' in its own right.

The module was also situated squarely in the context of debate on 'academicism' versus 'operational competence' (Barnett, 1997, p. 25) and the question of generic 'bolt-on' versus integrated (embedded) programmes (see e.g. Hodginson, 1996; NCIHE, 1997; Barnett, 2000, 2009). My institution had been developing its learning and teaching strategy, a required activity following on from Dearing (1997) and a process in which I myself had participated in my capacity as 'head' of the English Language Unit, later to be renamed the 'Learning and Teaching Unit' in at least a nominal recognition that our work was concerned with more than 'just' English and, perhaps more pragmatically, that there would be a group explicitly identified with learning and teaching issues.

With this in mind, I hoped that the module would provide students with the opportunity to explore different communicative practices through considering different communicative events. I wanted them to analyse how different 'texts' are made, including academic texts, and to encourage them to explore how the intended ideologies and agendas are promoted by the textual materials used as in Fairclough (2001). And inevitably, since the content of my module was the means of production for the students' other modules, what they learned on Language Power and Ideologies would, I thought, be transferable to their other courses, thereby fulfilling the remit that I had initially been given.

1.5 The Module

The module was called 'Language, Power and Ideology: an exploration of texts and criticality' and had the following stated aims:

- To encourage students to look critically at texts across a variety of media – including written texts, visual texts
- To provide students with the opportunity to explore the different ways in which texts are constructed to convey meaning(s) and how they can be interpreted or read
- To help students develop their own writing and research practices within the School context
- To develop students understanding of how language works

The plan was to introduce students to a variety of different types of texts, images and other media to explore how they had been constructed and how they could be interpreted. The module timetable was ambitious but, apart from the final topic, ultimately achieved:

- Social Semiotics – introduction to the concept of texts as communication, language as meaning maker (not conveyer) – and a brief visit to elements of semiotic theory (Hodge and Kress, 1988)
- Discourse as Social Practice – 'reader/writer' relationship, meaning and interpretation as a social (negotiated) activity
- Language Awareness – grammatical choices, lexical choices, reader/writer positioning – language in the construction/maintenance of ideology
- Doing Critical Discourse Analysis – understanding discourses and 'discourse communities'
- Interacting with the University – the university as a discourse community
- Interacting with the discipline – disciplinary communities – insider/outsider

- Multimodality – the visual and the verbal in the construction of meaning – the grammar of visual design – the grammar of verbal language – texts, media and the construction of information
- Performance as Text – dance, drama and criticality

Unlike most of the other modules on offer, which were assessed mainly by exams, this one was assessed by coursework only, with two differently weighted assignments.

The module attracted a small group of eleven students from across the range of disciplinary fields within the regional specialisms of the institution including political science, social anthropology, economics, religious studies and African linguistics. Only two of the students came from what might be considered non-traditional backgrounds as first-generation university entrants. The others were all from university-educated families. None of the students appeared to be 'marginal' in the sense that they might experience fundamental difficulties in dealing with academic study. But many revealed in later interview that they had been worried about their studies, although most received high grades on their early coursework in their other modules, suggesting that they should have had nothing to worry about. This highlights the degree of anxiety students all have, regardless of background.

In interview, the students reported a variety of reasons for choosing this module. It sounded interesting:

> *I was interested in the way people in general use language and methods of communication to impose – reflect ideas ...* (Dan)

They wanted to help with academic tasks:

> *Didn't have any real idea except that it would probably help me reading texts and different texts – we'd work with variety of texts and images and develop some critical methods.* (Anya)

One student admitted that he chose it because it didn't have any final exams and another because it was the only module available that didn't clash with his other ones:

> *I didn't know anything about it until about the second week when all the things I'd wanted to do all clashed and so I started asking people in my class what they did 'cos I thought that obviously they were going to do something that doesn't clash*

and asked Sonia and she said come and try it out. So I came to that lesson and tried it out and stayed. (Peter)

No one really knew what to expect, and indeed, as it was the first time for the module to run, neither did I, so in some respects the module developed organically. In its focus it was unlike the other modules that the students were taking in that it did not specifically deal with their own disciplinary fields but rather with what could be considered the *means* of disciplinary production. Of course, what they were learning was disciplinary, just like any other field – it was just that in our case the body of disciplinary knowledge was also the means of production. A further difference was the approach we used, which did not follow the conventional one-hour lecture format followed by a tutor group class. This was because my experience was not as a 'lecturer' but as a 'teacher' whose normal practice was to combine the different aspects of class activity in a discursive and interactive framework. I did not expect or want the students to try to note down everything I said and actually had to stop them from doing so in the first session when as soon as I opened my mouth to speak they had their pens ready to take down every word that came out. This took the pressure off them and gave them the chance to develop a different approach to their learning, which was something that the students commented on.

I think we were more of a group than teacher–students – and just taking notes. I mean everybody's ideas were valid and it was a nice way to study I think ... (Nat)

Another factor in generating the kind of atmosphere Nat referred to was that the materials we used to explore the different aspects of the module were extremely varied in terms of mode and in terms of content.

We analysed political speeches of the day, using tools developed by Fairclough (2001), we drew on social semiotics (Hodge and Kress, 1988) and multimodality (Kress and Van Leeuwen, 1996, 2001) to explore news media and documentary texts before turning our attention to academic texts. Genre was one of the module themes and in the context of academic genres we examined two 'subversions': a spoof article on remote geo-location systems and 'fuzzy logic', published in a professional academic journal (McNoleg, 1996), and an assignment written for an art and design course led by John Wood at Goldsmith's College, London, produced as an illustrated children's story. In our discussions we discussed, in the case of the former, the role of academic conventions and disciplinary discourse in the 'acceptability' of the spoof article where linguistic 'form' served to disguise the implausibility of the content. Referring to the latter, we considered how disciplinary knowledge had been reflected through the medium of the alternative genre – a children's fictional story. The idea of comparing these two productions was to explore some of the issues surrounding the relationship between 'content' and 'production' and the positioning of students, their knowledge and that of the disciplinary field.

As the students began to develop an 'eye' for this kind of analysis, they began to bring in texts that they had come across and had found interesting. The combination of these different aspects of the module and the students' active participation allowed them to begin to make connections between the ways texts are made, their social and cultural contexts and the meaning potentials they offer. In other words, on this module we did not consider language as a 'transparent medium' through which meanings are *conveyed*, typical of the skills approach so strongly challenged by Turner (1999) or Lea and Street (1998). On the contrary, we viewed language as meaning making, as knowledge, as system; literacies as practices (Street, 1984, 2001); and communication as multimodal (Kress, 2010).

For the final assignment I wanted to give the students the opportunity to experiment with some of the concepts we had been exploring and gave them three options. Two of the options were analytical tasks involving the students working with pre-existing texts from print, audio, film or digital media and five of the students chose one of these. The other option, chosen by six of the group, entailed rewriting, in a genre of their choice, an essay they had already produced for one of their other modules and it is this option that generated the work at the heart of this book.

1.5.1 Regenring

When I designed the 'regenring' assignment, I was not entirely sure of what I was aiming for or how it might impact on the students' own understandings of what we had been talking about. I felt that it would be an interesting task, certainly playful, but also a chance for the students to bring their other study content into this module in a way that might encourage a reflection on language and its centrality in knowledge making.

I gave them the instruction to include the same references to works cited in their original essays and asked them to deal with the topic in a way that reflected the original essay question and content. I also, fortunately as it turned out, asked them to submit a copy of the original essay alongside the regenred work. My rubric was as follows:

Take an essay that you have already written from one of your other units and rewrite it for a different reader. In other words, reproduce it as a different genre. You could, for instance, write it as a story, a newspaper article or even in play form with dialogue. Think about the conventions surrounding academic writing and take account of how you will ensure that the piece is properly referenced etc. When you submit the assignment, please make sure you include also a copy of the original essay.

What the students produced far exceeded any expectations I might have had and I became very excited as I read through the work. The genres chosen included a newspaper report, a play, a simulated radio phone-in and a children's expository text. All were exceptional in their own ways, faithful in themes and topics to the original essay versions but substantially different in how that information was (re)worked. Most importantly, this work raised questions about the effect of the new genres on the 'old' knowledge that had been represented in the original essays. What had this exercise in regenring allowed to happen that hadn't happened in the essays themselves? What opportunities had the 'regenring' offered the students regarding *what* they could write and *how* they could write it?

1.6 From Practice to Research

As an assessor, in my capacity as module tutor, I could see that these productions were successful and effective. But it seemed to me that there was much more going on in the process than could be seen with the naked eye. My previous experience as a researcher on a large-scale project into language across the school curriculum (Gorman et al., 1990) had demonstrated the impacts of genre and language 'performance', which I might now gloss as 'contextual expertise', on the attitudes of educational assessors towards pupils' productions. In that study we worked towards developing frameworks for analysing those texts, both spoken and written, based on the initial assessments made by teachers involved in the surveys. My present aim was similar in that I wanted to reveal what effect the regenring had had on the work and why it had made such a strongly positive impact on me as reader–assessor.

Having made an analytical start with some initial comparisons between the paired texts in an attempt to see the different effects the regenring had had on the students' understanding of the essay topics, I could see not only the obvious changes in terms of register, for example, but also changes in what they paid attention to, how they viewed the disciplinary content and in some cases how they viewed themselves working with that content. I decided to talk to them to find out more about their experience in doing the work and because I could see the beginnings of what turned out to be for me a fascinating and illuminating study.

I used the opportunity for 'course unit review' to initiate the feedback process by distributing the standardized institutional feedback form, which I swiftly followed up with a request for further feedback specifically on the students' assignment choices. This could be undertaken either with written e-mailed responses or face-to-face discussion. The questionnaire was as follows:

Questionnaire

As you know, my research involves looking at writing practices in academic contexts. I'm very interested to know what your experience was of doing the re-write assignment for the LPI course.

What I'd like to do is interview you and record the discussion and the questions below are the sort of thing I would like to talk about. I'm sending them out so that you can think about it – but also, if you feel like it you could jot down some responses and mail them back to me as an attachment.

Questions

- Why did you choose this assignment of the three?
- What made you choose the particular essay?
- What determined your choice of rewrite genre?
- Talk about the process involved in the rewrite (e.g. thinking, interpreting, repositioning etc.)
- How did it help you in your understanding of the topic?
- What impact did it have on your feelings towards your discipline?
- What was your feeling in doing it (e.g. fun, chore etc.?)
- How did it differ (the experience) from writing the original essay?
- Do you think it would have worked the other way round – i.e. writing in the different genre, then writing the essay?

This approach gave the students time to focus their ideas and during the interviews, which I audio-recorded, the questionnaire served as a thematic guide rather than a set of discrete questions. In total, five students came along for interview: four who had done the regenring assignment (Anya, Andy, Peter and Dan) plus one other (Nat) who had chosen a different task but who had wanted to participate in the process by giving direct feedback on his experience of the course unit. Sonia, who had also done the regenring task, e-mailed her responses to my questions, whilst Assif, another of the regenring group, only completed the standard feedback form.

As I had hoped, the approach facilitated an open and wide-ranging discussion while also maintaining a general consistency of focus between each of the interviews. As can be noted from the questionnaire itself, I was hoping for insights into the motivations and experiences of the students in choosing and doing the assignment and to shed light on key aspects of the work that I might miss in my analyses. As Hammersley points out, interviews serve:

> as a source of witness accounts about settings and events in the social world, that the ethnographer may or may not have been able to observe her or himself; and as supplying evidence about informants' general perspectives or attitudes. (2006, p. 9)

There would be no conflict of interest in my being their tutor, or at least the risk was minimized, because all the marks had been submitted and I no longer had any assessment role in their studies. In fact, the students were very willing to talk about the process and to admit that even though they'd enjoyed it, this didn't necessarily mean that it was all fun or even easy, despite being what some might consider as 'unacademic' work.

> *It was really fun at first but then I found it – well, with an essay if you've done the reading then I mean you don't really have – you can just write it in a really flat way because it's not really what you're going to be marked on whereas with this, well because I was doing it in essay circumstances, then it was – I felt it was a real pressure …* (Anya)

The insights that emerged during the interviews were extremely perceptive. The students' comments confirmed things that I could see from my initial analyses of the texts but more importantly helped me to look at the texts not only from the perspective of the linguistic and thematic resources they had used, but also how the work had enabled them to experience their disciplines differently. This was particularly so in relation to how they felt able to articulate their knowledge with a greater sense of confidence and ownership:

and I felt that by using the characters ... I found myself free or freer to express my opinions or my ideals of my feelings towards the subject in a way that the purely conventional way of writing didn't or wouldn't allow me. (Dan)

Or:

Because I already had the information in front of me from the original essay it was much more fluid and I could be more confident in presenting ideas because I started to understand them better. (Sonia)

The interviews confirmed me in my resolve to explore the work more deeply to see what kinds of transformations had occurred and how the 'old' information had been reconstituted into 'new' knowledge. I felt that I needed to find a way to be able to say something about their work that would enable a more coherent response than simply 'this is excellent' or 'this is very good', as had been the case in my somewhat feeble earlier attempts at meaningful feedback on the assignments as assessment. I wanted to be able to say something about what was going on so that I could provide a persuasive argument to justify what had clearly been a fruitful and challenging activity. The 'regenring' exercise had undoubtedly enabled the students to bring different perspectives and develop new insights in relation to the disciplinary knowledge they were working with. My task was to reveal these through an analysis of the work itself to begin to understand what these different genres can do and how this kind of work might introduce a new approach to students' disciplinary learning.

The next section introduces the work of the six students who chose the regenring assignment task. It summarizes both the original essay and its new counterpart and considers both the anticipated as well as the actual outcomes of the work. It is important to note here that both versions were produced within the same academic term so the time gap between each was only a matter of a few weeks.

1.7 The Students' Work

Before moving on to descriptions of the student work, I first want to clarify a couple of points. The first is that when I use the term *genre* in connection with my data, I am referring to 'big genres' such as a play or an article, corresponding to what Bakhtin (1986, p. 62) called 'secondary' or 'complex' genres and what Martin (1993, p. 121) calls 'macro genres'.

When I talk about *regenring* I mean turning a text which has been produced using one 'big' genre (a student essay) into a text using a different genre (*not* a student essay). When I talk about *genre shift*, I mean the effect that regenring has on the textual product and the textual producer. I provide a full explanation of my use of genre in Chapter 3 and develop the concept of genre shift in subsequent chapters.

The second point is that the regenred work can be divided into two broad categories. These are not genre categories as such, but categories that distinguish what I am calling 'imagined' or **as if** genres and those that are 'authentic' or **as** genres and those that fall between both. The as if genres comprise a radio phone-in, an extract from a children's textbook and a newspaper article in which the students imagined specific contexts for their work. The newspaper report is not a real newspaper report, nor is the radio phone-in a real radio phone-in. By contrast, the as genres, both of them plays, are not simulations but are real plays in their own right. The last one, combining aspects of each, is a kind of bedtime story (which clearly it is not) using dialogue resources which turn it into a play (which clearly it is). The main difference that these distinctions make is that in the case of the 'as if' genres, the discussion remains external to the students' own experience, reflecting mainly on the content itself, whereas the 'as' genres, including the 'bedtime story', tended to encourage a greater degree of reflexivity, as is discussed in Chapter 8.

The original essays from which the regenred versions were derived were all part of the first year undergraduate portfolio of work in the different disciplines the students were studying and all were more or less successful in terms of the marks they were awarded. All the essays dealt with key debates in the respective disciplinary fields: history of political systems, evaluation of anthropological methods, classical versus Keynsian economics, origins and sources of African lingua francas, advantages and disadvantages of phenomenology in the study of religion. As regards the feedback from the respective module lecturers, all were considered acceptable as first year essays and two were considered extremely successful, notwithstanding the dissatisfaction expressed by the students regarding these essays encapsulated in the quotation that opens this chapter.

I take each pair of productions in turn, starting with the original essay version. I provide basic interpretations of the essay questions themselves, considering both the stated and implied expectations they contain. This provides a backdrop against which to consider the students' responses with both the essay and their alternative genres. In some cases, the students maintain the original 'title' of the essay for their regenred work, while in others the title reflects the regenring experience itself.

1.7.1 **Peter** (discussed in Chapter 5)

The essay

Peter was doing a degree in African Language and Literature and the essay he chose to regenre was from the module on African linguistics. The assignment was:

> *From a set of Swahili loan words, establish the linguistic source of each word and suggest the probable period from when it was borrowed.*

The assignment is presented as a series of three seemingly straightforward, logically linked tasks: 1) select a set of Swahili loan words, 2) establish their linguistic source, 3) suggest the probable period from which each was borrowed. In this context, the disciplinary topic appears to be *loan words*. This is what the essay is 'about', while the limitation to that topic is *Swahili*.

In order to produce a successful essay the student needs to have developed specific disciplinary knowledge so as to recognize the disciplinary meanings of the three central elements: what are 'loan words', what is meant by 'linguistic source' and how do linguistics understand the term 'borrowing'? The assumptions behind this question are that Swahili has loan words which have different linguistic sources and there is a relationship between the linguistic sources and historical events, and if you are doing that module you should know all this. To the outsider – that is, someone who has not done that module – there is nothing to suggest that there might be any disagreement about these loan words and their linguistic and historical origins, although the use of the word 'probable' could be an indication that there is. Furthermore, there is no specific instruction to define any of the disciplinary concepts, even though it is likely that this too is part of the task.

Peter's essay succeeds in fulfilling all the above aspects. It provides a general definition of the loan words and later clarifies the linguistic conditions under which loan words are retained or not. He specifies Swahili as the site of his discussion, noting that it is a lingua franca, thereby further emphasizing his disciplinary knowledge, and then proceeds to offer a chronological account of the different waves of foreigners who came to East Africa, why they came and the different languages they brought with them. For each wave he provides examples of modern Swahili words whose origins stem from these other languages and gives examples of their derivational process – again, a disciplinary activity. The whole essay reads as a history of language contact in a specific region and focuses mainly, though not only, on lexical borrowings. It is framed, however, with an introduction which challenges assumptions about language purity and a conclusion which challenges assumptions about the 'bastardization' of languages. These aspects of the writing go beyond the instructions provided, though they may well have been module themes.

The Alternative

Swahili Loan Words

Peter chose to reproduce the essay in the form of what he called 'a kids' book', which involved refocusing the essay to make it suitable for a younger readership. He retains the organizational structure of the original and deals with the same themes in the same sequence but the new work makes use of a different range of linguistic resources and introduces different explanatory examples to take account of the younger readership.

1.7.2 Sonia (discussed in Chapters 5 and 7)

The Essay

Like Peter, Sonia was also following the African Language and Literature degree and, like him, chose an essay on Swahili from the African linguistics module to regenre. Her assignment was as follows:

> *Give an account of the origin and present day function of one African lingua franca.*

Despite its seemingly straightforward wording and the free rein it suggests, this kind of assignment can be extremely difficult to manage. On the surface, the question appears straightforward in its three explicit tasks: 1) choose an African lingua franca, 2) explain its origin, 3) explain its present-day function. However, the frames of reference in these three tasks contain implicit disciplinary meanings which the student has to recognize in order to fulfil the assignment successfully. For instance, it is necessary to know what is meant by 'origins'. Does it mean historical, linguistic or both?

How is the term 'function' to be used? Unfortunately, the stated instruction 'give an account of' does little to help in determining what direction the student is supposed to take. Given that this was a module in African linguistics either a linguistic or a sociolinguistic response could have been intended and Sonia chose to take the latter approach, offering almost no reference to linguistic origins, unlike in Peter's essay above.

As discussed in the Introduction to the book, her essay is organized in a list-like sequence of loosely connected paragraphs, as in an encyclopaedia and follows the structure represented in the assignment task, dealing first with origins and secondly functions. Each paragraph represents a different topic: the linguistic origins, socio-historical origins, geographical origins and spread, colonial impact, written form, resistance to its spread, regional variation in form and function, number of speakers and spread, standardized variety, competition with English in certain countries and regional dialects. Finally she refers to Tanzania, which she uses to consider the present-day functions of the language, in different domains (my term not hers), as part of a wider linguistic repertoire and code switching. She completes the essay with a paragraph that attempts to draw this all together, concluding with a valedictory comment about the robustness of Swahili in continuing to grow in importance despite the dominance of English globally. At no point does Sonia provide any actual examples of what she is describing and nor does she offer any comment on what she writes.

The Alternative

Culturally Confused

Sonia chose to render the 'content' of the essay accessible for a younger audience for much the same reasons as Peter above. However, she felt that the topic lent itself to being 'told' rather than 'written' and so decided to reproduce the essay as a dramatized account of a father telling a bedtime 'story' to his two children aged eight or nine. The device that enables Sonia to present the information from the essay is that the father, who is described as 'politically correct to the extreme', uses the 'bedtime story' as an educational opportunity, much to the chagrin of his children. Only a selection of the actual information from the essay is used, filtered through the characters that Sonia has created; the to-ing and fro-ing of banter between the children and the parent. Rather than the listing of factual information that typifies the original essay, these are, in the regenred version, grounded in a 'real-world' context where things need to be explained rather than announced.

1.7.3 Assif (discussed in Chapters 6 and 7)

The Essay

Assif's essay came from the module 'An introduction to economic analysis' as part of his BSc Economics. The essay is titled 'Interest Rates Determinants' followed by two oppositional assertions presented as quotations:

> *'The rate of interest is a real phenomenon, determined by the twin forces of thrift and productivity.'*

> *'The rate of interest is a monetary phenomenon, determined by the interaction between the supply of and the demand for money.'*

As with the other essay assignments, this one also invites students to deal with a key disciplinary concern, in this case the opposing theoretical stances represented in the two quotations identified in the essay as, respectively, classical and Keynsian economic theory. The site for the discussion, the limitation, is 'interest rate determinants' and the student tasks are to 1) explain the competing theories and 2) use the topic of interest rate determinants as the context for the explanation.

The essay more or less follows the structure as suggested by the quotations, moving from 'classical theory' to 'Keynesian theory'. However, Assif also integrates the discussion of 'interest rates determinants' into the discussion of each of the two theories. The essay provides an exposition of Classical theory and its understanding of interest rates determinants and then moves into an oppositional account of Keynsian theory on the same topic, contrasting this, in an argument, with the classical position. As this is an economics theory essay, Assif employs numerical and graphic representations of equations to express the respective theories, but these are also interpreted verbally. The essay is both an account of the theories in relation to the topic and an argument but one which does not proffer much in the way of 'siding with' one or the other.

The Alternative

Debate Time: A radio debate between M. Friedman and J.M. Keynes

Assif's decision to present this essay as a radio discussion on the topic of Interest Rates Determinants gave him the opportunity to present the information from the essay, which was essentially an argument between opposing political as well as economic points of view, in a naturally argumentative context. The radio debate conceit allowed him to put two proponents of the respective theories in direct opposition as in a debate. However, rather than have Adam Smith, who was explicitly referred to in the essay, Assif chose instead the modern day classical economist, Milton Friedman, to represent that particular point of view, even though Friedman does not appear at all in the essay. The radio programme has a 'host' who mediates between the two opponents and manages the callers who phone in questions after each of the guests has presented a three-minute presentation of his argument. In this way, Assif covers the content of the essay through the presentations and through the phoned-in questions. To highlight the contentions between these two theories, Assif provides incidents where the sparring guests descend into antagonistic remarks.

1.7.4 Andy (discussed in Chapter 4)

The Essay

As with the other students, the essay that Andy chose to regenre relates to a key aspect of the study of politics, namely that of the classification of political systems. The essay title was:

> *Discuss some of the different methods of classifying political systems with their advantages and disadvantages.*

The essay task invites the student to do three specific tasks: 1) select from among a variety of methods (*some* of the ...), 2) say what they are (*discuss*) and 3) evaluate them (*advantages and disadvantages*). The assumption underlying this question is that the student will know from which pool of methods he is supposed to make his selection, though how many he should choose is unclear. The invitation to evaluate them is the most challenging aspect of the task as he has to know how to use disciplinary arguments to achieve this. He is not, for instance, being invited to give his own opinion, even though this may appear to be the case, but rather negotiate an opinion from what he has learned so far in his studies. It may even be that there are 'preferred' opinions, which he needs to be aware of.

In the essay, Andy chooses the classificatory methods of Aristotle and Montesquieu, offering these not only as examples of the ways in which political systems can and have been classified but also as a means to discuss the weaknesses of such classificatory systems, with particular reference to the approach, deductive (Aristotle) versus inductive (Montesquieu), historical change and historical relevance. He has clearly chosen appropriately. He then moves on to discuss more generally the difficulties of attempting to classify systems, citing various commentators, until he introduces a contemporary theorist whose model, according to Andy, is the most useful. The essay is framed within a problematization of the topic, attempts to provide classification models and a conclusion which offers a preference, but one which is open and flexible.

The Alternative

Classified!

The genre Alex chose for his alternative version was a newspaper article, or more accurately report. It uses a tabloid press discourse full of hyperbole, scandal and actions. Andy himself is the reporter and the setting is an 'international time-travelling conference of political philosophers and theorists' held in fourth-century Athens. The reporter interweaves his report on the conference and its speakers with snide journalistic comment and critique in true tabloid style, although I must say I have never read a tabloid reporting such intellectual debate! In much the same way as Assif's rewrite, above, put the exponents of particular points of view in direct contact, so does Andy with his cited sources. The conference delegates are those referred to in the essay and he, the reporter, links the ideas to the critiques offered by the various commentators. In this way the different theorists are enabled to interact and argue amongst themselves.

1.7.5 Dan (discussed in Chapter 7)

The Essay

Dan's essay was chosen from his Introduction to the Study of Religions unit as part of his Religious Studies BA. The question under consideration, in his case, was:

What are the advantages and disadvantages of a 'phenomenological' approach to religion?

This is a classic essay question which asks students to consider a disciplinary theory, in this case 'phenomenology' within the context of a specific field, here 'religion'. The tasks can be broken down into the following questions: 1) what is phenomenology, and, 2) how useful is it in discussing religion? Implicit in the question is that there are advantages as well as disadvantages in applying this approach and these need to be identified, although there is no apparent preference suggested one way or another. As with Andy above, Dan is expected to know the 'preferred' terms of reference for dealing with the task.

Dan's essay was extremely thorough, very lengthy, and submitted late, a fault for which he had marks deducted. It provided a detailed review of key literature representing both proponents and critics, and in so doing provided or clarified the usefulness or not of phenomenology as a methodology. The essay took a chronological approach, tracing the history of the methodology, but it was framed, unusually, by quotations from the religious text associated with his own faith, the Bhagavad Gita, which he employed to highlight the paradoxes involved in the kind of methodology being discussed in the essay itself. Hence he provides an overarching critique of the whole process from his own rather than a disciplinary perspective. It is undoubtedly an erudite piece of work and would have been awarded a very high mark had it not been submitted late.

The Alternative

Dan chose to reproduce the essay as a play, a two hander set in some distant future described as a 'golden age', a 'God-centred' utopia where 'the highest truth is that of reality distinguished from illusion for the welfare of all', reflecting the personal beliefs with which he introduced the original essay. The conceit is of a student who is working on an essay evaluating twentieth-century understandings of 'religion' with specific reference to 'phenomenology'. There are two main characters, the student, Josh, and a speaking computer very much in the mould of science fiction constructs such as HAL in the film *2001*. The computer provides the information required for the essay and the student provides the questions, interpretations and evaluations of that information, although, at times, the computer is drawn into an evaluation based on the critical sources being used. Many of the various writers referred to in the essay are evoked as holograms to 'speak' their own words, although they appear merely as embodiments of the ideas: a bit of fun, as the computer suggests, rather than as participants interacting in a discussion.

1.7.6 Anya (discussed in Chapters 6 and 7)

The Essay

The essay was from a particular unit on Anya's Social Anthropology course, 'Voice and Place', a module where the lecturers talk about their own research practices and activities to contextualize and exemplify anthropological research methods. Each week a different lecturer talks about his or her recent or current work and Anya chose an essay question linked to the session on anthropology of the built environment.

How might anthropological considerations of the built environment lead to better understandings of issues such as social status, identity construction and nationalism?

Like Dan and Andy's essays above, this one deals with a key problem in the field, that of anthropological 'methodology'. The question asks the student to fulfil the following tasks: 1) explain the phrase 'anthropological considerations', 2) define the 'built environment', 3) choose from among the topics suggested ('social status, identity construction and nationalism') or others of your own ('such as'), 4) use 'anthropological considerations' as a lens with which to discuss the 'built environment' in relation to the topics chosen and 5) evaluate the whole process.

Despite the apparent straightforwardness of the direct question, this assignment is extremely challenging, as not only does it concern a controversial debate, but the disciplinary connotations associated with the terms of reference make it even more tricky. What exactly is understood by 'anthropological considerations' and who it is understood by? Is it necessary to define the concept of the 'built environment' and the other 'disciplinized' terms of reference? Finally, as with the many of the questions above, whose evaluation is being requested? The student's or other anthropologists'?

Anya's essay covers all the topics suggested in the question, but adds also another big anthropological issue – gender. She frames the discussion in what is presented as an ongoing debate about the value of ethnographic study, Anya's gloss of 'anthropological considerations' in understanding different contexts, specifically the built environment. The essay moves along taking each topic in turn, considering it with examples from reading and from the relevant module lecture. She starts off with discussion of the domestic space with reference to different types of housing and their meanings, then moves on to the workspace and the design and purposes within changing societies. She moves on to consider the role of architecture and design in the construction of environments in different cultural and social settings (traditional, industrialized and post-industrialized), then contrasts urban space with 'savage' or forest environments, particularly from the perspectives of social identity and the construction of the other. She then draws on the work of the academic whose lecture the essay is based on by discussing traditional methods of building using Sa'ana, Djenn and Istanbul as examples and ends up by focusing on the role of monumental architecture in the construction and preservation of national identity. She concludes the essay with her evaluation of 'anthropological considerations'.

The Alternative

Snails and Other Gastropods

Anya chose to rewrite the essay as a play with eight scenes, presented as a quest in which the protagonist journeys through space and time encountering other characters on the way. Adventures happen, experiences are had, lessons are learned and the quest is successfully accomplished. Like Dan's above, Anya's regenred work is an account of doing the essay, or rather doing the research for the essay.

The play tells the story of Boris, an intergalactic snail, who has been referred by a careers advisor to try out being an anthropologist to see if he would like that kind of work. The 'snail' metaphor clearly has a strong resonance in the discussion of the built environment. He is sent to Earth to study at the institution where Anya herself was a student. Boris is given the assignment (*How might anthropological considerations ...?*) and sets off on his quest to find the answer to the question. In this case, instead of using the library or attending the lectures, he engages in an ethnographic study of the built environment, starting with the environment in which he finds himself. He wanders around London, meeting people who have issues relating to social status, identity, nationalism and gender, all of whom join him in his quest, representing the 'travelling companions' common to most 'questing' narratives. They travel to different locations, eventually arriving in Yemen to observe, in research action, the lecturer whose talk inspired Anya to choose the essay. Other devices are used to bring in the anthropologists cited in the essay: an internet café and an on-line discussion with the key writers on the issues within the 'built environment' context. Finally, in true quest style, the story ends with Boris and his band of friends realizing that they had had the answer to the question all along: they just didn't realize it.

1.8 Conclusion

My purpose in this chapter has been to provide an understanding of the circumstances in which the research used in this book emerged. It offers a contextualized account of the events which took place within a very particular context, the module, and which involved a small group of people, the students and me, working within a framework that I established through the pedagogical decisions I made. The work that the students produced in response to the assignment I set them led to the investigation that I have described here and the subsequent development of a theory-generating analytical framework as will be discussed in Chapters 3 and 4 and exemplified in subsequent chapters.

I have also used this chapter to introduce the narrative 'plots' of the student work itself so that readers have something tangible against which to place the discussion that follows. I have not been able to do justice to the work in these brief summaries. This could only be achieved through a reading of the productions themselves. However, throughout the book, particularly in Chapters 5, 6 and 7, I provide examples of the different pieces of writing and comments from the writers themselves. Suffice it to say for now that the range of possibility afforded by the new productions resulted in both more and less than the sum of the parts of the original essays.

The next chapter offers a discussion of what I am calling the communicative landscape. It examines the interactions between students and their teachers, particularly in relation to assignments, and investigates the desires and goals of both parties in establishing whether and where the work that my group of students produced might fit in the disciplinary repertoire.

Chapter 2

The Communicative Landscape

And sometimes when you're writing essays for your other courses, even if you do write quite a good essay you're probably boring the reader to death because it's the same old essay that's been churned out year in year out by the students. (Andy)

2.1 Introduction

Communication between students and lecturers involves often quite intense interactions, sometimes extremely positive and sometimes less so. Whatever the experience, however, there is no doubt that the relationship between the participants is a complicated one, as has been discussed by Lillis (2001). Unlike regular schooling, and indeed many other institutions, where relations are defined by visible rules and explicit hierarchies, the university offers a less obviously regulated environment where relationships appear far less rigid and formal. However, despite this apparent looseness and the informality of many of the interactions, the relationship between lecturers and students is not an equal one, not just in terms of practical authority, as in awarding marks for assessments, but in disciplinary authority: knowing more than the student. The genres which typify university interactions reflect this ambiguity with lectures and assignments promoting 'authority' and seminars and tutorials promoting a kind of 'equality'.

This is obviously an oversimplification of the relationship, but it gives some explanation to the contexts in which participants work and indicates why the relationship is complex. Andy's comment, which considers not only his own position as a writer but that of his lecturer as a reader, shows how students (re)construct the practices they are involved in to explain, perhaps in this case, the sense of frustration that the experience produces. While he may or may not have been accurate in his construction of the lecturer concerned, for Andy, writing an essay was 'only' a display of the already known, or, as Bourdieu and Passeron (1994, p. 14) put it, 'the practice of an *ars combinatoria* of the second degree and at second hand'. Implicit in this construction is the idea that everybody engaged in the assignment process was somehow powerless, caught up in the round of reproduction; reproduction of the same old questions, which inevitably lead to the production of the 'same old essays', and being endlessly 'bored to death'.

Essay writing is, as already discussed, central to the educative process at university. Lecturers expect to set essays and students expect to write them. Handbooks and study guides are produced on how to write a good essay and models of the genre are provided, implying, perhaps unintentionally, a template that has only to be filled with information. However, successful writing is more than the sum of its parts, and a 'how to' approach can disguise the complexity of what is involved in writing the discipline, as has been widely discussed (e.g. Scott, 1999; Lillis, 2001).

The following extract from a departmental handbook demonstrates the problems inherent in attempts to describe.

> Essay writing is a way of mastering a body of facts or ideas. You accumulate knowledge on a particular topic by reading the relevant literature, and then present what you have found in your own terms and in your own way. You thereby retain the material more effectively than merely reading.

While well meaning in its attempt to clarify the purposes of an essay, the 'no nonsense' terms of reference used ('a way of *mastering a body of* facts or ideas', 'you *accumulate* knowledge', 'reading *relevant* literature') give the impression that these are simple, straightforward activities, rather than the complex work involved in learning and participating in a discipline. Even more confusing is the curious invitation to present what is found *in your own terms and in your own way*. Of course, students can easily find out what an essay *looks* like and learn very quickly that this process of presenting in your own terms and your own way is limited to *particular* kinds of terms (academic, disciplinary) and *particular* kinds of ways (essays, presentations). Failure to do so can result in the kind of response that this student refers to.

> '*Cos when I got one essay handed back ... there was one thing that I said that I thought, well that's how **I'd** interpreted it – so you know, it was a bit much for him to write 'This is not the case.'* (Peter)

Peter's comment encapsulates a key problem inherent in the interactions between lecturers and students: that of who can say what, when and how. In this case, the student had given a personal interpretation of a disciplinary issue only to have this invalidated by his tutor's, albeit possibly casual, comment. Of course there is a lot of missing information here, in that we do not know what the student actually 'said' and how it was said, but the point is that the feedback from the tutor ('This is not the case') is presented in such categorical terms as to deny any space for the student to find his own understandings. What is suggested by the feedback comment is that the student was wrong, not necessarily in the factual accuracy of what he was saying, but in his personal interpretation, and it was this that led to Peter's indignation.

This chapter explores the relationship between students and lecturers and considers how each are positioned and position themselves. It problematizes the apprenticeship model that is sometimes used in relation to students before moving on to consider interactions between the participants, particularly those that occur around essays and assessment.

In the course of this discussion, I draw on interviews with a small number of lecturers, some of whose students were involved in the module described in Chapter 1, in order to explore the expectations around student work with the aim of discovering how the regenred work might fit within their criteria. I include my own reflections in this discussion because, having moved myself in terms of both university and job description (academic literacies specialist to senior lecturer in applied linguistics), as happened a year after the events in this book took place, I am acutely aware of how my own perceptions are now differently shaped. I also use examples of interactions from my current teaching context to illustrate the communications and miscommunications that occur around essays. The combination of these additional sources helps to shed light on the aspirations of lecturers in relation to assignments and student work, and the difficulties in articulating those aspirations in 'transparent' ways.

2.2 Constructing the Student

You know – this is a group of young novices looking to engage in the predominant discourse of the discipline . . . (Thierry, a lecturer)

In his discussion of the 'metadiscourse options' of the textbook, Hyland (2000) considers how these books (and their writers) position the student as novices through the linguistic choices of their writers: for example, the inclusive 'we'. He argues that 'The texts establish clear role relationships, with the writer acting as a primary-knower in assisting novice readers towards a range of values, ideologies and practices that will enable them to interpret and employ academic knowledge in institutionally approved ways' (p. 121).

So how are students perceived within the university setting? The metaphors of 'novice' or 'apprentice' are often used in describing students in relationship to their lecturers ('expert', 'master') and to the disciplines they have chosen. Both metaphors are associated with vocation and conti- nuity as the novice/apprentice is inducted into the world and work of the expert/master. Hyland's discussion shows how textbooks, for instance, emphasize the distance between the knowing lecturer and the unknowing student in the same way, I would add, that lectures and other pedagogical genres do. They establish the participants as 'teacher' and 'student' by employing a pedagogized discourse characterized by particular metadis- course options (see also Candlin and Plum, 1999). These metadiscoursal strategies, combined with a display of 'institutionally approved' knowledge (Hyland, 2000), help to maintain the relationship.

However, unlike apprenticeships, where the master models the relevant practice using particular procedures which the apprentice is supposed to follow exactly and unquestioningly, as Marchand (2000) shows in his study of traditional crafts apprenticeships, lectures and textbooks do not model the kinds of texts that student are expected to produce. In fact, if students were to write as textbook writers write or to present as in a lecture, using similar metadiscoursal features, they would be positioning themselves as expert and their readers as novices, thereby disturbing the institutional relationship. I return to this in Chapter 5 when discussing the effect of regenring on the students' authority as writers.

Understandably, lecturers want their students to engage with the disci- plinary epistemologies, practices and knowledge that they themselves love and from this perspective the analogy of apprentice or novice is appealing. But for most students a university degree does not imply an academic career and students do not necessarily see themselves as becoming 'full members' of the academic disciplinary community in the same way that an apprentice builder might. In this sense, it may be more appropriate to consider students as 'legitimate peripheral participants' (Lave and Wenger, 2002), engaged and interested and involved in community learning and practices without the 'obligations' associated with apprenticeship.

Some students do, of course, continue into academia, though this may not necessarily be an immediate process, but for the most part graduates continue on into other fields of work often not even associated with the studies they have undertaken. This fits with the notion of transferability referred to in the previous chapter, although it also is important to say that such transferability had been going on long before the skills ideology emerged. In fact, learning 'employment skills' has far less to do with a university education than it does with a student's eventual job, which is where the real apprenticeship begins.

Clearly, then, students do not necessarily see themselves as apprentices in the sense described above nor do they necessarily consider themselves novices, at least not in all areas. A growing number of young students take a year out before starting their degree studies, using the time to earn money or travel or do voluntary work. In addition is the large number of 'mature' students whose experience may well include levels of expertise that sit somewhat uncomfortably with apprenticeship constructions which assume a vertical power relationship of 'master' and 'novice'. This can sometimes lead to difficulties in the interactions that take place between the participants, as the following example from a previous study (English and Fusari, 2002) illustrates.

We built our discussion around a case which concerned the feedback and assessment of a disputed essay assessment. The following extract is from the lecturer's e-mail responding the student's query about the feedback.

> *Reading it again, I feel that you almost wrote it for yourself, not for the reader; that is, that you wrote it with the assumption that the reader would have all the same references as you and would be able to draw all the inferences you saw in the material.*

In this case both parties had misjudged the relationship they were engaged in. On the one hand, the lecturer, who was correct in recognizing that the student assumed certain shared understandings, had (mistakenly) positioned him as a novice. As such he expected the student to demonstrate his learning rather than allude to shared assumptions in the way professional writers might do when engaged in close community discussion. The student, on the other hand, had misjudged his own position and (equally mistakenly) assumed that he was considered as a full (and equal) member of the disciplinary community rather than as a novice displaying his learning.

This example shows how conflict can arise when there is a disruption in the conventional positionings as the result of a misalignment of expectations about identity and status. In this case, the student appealed against the allocated grade and other members of the department received the essay very differently, reading it with a smaller power distance than the original lecturer. It also shows that it is not only students who experience problems in knowing how to situate themselves. Lecturers also have to find ways of positioning themselves in relation to their students and their students' work. This necessarily involves how they position their students, as has been shown in the case above, but it also involves how flexible they are in adjusting that positioning. The following observation, made during my interviews with lecturers, expresses this very clearly.

You know I get a little bit tired of, you know, Edward Said's polemical discourse on orientalism. It's important but it's been stated so many times now that it's almost an obvious – and I sometimes have to step back and remind myself that – ok it is really important for this student to be hyper-critical about the post-colonial context and can even go on about it at exaggerated length because in fact they're coming from a different perspective than myself – and I think too, the um – this comes into play. (Thierry)

These remarks, with the example given, capture precisely the experience of reading students' work. As I discuss later on in the chapter, it is a rollercoaster of experience ranging from feelings of delight to feelings of desperation. Thierry's awareness of 'who' the student is leads him to reflect on his own identity as a reader and make the necessary adjustments. It is a delicate balance.

For the rest of this chapter I move on to consider the interactions that occur specifically around essays with a focus on the design and interpretation of essay tasks. The next section discusses issues associated with assessment criteria and the problem of explicitness, particularly in relation to institutional frameworks.

2.3 Assessment and the Transparency Myth

Assessing student essays is not difficult if by assessing we mean grading. Lecturers invariably have a sense of the quality of a piece of work from a holistic perspective and would probably find it fairly easy to classify. Provided the assessor is an experienced teacher in the field, holistic marking has, in fact, been shown to be a reliable assessment methodology (Gorman, 1986;

Thornton, 1987). However, what makes the process challenging is the pedagogical dimension, the task of articulating what constitutes quality, or lack of it, in justifying the grade: in other words, feedback. Moreover, feedback works both ways. As the lecturer, Thierry, put it:

> *Well, it's a good telltale for us as well – you know you get one or two bad papers and you can say that was one or two bad papers but the rest of them are good. But if all of them seem to be missing some kind of a key issue then you have nobody to question but yourself.*

This is a dimension that is not always understood and further exemplifies the complexities involved in the processes involved in assessment. However, along with the bureaucratization of higher education, as mentioned in the previous chapter, a plethora of institutional documentation has emerged with the intention of opening up all activity to public scrutiny and evaluation under the aegis of what is known as the Quality Assurance Agency, a non-governmental 'watchdog' organization. While it is perfectly appropriate for universities to be publically accountable and to ensure that provision is of a high quality and standards are robust, it is also the case that attempts to describe and quantify university activity lead to difficulty. Similar problems have been experienced throughout education in the UK all resulting in similar often deeply unsatisfactory compromises in terms of the descriptions that are produced.

The main problem is that the process of quantification leads to attempts to itemize something that is eminently un-itemisable. This results in a reductionist impression of what is involved which, in turn, creates false expectations about things like transparency and accountability. This last point is particularly true in relation to documented assessment criteria with the result that what is intended as description aimed at helping students can easily evolve into prescription, as has been found in UK primary and secondary education following the introduction of the National Curriculum and SATs. There is nothing intrinsically wrong with attempting to articulate what it is that students are expected to do and how they are being judged on their work. However, expressing what 'we' want in clear and uncertain terms is not as easy as it might seem and despite the many attempts that have been made to establish assessment criteria, all are intrinsically flawed.

The following effort by Brown et al. (1996) of the organization established to 'accredit' learning and teaching at university, now known as the Higher Education Academy, demonstrates the problem. They offer what they call their 'Ten Point Assessment Manifesto' as a specification guide to what constitutes 'good' assessment. At a first glance, few educators would disagree with inclusions such as 'assessment should play a positive role in the learning experiences of students' or 'assessment processes and instruments should accommodate and encourage creativity and originality shown by students' or 'assessment needs to be valid'. However, on closer inspection, the 'manifesto' reveals itself to be contradictory, deterministic and ultimately counterproductive to university learning. Take, for instance, the following, which is number four of the ten points provided:

> 4. Assessment needs to be valid. By this, we mean that assessment methods should be chosen which directly measure that which it is intended to measure, and not just a reflection in a different medium of the knowledge, skills or competences being assessed. (Brown et al., 1996)

Even ignoring their unproblematized use of the terms 'knowledge', 'skills' and 'competences', this attempt to clarify what they mean by 'valid' immediately falls into vague and solipsistic expression. The exhortation that assessment 'should directly measure that which it intends to measure' indicates an approach strongly oriented towards above, "competences" models of assessment with describable and measurable discrete items. This, however, does not fit with their earlier demand that assessment should 'accommodate and encourage creativity and originality'. In fact it serves to militate against those aspirations in its sidelining of the *qualitative* (reflection on knowledge) in favour of the *quantitative* (measurable items).

Such guidance criteria are based on assumptions that there are universal understandings of the terms of reference being used. Moreover, as has been pointed out by critics such as Lea and Street (1999), because the frames of reference in which such documents are produced are essentially political, the approaches they promote are inevitably prescriptive and ultimately pedagogically inadequate. O'Donovan et al. (2004) argue that explicit assessment criteria, which derive from outdated positivist notions of what knowledge is, fail to work because knowledge of 'what we want' is largely tacit, contextual and based on professional experience and personal preferences. They warn against a culture of bean counting.

> We must refrain from the temptation to give yet more and more explanatory detail and guidelines to assessors and students lest the whole edifice crumbles under its own weight and is replaced with a stark realisation

that no meaningful knowledge has been transferred in the unwieldy process. (p. 333)

In the end assessment criteria and their more institutionally official versions, benchmarks, always confound what they seek to clarify because, as I shall show later on, no matter how 'transparent' they try to be they are subject to the complicated kinds of interaction I have discussed above. Transparency and quantifiability do not offer pedagogically plausible approaches to learning precisely because they cannot capture the complexities involved in the kinds of tasks students are expected to engage in and the modes of assessment – specifically writing – only serve to reinforce 'transparency' myths. Transparency is a variable thing and explicitness can lead to an expectation that, firstly, the things made explicit have the same meaning for everyone and, secondly, that if you can show that you have 'done' the things you will succeed, which is not necessarily the case.

In the next section I show why transparency is not only unattainable but also undesirable when it comes to assessment. I examine examples of interaction that occur around assessment to illustrate this point and to suggest that it is in the gap between the design of the assignment and the student's production that learning can occur. In this discussion I draw on my lecturer interviews in exploring what is expected from a student essay and how this corresponds with documented criteria.

2.4 Design and Redesign

As anyone who has ever been a teacher knows, what takes place between what is 'taught' and what is actually understood is often something of a mystery. A glance at a page of notes that a student has taken during a lecture that you yourself have given or at a student's summary of a familiar article confirms that what 'goes in' is not necessarily what 'comes out'. This is because communication is always a process of making and remaking, as has been pointed out by Kress in much of his writing (e.g. 1989, 2003, 2010), and part of what influences what we 'understand' depends on what we have decided (or been able) to pay attention to. In the case of a student assignment, where the response is intended to be public in so far as it results in a product, such as an essay, which will be evaluated by someone who has the authority to make judgements, this can have important consequences for the producer.

As an assignment designer myself, I have come to realize that even the most explicit of instructions do not lead to task demystification, as the following example from a module on language teaching methodology illustrates. It concerns an assignment for a Master's programme in TESOL and involved the students evaluating a coursebook. We had discussed the assignment in class and had spent time analysing coursebooks along the lines of the assignment itself and the task instruction, below, was extremely detailed in its attempt to be explicit and 'transparent'.

The aim of this assignment is for you to consider the relationship between the ideas behind ELT practice and to see how these are encouraged by certain published syllabuses and materials.

Task

We want you to analyse and evaluate a published coursebook with particular reference to the underlying theoretical and pedagogical principles.

The discussion should be of around 3,500 words.

Analysis
Use these questions to help you focus your analysis of the coursebook itself.

Pedagogical aspects
How are the materials organized and staged both between units (syllabus) and within units?
Is there a particular 'methodological' approach which informs the coursebook?
How are the different activities linked/integrated?

Linguistic aspects
What kind of linguistic elements are evident and how are they presented?
    language input
    language analysis
    language awareness
    skills development

Socio-cultural aspects

Who is the 'ideal' user-group?
How widely usable are they beyond the 'ideal' user-group?
What world view is represented by the book?
How suitable/relevant is the approach implied by the book in different teaching contexts?

Writing

After you have analysed the book, think about how you're going to write your assignment. You may wish to give an account of the coursebook itself first and then discuss the ways in which it links into the theories and research we have looked at. You might want to talk about the theories first and then discuss the book. Whatever you do, you need to contextualize your discussion and make it relevant to your own situation and your own learning.

What we're looking for

Your work will be assessed for the analytical content of your discussion and for the ways in which you bring together different and relevant elements from the course. We expect you to incorporate your own understandings of language teaching based on your reading and on your own experiences as a language learner and teacher.

Example 2.1

The following e-mail correspondence, however, demonstrates how even though I had thought I had covered all bases, this was clearly not the case.

28/4/2004 Assignment

Hi Fiona!

Hope you are fine. Here are my questions for the assignment.

Could you give me a brief recommendation about how much I should value the different parts of the assignment.

For example approximately how much percent of it should be the analysis of the materials, how much should be analysing the theories, and how much space should I use for considering the usefulness of the materials in my context.

I had not anticipated such questions but I am convinced that even if I had allocated precise percentages as to the 'amount' of effort to be spent on each 'component' this would undoubtedly have caused a different kind of consternation. From the student's perspective her questions were perfectly reasonable given the way in which the instructions had been formulated and, more importantly, in her own concern to make sure she got everything 'right', in the way I wanted it. I will return to this below when discussing the problem of what lecturers want. For now, I use this example to illustrate the way in which even the best laid plans fail to provide the kind of transparency referred to above and the pointlessness of expecting direct correspondence between what is uttered and what is understood. This has little to do with the 'clarity' of the utterance itself but rather more to do with the positioning of the participants.

On discussing this further with the student group I was fascinated by the responses I got. Some students said they hadn't read beyond the general overview instruction – the essay question itself. Others said that they had analysed the question sheet in a group, deconstructing each phrase until their heads were spinning and their confusion was complete. Yet others reported being so overwhelmed by the amount of information that they reverted to old, familiar approaches to essay writing rather than take any of the 'risks' implied by the rubric. But what is clear is that in all cases, the intended explicitness of the rubric confused rather than clarified.

What then happens between the design and the production of an essay? Using the terms of reference proposed in Kress and Van Leeuwen (2001) the following chart offers a schematic representation of this particular interaction drawing an analogy between this and other forms of transactional relationships.

INTERACTIONS			
Design	Redesign	Production	Distribution
What the teacher wants/envisages/desires – and why	How the student understands and (re)interprets – and why	What the student produces – how and why	How the product is 'delivered' and 'received' and what is done next

FIGURE 2.1

Here the student assignment task, whatever it is, corresponds to the category of *design* – in other words, what stands between content and expression. In the case of an essay, it involves the expectations of the designer, what she has in mind based on her own disciplinary knowledge, her experience of other essays she has read and even done herself, and on the ambitions she has for her students to work with the disciplinary material in certain (though not necessarily expressible) ways. In this sense the lecturer is something like the client in a contractual arrangement with an artisan; someone who has a particular design in mind but who is not actually going to produce the item. In some cases, the lecturer who will evaluate the essay may not be the actual designer; that may fall to an architect, for example, a course leader, in which case there may be an additional level of interpretation.

Following the analogy, the artisan student interprets the 'design blueprint', that is the essay instruction, so as to put it into production. This corresponds to the category of *redesign* in the chart and is influenced by the kinds of things that the student has understood and prioritized in relation to both the content and its expression. However, it also involves the kinds of issues that are connected to positioning discussed earlier. *Production* is the realization of the 'new' design, that is the essay itself, and *distribution* corresponds to the delivery of the goods and how the goods are received. In the analogous situation, distribution will involve payment or occasionally not, depending on the acceptability of the work done itself. In the student situation, it involves the mark and the feedback, which depends on the degree of fit to the original design and/or the possibility, or otherwise, of the lecturer being willing to accept the new design. This last aspect of the interaction relates to the concept of agency. In other words, it concerns the way in which the reader constructs the writer, as discussed earlier and, in a different sense, how the writer has constructed the reader, a topic I return to in Chapter 5 when considering discursive identity.

2.5 What on Earth do 'We' Want?

A key factor in the relationship sketched out above is the fit of the product to the design: in this case, the degree to which the essay accords with the sort of thing the lecturer wants. What lecturers want, and equally students' attempts at trying to work out what lecturers want, plays large in the university student–lecturer relationship. In her discussion on agency and subjectivity in student writing, Scott (1999) points out that students have a general awareness of what is required of university writing. Her conversations with students indicate that they are well aware that they will have to be critical and creative and not simply reproduce information. But, as she goes on to argue, and as I myself have pointed out (English, 1999), being aware of expectations is not the same thing as knowing how to fulfil them or, indeed, knowing how they are realized in an essay.

Students know very well that they are writing for a very specific and narrowly distributed readership. They sense that different readers might like different things or rather different ways of articulating things, as has been noted by Lillis (1999) among others, and it is something that often comes up in my discussions with students. Rumours abound about how 'so and so' likes 'this' but not 'that', or 'this' is allowed but 'that' is not, as the following e-mail demonstrates.

Hi Fiona!
Just a brief question, is it possible to use bullet points in assignment.
Talked to a friend who said that they weren't allowed?

Sometimes rumours can even send students completely off track, despite all the 'clear' guidance provided.

In order to find out more about the expectations that lecturers have of their students, the different elements they look for in an essay and the priority they give to those elements, I interviewed a small group from the institution involved in this study, some face-to-face and some by e-mail. The issues I wanted to explore concerned not only their aims and expectations in designing assignments but also the experiences and attitudes they had when reading the submitted work. The lecturers included those involved in teaching the students in the study and represented a range of disciplines. The interview questions were as follows:

- What influences you in your design of assignment tasks?
- What sort of things do you want – do you have an expectation of what they're going to produce for you?
- What kind of anticipation do you have when you sit down to read an assignment (dread? excitement? etc.)
- At what point might you relax while reading student work?
- What 'qualities' do you like to see in a student production?
- What don't you like?
- Who are you when you're reading student essays? How do you position yourself – what is your identity?

- Do you read student writing differently from other academic writing and in what way is it different? Is there ever a crossover?
- Do you, in your own teaching, ever discuss your own writing with the students?

I also include some reflections of my own as I myself am involved in the process of assessment and have my own attitudes and expectations. A further reason for including these is that I wanted to see how closely the lecturers' aims and desires matched those expressed in the institutional handbook mentioned at the beginning of this chapter.

I do not claim that this small survey is statistically valid or that strong conclusions can be drawn from the interview responses. However, they exemplify the kinds of assessment values that university lecturers have and as such are interesting from the perspective of the circumstances in which students write and lecturers read.

I start with the lecturers' responses, focusing first on their thinking behind the assignment tasks they design and then moving on to the qualities they look for and how they position themselves as readers. As with the students involved in my research, I have used pseudonyms for the lecturers: Thierry and Dalia (social anthropology), Lorenz (African linguistics), Bernard (religious studies), Elizabeth (development economics), Maurice (contemporary media), Walter (comparative law), Belinda (Japanese linguistics).

2.5.1 Assignment Design

The first topic concerns the design of essay assignments, which they all agreed were chosen with the intention of getting students to show their familiarity with module content and readings. The following is typical of the sorts of things the participants expressed.

I try to set questions that actually respond directly to key texts that I've asked the students to read. I usually try to set a question that's fairly general both in my written assignments and also on my exam papers. I like to leave the question broad enough so that it gives the student the opportunity to demonstrate what it is that they know and to bring in salient issues ... I like to give them the opportunity to bring in their own regional interests into the essay question, but at the same time the essay question is specific enough that it is addressing key theoretical concerns that were taught ... (Thierry)

All of the responses demonstrated strong pedagogical motivations in the design of assignments and a clear desire to help students succeed. Some referred to using previous exam questions to help students prepare for their exams.

> *I often assign old exam questions as essay questions so that students can begin to think about how to deconstruct a question and how to construct an answer – skills they need for their exams.* (Dalia)

Others to encouraging students to use disciplinary 'tools':

> *To show an understanding of the conventions in the discipline, for example the adoption of a certain type of discourse in discussing a topic, which departs from everyday conventions or perspectives.* (Lorenz)

Most referred to involvement with disciplinary debates as a design motivation:

> *I want them to deal with the debates and find where they themselves stand in the debate …* (Elizabeth)

and to write about things that interested them:

> *For essay-type assignments, I don't set assignment topics, but rather ask people to choose a topic related to the course content … That way, students can work on things they find interesting. It also means that students have to think about what they find interesting or curious, or how course content related to their own background and experience …* (Lorenz)

How then do these intentions fit with the advice about essays and assessment set out in course documentation and the demands for transparency and objectivity discussed earlier? The following extract is from the handbook I referred to at the beginning of the chapter, reproduced here for ease of comparison.

> Essay writing is a way of mastering a body of facts or ideas. You accumulate knowledge on a particular topic by reading the relevant literature, and then present what you have found in your own terms and in your own way. You thereby retain the material more effectively than merely reading.

It goes on to clarify these points as follows:

> Essay writing develops skills of selection, analysis and condensation. Out of the mass of information available, you have to decide what to include and what to leave out. You have to be alert to contradictory arguments and points of view presented by different authors and you have to present your answers in a succinct form without over-simplifying.

Although on one level the lecturers and the guide anticipate similar things, they differ substantially in tone and in focus. Both are interested in course content, literature and debates, but from different points of view. In the interviews the lecturers couched their intentions in a pedagogical frame, particularly in relationship to supporting students' interests, their participation in the debates, their thinking about things, their use of the material, not 'mastery'. By contrast, the guide comes across as regulatory and potentially intimidating, despite its intentions to the contrary. Phrases such as 'mastering a body of facts', 'accumulate knowledge', 'relevant literature', 'retain material' are all rich in anxiety-producing emotions because despite their regulatory tone, they are in fact very open and vague. How, for instance, can we understand '*accumulate knowledge*'? Does it mean an additive collection, like an encyclopaedia, or does it mean that you process it in some way? What exactly is meant by '*relevant literature*'? Is it what's on the reading list, is it something that can be found on the internet, is it something specific to the topic or is it something that the lecturer values?

Furthermore, unlike the comments from my interviews, which were more about *learning*, the guide is more closely connected to *acquisition* precisely because it is produced with the kind of discourse associated with competencies and skills. Of course, as we have seen with the detailed assignment task in Example 2.1, even when more pedagogically oriented discourse is used, students nevertheless reinterpret it, assuming that there are hidden agendas that are being kept secret.

2.5.2 Qualities Desired

The lecturers all referred to issues closely related to disciplinary factors in talking about the qualities they were looking for in a student's essay. They were particularly concerned that students would use what they had been discussing on the module and that they had understood the basic concepts.

They have to show that they have understood the major concepts and can express them in writing … and be thoughtful about key issues. (Walter)

However, what they were particularly looking for revolved around students doing something with the disciplinary material. They wanted them to interpret rather than restate what they had discussed on the module, backing this up with evidence.

[I don't like] *Too strong judgements, based on insufficient evidence; re-stating others' points of view without properly thinking about them.* (Bernard)

They also wanted them to use disciplinary concepts and discourse in framing ideas:

I appreciate it when they show an understanding of the conventions in the discipline, for example the adoption of a certain type of discourse in discussing a topic, which departs from everyday conventions or perspectives. This for me constitutes evidence of learning in a broad sense (as opposed to automatic memorization of data, so to speak). (Belinda)

or to offer new insights into old topics:

A coherent piece of writing which is grounded in the course discussion, i.e. starts from some common background and uses this to introduce something new, i.e. something which I don't know. I also expect appropriate use of technical concepts and related terms, and awareness of the context in which the essay is placed. (Lorenz)

Evidence of originality of thinking was sought …

New ways of looking at old questions. (Bernard)

as was evidence of personal commitment …

When I come across some evidence that the student actually sat down and gave the task some thought, and engaged with it and produced a personal reaction to it, I feel like giving them a first just for that. (Belinda)

Everyone mentioned language and structure, usually in connection with coherence:

> [I like] *Evidence of care taken over expression and structure of argument ...* (Elizabeth)

but also in terms of the impression, either of care or carelessness, that was produced:

> [I like] *Good organization and clean presentation. I hate messy work because it is unprofessional.* (Walter)

Poor use of English was also remarked on as a serious factor in how the lecturer responded to an essay:

> *I dread how much English I will have to correct. That's one of my biggest concerns ...* (Dalia)

as was poor editing:

> [I don't like] *sloppy editing especially when this gets in the way of understanding what a student wants to say; a feeling of reading something not thought through, inconsistent and written with a lack of interest.* (Lorenz)

In relation to work of the highest quality, attributes such as 'excitement', 'sincerity', 'elegance', 'playfulness' were used to distinguish this category of work from the rest.

> *Those students who can playfully manipulate these kind of things* [personal anecdotes, newspaper articles etc.] – *bring them into their argument and bring the whole theoretical discussion on to a new tangent – those are the essays that I think merit the higher* [grades] ... (Thierry)

As previously, it is interesting to compare these comments with the criteria associated with the 'best' essays expressed in the guide referred to above, but unlike before, where there was a clear difference in terms of attitude and approach, here there is a greater synergy.

- Shows clear evidence of wide and relevant reading and an engagement with the conceptual issues

- Develops a sophisticated and intelligent argument
- Shows rigorous use and a sophisticated understanding of relevant source materials, balancing appropriately between factual detail and key theoretical issues. Materials are engaged directly and their assumptions and arguments challenged and/or appraised
- Shows original critical thinking and a willingness to take risks

Both the interview comments and the guide use similar qualitative attributes ('sophisticated', 'intelligent', 'rigorous') along with descriptions of the kinds of activity students would be expected to have engaged in. Interestingly, the criteria have moved away from the skills approach suggested by the general guidance referred to above. Perhaps it is indicating that, after all, academic success is not about skills but about knowledge and understanding.

My own reflections on what I particularly like correspond to many of the things mentioned during the interviews.

I like a discussion that is contextualized. I like it to be political in the most general sense – for instance a challenge to something or an acknowledgement that things may not be as they seem. I like students to argue and interact with their readings in some way. I like personal anecdotes and examples to illustrate or situate the work. I like assignments which make me smile or laugh – where students have been candid and natural through referring to some incident or other, provided it is made relevant. This kind of inclusion lends a quality of authenticity to the discussion and reassures me that the student feels some kind of ownership of the work. I like there to be further possibilities stemming from their work. (Fiona)

In retrospect, I wonder what my students would make of these reflections. Would they find this more accessible than the guidelines I myself produced for our own course handbook or would they (over)analyse them into a new series of mysteries, redesigning them as I am sure they do with the 'official' document? I have had sight of several of the students' copies of the handbook when they have come to ask for further clarification and have seen the highlighting and underlining of what they have decided to be the 'key' attributes for 'excellent' work and the annotations which reframe them, hence turning them into something else. Unfortunately, no matter what 'assessment manifestos' and competencies agendas might suggest, there is no quick fix. The 'qualities' sought by lecturers and by institutional guides are a mix of explicit and implicit criteria which combine the describable (e.g. use of disciplinary terminology) with the indescribable (e.g. sophistication, playfulness, excitement) in ways that can never be wholly captured by lists of assessment criteria.

In the end, students cannot know 'what we want' until they write, and the problem then is that if they have not done 'what we want' and the mark counts towards their overall result, then they feel devastated. However, it is actually somewhere in the gap between the lecturer's design and the student's interpretation that learning takes place despite the pain that it causes. It is the gap that gives a space for students to be different from each other and, more importantly, it is the space where they can (or must) try to make sense of the material.

The next section explores the frames in which lecturers actually read their students' work and their emotions as they do so. I start with my own reflections because they represent a very different identity from the one I used to have as an academic literacies tutor. In fact, I wrote these comments shortly after a year in what was then my new job as a 'subject' specialist in a different university and it was that experience that made me rethink the lecturer's position. As an academic literacies specialist, I could comment, critique, suggest and so on without either the pain or the regulatory authority of having to give a grade. For the student, in that relationship, there was no risk. An academic literacies specialist, as one student put it, provided a 'safe haven' where the anxieties associated with the disciplinary lecturer's authoritativeness (real and imagined) were absent from the interaction.

The title that I have given this next section is intended to problematize the constructed identities that students, and others, including ourselves, ascribe to lecturers, mirroring the ways that lecturers, and others, construct their students. I start off with some of my own reflections.

2.6 Constructing the Lecturer

First of all, I want the writer to do well. While reading, I'm urging them to explain, clarify, interpret and exploit all the bits of their work – and to answer those questions that I have about what they're saying as I read along. I may have a doubt about something or feel that something could have been developed better and as I read, I look out to see if it has been done later on. At times it is a bit like being on a rollercoaster with peaks and troughs of reaction.

I engage as if in conversation – commenting verbally or non verbally, nodding or shaking my head, laughing, groaning, sometimes noting in the margin for my reference and as an aide memoir for later written feedback. I tend to use pencil so that I can rub things out if I change my mind later on or the student changes it for me.

I can be overly critical and have to rein in my critical comments. For instance, I may see something in the discussion, based on my own personal preferences, experiences, interests and prejudices, that they don't see or they don't feel important. It might be an omission of a particular perspective or it might be what I might consider a naïve response to something they've read. In such cases I have to decide whether it's worth mentioning or whether I should leave it alone. Sometimes the omission may influence my marking when I feel they should have considered it, and sometimes it may not have any grading impact, when I feel it is something that they have no reason to have thought about.

Do I treat students as peers? Not usually, as I am also expected by them and by my agreed position (lecturer) to give them a grade, to provide teacherly feedback, to evaluate their work in the process of validating them as successful (or otherwise) students on a given course of study. However, it also depends on how I feel about the work and the level of expertise of the writer. I am not an expert in all of their areas of choice so cannot know everything. I certainly look out for new and interesting points and in that case treat them as having expertise and knowledge which I might not have. But still – I am marking it all and am having to respond to how much or little of the course input – content, perspectives, issues – is evident. With really excellent work – that is work which is expert and professional – it is difficult to allocate a mark as the process almost demeans the quality of the piece. It is a very strange position. (Fiona)

From the interviews with the other lecturers, it is clear that they reflect similar feelings and attitudes to my own: the same ambiguities, the same fluctuations and the same reluctance in relation to 'official' judgement, as the following comment confirms.

I am a discussant and a sounding board. I am a senior member of the community of students. Sadly, I am also a judge or a gatekeeper. (Belinda)

It is not necessarily that we are unwilling judges, but that the job of judging makes the job of reading different from other kinds of reading that we do. As Thierry put it, somewhat regretfully, '*I think we land up reading our students' work expecting there to be problems with it …*' This was also noted by Belinda, who suggested that she was more critical with her students' writing than with that of other academics.

In a way I am more 'alert' (this really is not the right word, but can't think of another: more 'picky?') when I read my students' essays than pieces of more experienced scholars – I feel responsible if my students write rubbish. It could also be that I assume other scholars to imply things I cannot see even when I have a sense that a piece of writing is not that good. (Belinda)

What is particularly interesting about her comment is the reference to her own responsibility with respect to her students as opposed to the tolerance she has towards other scholars whose work she assumes to be 'good' even if it is not well written. This in itself is a strong indication of power and positioning, not only between academics and their students, but also between academics themselves. The pedagogical responsibilities associated with reading student work, the explicit attention to the 'writing', to the use of materials or to the arguments developed is very different from other kinds of reading where even though we may judge those elements we are not doing so with responsibility, least of all pedagogical responsibility.

All the lecturers in my survey wanted students to do well and read their work with that in mind. They often used expressions of emotion when talking about this.

I may get upset with the writing, or be intrigued, or think 'well done!' or 'not again!' (Belinda)

There were several expressions of hopefulness and supportiveness, as in 'hoping to be convinced by' or 'I'm kind of rooting for them' and even excitement and curiosity:

I think it's [the anticipation] *excitement. I usually know about the topics student write on (as I usually discuss topics in advance), so I ask myself, mmmm, I wonder what X made of this and this problem.* (Lorenz)

Such anticipations, however, have their corresponding disappointments and the worst kind of disappointment, as it turned out from the interviews, concerns the issue of 'effort'.

I think that when I'm reading them I'm truly concerned that they have grasped the material and I think, unfortunately, and it's probably not good for my heart – but it does upset me when I read something bad or when I read something that just doesn't make sense or no – worst of all is when no effort was put into it. That I find extremely disheartening when I'm putting the effort into teaching and grading this and you're not getting the return. (Thierry)

This is particularly sensitive, as the above comment makes clear, because of the notion of reciprocation which is here viewed from the perspective of the lecturer. However, the experience of reciprocation can be viewed in the reverse with the student experiencing disappointment from a meagre grade despite, from their point of view, having put all that effort into the work. The rules of engagement are extremely complicated, as has already been pointed out here, and in numerous studies (e.g. Ivanic, 1998; Scott, 1999; Lea & Street, 2000; Griffin, 2006). The concerns about 'effort' link back to my earlier discussion about different perceptions of students' affiliation to the discipline, the problematizing of the 'novice' identity that their lecturers like to imagine, a theme which Ivanic (2006) develops in her discussion of the relevance of identification and community affiliation in learning.

From my interviews, it is clear that lecturers want their students to do well, that they want them to be interested and they want them to be engaged. They also want them to show affiliation and to show that they care about the things they are writing about. It is this kind of engagement that leads lecturers to relax, enjoy their students' work and view them as scholars in their own right:

> *And it's real fun when you look at it and think, right, I'm now reading this as if I were reading a professional article and you actually – and then I actually move physically in my chair – and I tend to – and you say 'right' ok – this is serious and I'm going to enjoy this and you're immediately giving a new kind of respect to the student. You're saying, I'm now switching on my intellectual faculties full because you have persuaded me that I have to.* (Maurice)

Such shifts in approach can happen as I mentioned in my own reflections above, but still, the pedagogically framed context in which the work is produced means that the reader has to say something about it to explain the grade itself. And it was precisely that position that I found myself in with the regenred work, reading not as a teacher, but as someone reading for the pleasure of it.

2.7 Conclusion

The interactions that take place between students and their lecturers around essays are clearly complex. They can be intensely frustrating on the one hand and intensely rewarding on the other, with all the shades of experience that fall in between. The interactions are not unidirectional, even when the 'subject' of the interaction is an essay and one of the participants is physically absent: they are dialogic, as was stated quite explicitly by one of the lecturers (*The process of reading is like that of a dialogue and it is dynamic*). It is not just that the participants concerned have a multitude of identities and emotions, all of which interplay in the different interactions which take place: it is how these factors play out in the context of the work the parties are engaged in, namely essay assignments. As Ivanic (2006) points out:

> people's identities are in a continual state of flux, co-emergent with the ongoing activity in which they are participating and secondly, people bring with them to any activity a history of identifications which are textured into their current sense of self. (p. 24)

The demands for explicitness and transparency have been shown to be futile as the terms of reference in which pedagogic and disciplinary goals are expressed will always be subject to a reinterpretation, or redesign, on the part of the students. The desires and dreads of the lecturer readers are clear at the conceptual level, but once articulated they become stereotyped into platitudes or regularized into prescriptions.

The difficulty in knowing more than we can tell, to paraphrase Polanyi (1997, p. 136), is part of what creates the tension between what the lecturer wants and what the student thinks he or she wants and it is only through the exchanges that occur in the process of dialogue that no amount of up-front explanation will help. Students can never really be privy to the kind of understanding of 'successful essay writing' that O'Donovan et al. (2004) discuss simply because they are students. How then can they negotiate their way without experiencing difficulties? The answer is that they cannot. There is no such thing as a free lunch, to use a well-worn aphorism. University study is neither problem free nor, for that matter, risk free. Moreover, as I have already suggested, it is in negotiating the gaps between 'design' and 'redesign' and the interactions that occur about the 'product' in the process of 'distribution' that learning takes place.

In the case of the students involved in my study, the gap was of a very different kind. Unlike in the discussion above, where students try to 'fit' theirs to the original, that is try to work to the blueprint, my students did, if not exactly the opposite, something close to the opposite, something they were authorized to do. In the process, the very wide gap between the original essay design and the new regenred work gave them the opportunity to engage in their disciplines in the very ways that the lecturers above so desired. To do justice to their efforts and to explain my own reactions to their work, I inevitably had to investigate the category of genre itself. The next chapter, therefore, offers a discussion of genre and establishes the theoretical and methodological principles with which I analyse and discuss the students' work.

Chapter 3

The Affordances of Genres

And whether I think it's right or wrong I'm not going to moralize about the issue: it's simply about the parameters that are defined by discipline and I don't think that those boundaries are easily negotiated or easily changed. (Thierry)

3.1 Introduction

The lecturer whose words preface this chapter both problematizes and confirms established disciplinary practice that typifies the production of academic knowledge. Despite his very positive response to the regenred work that I showed him and his subsequent remark against the privileging of written forms over other forms of representation, he highlights the power of established ways (genres and discourses) of communicating, in this case, disciplinary knowledge.

Unfortunately as academics we are rather constrained to the spoken or the written word because that's the medium that we use to convey our knowledge – so we privilege that form of knowledge and in fact to the exclusion of all other forms of knowledge ...

As already discussed, in the context of learning and assessment the student essay occupies the default position particularly in the social sciences and humanities. As with other genres, it is considered stable and reliable due to the familiarity with which it is socially and materially experienced and regardless of what 'type' of essay it is (e.g. comparison and contrast, description of process) the student essay indexes a highly specific social practice within a particular set of circumstances using a particular range of textual resources and disciplinary materials. Students expect to write essays and lecturers expect to 'set' them, and in the process of this 'agreed' practice, both parties 'collude' in confirming their generic stability. However, after analysing the regenred work in relation to the original work, I began to wonder why essays are as privileged as they are and why, for so long, alternative opportunities for learning have been excluded.

The work that my students produced showed me that a substantive shift had occurred when they used the alternative genres. For one thing, the activity was a reworking of something they had already produced so there was more opportunity for reflection in the reworking process:

I think I was able to stand back a little further the second time around – I got a little distance between myself and the subject ... That distance did help to perceive the subject in a better way. You kind of get a better grasp, a better hold of it, a more homogeneous kind of all-encompassing idea of what the subject actually is. (Dan)

For another, it engendered a more profound understanding of the issues:

You know, I feel more flexible – I haven't looked at it in only one way. I feel like I could use that knowledge again quite comfortably. (Assif)

However, it was not just a case of revising the original work, as both they and I may have originally thought it would be. As the students themselves pointed out, the regenring was different in terms of how they were able to work with the disciplinary material. This was not only in terms of differences associated with disciplinary terminology, such as in not having to use '*big words*', as Anya put it, or in being able to use alternative resources such as characters, but in how those opportunities affected the students' own sense of agency in working with the disciplinary materials, as in Dan's observation:

by using the characters ... I found myself free or freer to express my opinions ...

or Anya's reflection on the degree to which the regenring forced her to engage with the disciplinary issues:

and I had to have a take on it – a position that I could get away with – not really taking in the essay ...

In fact, what happened was that the shift in genre led to a series of other shifts in terms of both the texts themselves and the experiences that the students had in making those new texts.

In order to be able to investigate these changes, it was necessary to develop a framework that would encompass these different dynamics and for this I needed to find a theoretical perspective that would support such a framework. In this chapter, I set out the theory that underlies my work and in the following chapter I explain the methodological approach that I use to analyse the texts themselves. In so doing, I propose the idea of the *affordances* of genres because what I am particularly interested is the impact of genre choice. For this purpose I want to consider genre as a social semiotic resource, so as to concentrate on what genres do, how they set off a chain reaction of choices, which in turn effect how we can experience the textual activity in which we are engaged. In this epistemological framing, genre works in much the same way that Kress and Van Leeuwen (2001) propose that mode works. In my discussion, genre can be considered a supra-organizing category that mediates between the idea and the articulation (or production) of that idea as an utterance taking into account the social context and the available material resources.

Viewing genre from a dual (social and material) perspective in this way is by no means a new idea. It was a central focus of the work that emerged from the 'Russian Circle' working in the earlier part of the twentieth century, which eventually found its way to the wider research community in the 1980s. As has already been indicated, their work has fed into several disciplinary fields, particularly because of this link between the 'social' and the 'utterance' (Bakhtin, 1986). In fact, Medvedev proposes an analytical approach in which genre has a double orientation: a contextual orientation, which relates to the social aspect of genres, and the thematic, which relates to the content (Medvedev, in Titunic, 1986). My approach, as I explain in the next chapter, adopts the idea of orientation and proposes two additional categories: semiotic orientation, which concerns textual materials, and discursive orientation, which concerns identity and agency.

In order to arrive at this point, I want first to clarify my terms of reference so as to work my way towards the understanding of genre that I use and the approach that I developed for analysing the work. I want to stress, at this point, that my discussion of genre is not intended as an exposition on the topic as is provided, for example, in Swales (1990) or Devitt (2004), but rather as the presentation of a different theoretical perspective which uses a social semiotic lens in unpacking the student work. It is this that makes the discussion different from those referred to above and from the approaches used by, for example, Martin (1993), whose work is strongly located in systemic functional linguistics, and from those developed from a sociocognitive perspective such as Berkenkotter and Huckin (1993) and Russell (1997), who use an activity theory framework. The value of the social semiotic focus, as will be seen in both this chapter and those that follow, is that it enables a multi-dimensional approach which combines both the social and the material in the analysis of the texts.

3.2 A General Definition of Genre

Genre, as Kress (1993) has pointed out, is a problematic term because it 'comes with a considerable baggage of accumulated meaning' (p. 31). Indeed, most discussions of genre identify this as a problem from the outset, Swales (1990) being a good example, with his five-pronged effort to reach what he calls a working definition (p. 45). As already mentioned above, I am not going to revisit the many arguments and debates about 'genre', although these will inevitably appear in the course of my discussion, but I do need to establish some general principles.

The term 'genre', of course, is a French word for 'type', but, in English at least it has acquired meanings beyond those that are captured by the word 'type'. This is because it is used to conceptualize things rather than to describe them. How we conceptualize things as 'types' was the subject of the work of Vygotsky and Luria in Uzbekistan. Their work suggests that human concept formation involves classification and that classification depends on what we pay attention to, the specific aspects or features of things that are most salient to us. This, they argued, is strongly influenced by the experience, social, cultural, educational, of whoever is doing the classification. In other words, the decision to classify this way or that is contextually determined depending on what is most relevant to the classifier at the time.

Anything can be classified into categories whether they are 'made' things, things which 'exist' in nature, such as rocks or vegetation, or even concepts, as in mathematics. For example, objects can by classified according to use as in types of furniture (chairs, tables, cupboards and so on). However, they may also be divided up differently, as in types of chair (armchair, dining chair and so on), and then the question arises about whether a stool might fall into the chair category. We sit on a stool, but it doesn't have a back to it. Equally, is an armchair in the same category as a wooden dining chair? The point is that we classify things because we want to say something about these objects. Classification means!

The special thing about *genre* is that it tells us that we are talking about 'texts'; that is, things that are produced with the intention of communicating meaning. I discuss this later in the chapter. It also tells us that these texts are in some way classified into particular types. The term can be used to refer to the conceptual framing itself as in 'genre theory' or 'genre pedagogy', but when referring to actual texts genre is associated with identification, both of the text and of the participants in the textual practice. Thus we arrive at specific named genres: novels, plays, poems; jazz, classical, pop; interviews, lectures, debates. Each of these names implies a kind of generic coherence which works on the assumption that 'everyone' knows what they are. If I say that I am reading a poem, I assume that whoever I say this to will be able to conceptualize not only the physical object, the words on the page, the way in which it is displayed, but also the experience of a poem, the feeling you get when reading a poem, its sound, its shape. Furthermore, I assume they also recognize it by what it is not, how it differs from other, perhaps related, genres such as novels, letters or reports. Genres develop socially and culturally out of production in practice, and, just as cultures have 'thick' and 'thin' descriptions (Geertz, 1973), so do genres.

3.2.1 Genre as a Classifier

Genre naming is useful in that it offers a shorthand means of referring to textual products without having to go into long and complicated explanations. So when we say 'jazz' the term 'jazz' conjures up a particular type of music, possibly a particular kind of place with particular kinds of people. If we are simply intending to categorize music in general terms, as in newspaper listings pages, then 'jazz' may be adequate, particularly when contrasted with 'pop', 'rock' and 'classical' under the larger category 'music'. However, one person's 'jazz' maybe another person's 'hip-hop' which may, in turn, be another person's 'rap' and another person's 'grime'. New genre categories emerge in ever-decreasing circles of specialism as a result of what Berkenkotter and Huckin (1993) suggest is the 'tension between stability and change which lies at the heart of genre use and genre knowledge' (p. 501). The distinctions between these genres may be visible only to some and invisible to others.

There is a sense of stability that a genre name gives to a text which can be helpful in that it provides a reference point but at the same time it can be misleading because it implies a kind of fixed solidity, suggesting that a genre actually exists as an entity. However, they don't actually exist, they communicate. They communicate a chain of expectations based on the participants' knowledge and experience of what that kind of text is. For instance, we (those who have experienced poems before) have certain expectation of a poem which concern things like organization – it will be differently organized compared to a novel or a short story. There may be certain expectations to do with the form or rhyme and rhythm which might influence, perhaps, whether it should be read aloud or silently. There are also expectations of the content of a poem, the sorts of things poems are about. These expectations can be further categorized into poetry genres like 'sonnet' or 'haiku' or 'ode', each with its own particular characteristics, in much the same way as the music genres above could be subcategorized. In other words, genres allow us to predict the kind of experience the text will provide. The degree to which those expectations are met depends on the degree of 'fit'. In the example of 'hip-hop', 'rap' and 'grime', the latter genre emerged partly to represent the different word flow, compared to other 'urban' genres, but also as a marker of social and cultural difference of the participants. From this it can be seen that genre is as much about exclusion as it is about inclusion. It all depends on who we are (or want to be), what we pay attention to and how the genre used both promotes and reflects these aspects.

3.2.2 Genre as a Linguistic Concern

Above, I discussed how genres are used in classifying cultural products such as literature or music. In contrast to this, the primary concern in linguistic approaches to genre has been in relation to spoken communication, specifically 'everyday' communication. This does not mean that linguistics is not concerned with written communication, as it certainly is, but generally in relation to literacy pedagogy, as I discuss in the next section.

The use of genre as a linguistic category emerged from what can be considered the social turn in linguistics (e.g. Hymes, 1974 and Halliday, 1978) where, in contrast to Saussurian and Chomskian structuralism, which focused on descriptions of systems and how they operated at the structural level, their interest was in language as communication. Blommaert (2005) provides a useful overview of this development. Although Hymes and Halliday adopted different approaches, Hymes ethnographic and Halliday social semiotic, they were both essentially interested in the same thing: that is a social linguistic approach to communication. For Hymes, genre became the framing category of his model of communication, providing the expectations of how a speech event would proceed. However, it was Halliday's work that used genre as a fully functioning linguistic category, not only used as a point of reference, but linguistically analysed.

In Halliday and Hasan (1989) genre emerges out of everyday social interactions and becomes an established set of textual everyday exchanges such as the 'service encounter' (see also Ventola, 1983). In the same volume, Hasan develops the idea of 'contextual configuration', which comprises a series of linked utterances that together enact a recognisable communicative event. Genre, in this case, is the social framing of the 'contextual configuration'. It is what makes the participants make their text in the way they do. Hence, a service encounter (e.g. buying and selling something) proceeds in certain ways and, according to Hasan, the genre, in other words the 'contextual configuration', can predict certain 'obligatory elements' of the textual structure and sequence necessary for the communication to work within the given genre. Her model also allows for 'optional elements', which can be accommodated in the course of the interaction precisely because the genre has provided the contextual configuration for the particular communication. Thus in a service encounter the compulsory elements are the purchase and sale which, in turn, involve particular communicative activities (the request, the offer/provision, the payment), all of which are enacted, in this particular approach, linguistically. Provided these 'obligatory' elements are present, other (optional) elements can be fitted in and understood as 'belonging' simply because they are located in the familiar frame of 'service encounter'.

In this case, genre is a socially experienced, socially made and socially determined frame that provides a kind of identity to the text. It is the particular frame which makes the text recognisable as belonging to a particular 'type' of communicative event. The text is recognisable as belonging to its type because of the precise combination of its (linguistic) elements and the circumstances (context, purposes and participants) in which it is used (Halliday and Hasan, 1989). In the same way that I explained how genres promote particular expectations from cultural products such as books and music, so do these 'everyday' genres. The framing which the genre provides prepares the participants for the communicative event itself and certain 'verbal phrases' (or motifs, or gestures etc.) come to be associated with it and serve as a *key* to the communicative event that is being enacted. This prepares the participants for their participation. It puts everyone in the 'right' frame of mind. It gives a sense of either reassurance if the genre key is familiar or confusion if the key is unfamiliar.

For example, the English phrase 'Excuse me ...' implies a certain communicative goal (request or favour), which anticipates a sequence of communicative practices (utterances and actions) which are carried out within particular contexts that recur within the societies and cultures from which they emerge. Furthermore, the choice of phrase ('Excuse me ...') indicates particular social relations between the participants (distance, formality). For 'successful' communication there must be a collaboration between the participants whereby they engage mutually in the practices that the social conditions expect. Berkenkotter's (2001) observation that genres 'instantiate structures of social and institutional relations' (p. 4) captures this idea of collaboration and the maintenance of cohesiveness genres. However, 'successful' interaction depends on whether the participants share the same genre understandings. If they do, all will be well, at least with regard to the communicative configuration. If they do not, there is the possibility of communicative 'failure' or disruption. 'Everyday (spoken) genres', such as those discussed by Hasan, involve the kind of instant feedback that is only available in speech so that where disruption occurs it is possible to make instant repairs. In the case of the student essay the feedback is always delayed.

This approach to genre has been of fundamental relevance to how genre has been used in pedagogical contexts, but one aspect that has led to a sometimes overly deterministic use of genre is that it promotes the idea of containment – in other words, the idea that genres contain specific features. This is something that I pick up in the next section.

3.2.3 Genre as a Pedagogical Concern

Since the early 1980s, genre has been a central concern of literacy pedagogy in primary and secondary education, particularly in Australia and the UK. This grew out of the early work of Halliday et al. (e.g. 1964), the development of Social Semiotics (Halliday, 1978; Hodge and Kress, 1988) and Systemic Functional Linguistics (Halliday, 1985). In the UK genre became a key focus of research and was used as a methodological tool in exploring children's use of language across the curriculum (Gorman, 1986; Gorman et al., 1990; Beard, 2000) feeding into the design of the national curriculum (DES/Welsh Office, 1988). This research was informed by the developments taking place in Australia, where Halliday was based, where a genre approach to literacy pedagogy was emerging, based on the theoretical principles established by the new linguistics. In this approach genres are seen as social processes which shape texts in particular ways to achieve particular goals and the teaching of genre literacy a means to empower students by helping them understand the social, cultural and political contexts in which genres occur: 'Genre literacy should open students' educational and social options by giving them access to discourse of educational significance and social power' (Cope and Kalantzis, 1993, p. 14).

This work has been extremely influential in shaping the ways in which genre has been used in the teaching of writing, largely because it offers an approach which can focus on particular types of writing for particular purposes. In other words, as in 'communicative language teaching', where language 'functions' have provided a pedagogical framework, so have genres in writing pedagogy. The approach allows for clearly guided teaching which scaffolds students' learning in very effective ways. Martin (1993), for instance, whose work explores the language of particular genres, their thematic and structural organization, shows how this can develop students' own understandings of how texts are organized and how their linguistic features work within the different ideological frames in which written texts are produced. An effective literacy pedagogy, which can offer students access to powerful literacy domains, needs to take account of this, and, as Martin and Rothery (1993) point out, teachers need to develop their own genre awareness before this can happen.

However, there is a particular problem associated with drawing such a close link between the 'features' of genres and genre pedagogy, as I have already indicated earlier. This is that it can produce an approach to the teaching of writing that relies on the idea of genre solidarity. This leads, in turn, to the prevalence of schematic writing frames which promote the idea that genres are a little more than templates to be filled. This is a concern that Kress (1982, 1994) expressed, even at the time when genre pedagogy was in its early stages, when he wondered whether 'mastery of the conventions' was enough. He continues:

> Effective teaching of genres can make the individual into an efficiently intuitive, and unreflecting, user of the genre ... The genre will construct the world for its proficient user. Is that what we want? (p. 126)

This is obviously not what was originally envisaged but, as already discussed earlier in the book, it is an inevitable consequence of reinterpretation, particularly during times of educational upheaval where 'quick fixes' are often used as the simplest option and form takes precedence over content. Nowadays, much genre-based writing pedagogy is, unfortunately, focused on producing different genres rather than on producing different kinds of knowledge, which is, after all, the reason that genres develop in the first place.

Examples of this kind of approach to genre in the teaching of writing are very common in literacy work at university, certainly in the UK, which is the context in which this discussion is located. Students on English for Academic Purposes (EAP) courses learn how to produce the genres associated with specific types of academic writing following the kind of staged processes inspired by Martin's work above. In this case, the focus is often on what he called 'small genres' (1993, p. 121), which combine to produce big or 'macro genres', such as a student essay or research paper. It is easy to see how this has come about. Students themselves are keen to have models to emulate for all the reasons of uncertainty and anxiety discussed in the last two chapters.

3.2.4 Genre at University

Before moving on to set out my own approach to genre, I want to refer to some of the other work on genre in the university context, most notably that in the North American context, specifically the USA. As already mentioned, I do not mean to provide an elaborate discussion of this, but want to acknowledge briefly some work with which this book has not been majorly involved but which offers some parallels to the present discussion.

In the USA, with its long-established college composition tradition, genre has been a central theme in studies in academic writing, most notably, and relevant to my work, in Bazerman (1988), whose work explores the ways in which disciplinary practices give rise to specific genres which, in turn, produce different ways of knowing. His focus on 'writing choices' has particular resonance in my work. However, with specific reference to student writing, Miller's (1984) article brought genre squarely into the domain of, as she called it, of 'rhetorical education' (1984, p. 165). Following on from this and reflecting her 'Genre as Social Action' approach are Berkenkotter and Huckin (1993). Drawing on Activity Theory (Engeström, e.g. 1999), their sociocognitive perspective offers a rich and encompassing approach to understandings of genre which shows how genre practices are enacted in the texts that are produced within specific disciplinary communities. Russell (1997) and Russell and Yañez (2003) also draw on activity theory in exploring genre and, like Martin above, despite the difference in theoretical and methodological perspectives, their work is also concerned with ideals of social justice and access. Russell discusses how genre can be used to explore why people write the things they write in the ways they write them. His approach, which uses a highly detailed and complex framework, aims to enable students (and teachers) to understand how genres relate to the activities that they occur in, or rather enact, and to negotiate those activities with the relevant genres.

Another important researcher in genre is Devitt (2004), whose comprehensive study of genre in both academic and non academic contexts proposes a pedagogy which, like Cope and Kalantzis above, raises genre awareness and expands students' genre repertoires. Her approach includes teaching students to understand how genres have developed, how they are formed and why they are used so as to empower them 'to resist those who try to dictate a genre too rigidly' (p. 212).

Whilst I have not particularly drawn on the above work in this book, it is important to note that despite the different theoretical lenses that researchers bring to bear on their analyses, similar issues tend to arise. Other genre researchers working in educational fields have studied genre in the context of professional textual products (e.g. Bhatia, 1993) or academic writing (e.g. Swales, 1990 or Hyland, 2000). They also argue, among other things, that genre awareness is crucial in understanding and participating in professional and disciplinary discourse communities and their work has contributed particularly to second language academic writing (e.g. Hyland, 2004). This work considers genre as a category which can subsume other analytical categories to provide a practical 'thicker description' (Bhatia, 1993) of language in use than can discourse analysis alone.

> In order to move towards a thicker description, discourse analysis needs a model which is rich in socio-cultural, institutional and organisational explanation, relevant and useful to language teachers and applied linguists rather than to grammatical theorists, and discriminating enough to highlight variation rather than uniformity in functional language use … Also, such a model needs to be more towards the specific end of the continuum than the general end, because in language teaching for specific purposes, it is more realistic, and often desirable, to find pedagogically useful form–function correlations within, rather than across, specific genres. (Bhatia, 1993, p. 11)

However, this attempt to find correlations between linguistic and discourse organization can, as Bhatia himself points out, lead to an over-prescribed approach to genre pedagogy. This kind of prescriptive approach was demonstrated by a draft of a proposed resource book on the 'grammar of genres' that I was once asked to review. In that case, while the idea was very interesting, it implied that genre was 'pattern imposing' (Hart, 1986, p. 88, cited in Bhatia, 1993, p. 40), thus illustrating how easy it is to fall into the 'template' problem that I referred to earlier.

I realize that in the above discussion, the issue of *discourse* as a category has arisen and needs to be clarified as it can be understood in different and often confusing ways.

3.3 Genre and Discourse

Theories concerning genre, particularly those I have just referred to above, interweave the concept of *discourse* as an integral part of genre discussion. For instance, Hyland's (2000) book foregrounds discourse as the main focus of attention while at the same time contextualizing this theme in genre settings and at times his discussion shifts almost seamlessly from one to the other. This is understandable if we understand, as I do, genres and discourses to emerge from social-cultural practices.

Both genres and discourses provide identity to a text – they locate the text as being of a particular type (genre) within a particular community (discourse). Some genres give rise to certain discourses. For instance, the textbook, as discussed in Hyland, is a genre which, he argues, uses a pedagogic discourse typified by the relative incidence of certain linguistic resources which function at a meta-discursive level when compared to other professional academic genres. Examples include textual metadiscourse such as logical connectives and interpersonal metadiscourse such as hedges markers (p. 111).

However, there are two main points that need to be clarified about discourse for the purposes of my discussion. First of all, the term discourse needs to be teased out. On the one hand is the use associated with linguistic pragmatics (e.g. Brown and Yule, 1983), where discourse is taken to mean 'language in use', the utterances themselves as linguistic entities. On the other hand is the use associated with ideological position, power and identity and although it is associated with philosophy and sociology (e.g. Foucault, 1972) it has come to be inextricably linked to theories of communication connected with, for instance, social semiotics, literacies and social linguistics (e.g. Hodge and Kress, 1988; Gee, 1999; Blommaert, 2005).

Hyland's 'discourse' as in 'disciplinary discourses' refers essentially to the linguistic features of the textual productions. However, his discussion also focuses on how these features mark out (academic) texts and their writers as belonging to and identifiable with particular social groups; specifically disciplinary communities and student–teacher (textbook writer) hierarchies. His conclusion that textbook writers construct their student readers as novices derives from an analysis of the 'language as used', including the organization and metadiscoursal features. This places his work between these two approaches to discourse.

Secondly, and in relation to the above, a particular genre does not *necessarily* give rise to a particular discourse as is suggested in, for instance, Hyland above. A play (as a genre) may have examples of a range of discourses depending on the circumstance enacted. Equally a genre such as a play may contain numerous micro-genres such as jokes, disagreements, greetings and these genres in their turn may also be positioned ideologically by their discourses (sexist jokes, ethnographic writing, mother's day greetings) and so on.

My choice in handling this terminological issue is to give each version of discourse a different referent. I will retain *discourse* for the ideological meaning while for the linguistic (or other modes) meaning I will use the term *textual materials*. This is because my analytical framework, as will be seen later, draws on a frame of reference which views communication as a cycle involving textual design, production and distribution (Kress and Van Leeuwen, 2001).

This now brings me to my own approach to genre, which I set out in the next section. It will become apparent that my use of genre is different from those mentioned above. This is not because I disagree with those approaches, which have, in many ways, provided a strong underpinning to my own thinking. Their work, for instance, has enhanced understanding about the social functions of written texts and the ways in which they work within different discourse communities. It has also highlighted the importance of understanding the structures and functions of genres in establishing, maintaining and challenging power through literacy practices. All these issues play a fundamental role in my discussion, but my analysis is differently focused. In my work, I do not use genre as a descriptive or even explanatory category in understanding how texts are made. Furthermore, although I refer to the ways in which certain genres promote certain material choices, I do not consider those choices as typifying a given genre in a descriptive sense. This is because my interest is not so much in genre as a linguistic category or as a pedagogical goal, but rather in genre as a social semiotic resource that can be used as a pedagogical resource in disciplinary study.

3.4 Genre as a Social Semiotic Resource

In this section I start my explanation of how I am using genre before moving on to discussing my analytical framework in the next chapter, followed by discussions of the students' work.

In a very general sense, I am using *genre* as a category which identifies the shape of a text, or better the framing of a text. It identifies what kind of text it is, that is what to expect from it, and at the same time, it shapes that identity. By *text* I mean that which is made in the process of communication, the material or, as Kress says, the 'stuff' of communication (2003, p. 47). It is the *semiotic product* of the interaction between the participants in a given communicative event. It has meaning, or rather meaning potential (Halliday, e.g. 1978). If it did not have meaning potential it would not be a relevant aspect of communication because it would have nothing to do. So now we can say that *genre* is a term which identifies texts as belonging to a particular type. This definition corresponds quite closely to the one with which I began Section 3.2 above.

The idea of conceiving of genre as a social semiotic resource derives from an understanding of communication as a process involving choices. By this I mean that the participants involved in any communicative event make choices about how best to express their meaning. In multimodal terms this is expressed as 'design'. Part of the design process involves the choice (or recognition) of the generic framing of the communication. This is determined by the circumstances and the social-cultural norms associated with the situation. This corresponds to Malinowski's (1923) context of situation, developed by Halliday into a functional theory of communication. I develop this idea below but it is important to mention it now as it helps to explain why I want to consider genre as a semiotic resource rather than an analytic category used for descriptive and explanatory purposes.

Derrida (1980), writing about the 'law of genres', complains that:

As soon as the word 'genre' is sounded, as soon as it is heard, as soon as one attempts to conceive it, a limit is drawn. And when a limit is established, norms and interdictions are not far behind: 'Do' or 'Do not' says 'genre'. (p. 221)

Of course, Derrida was not complaining about genre as a concept as such, but rather about the way in which genre theory had, at that time, developed into a kind of straightjacket whereby certain rules associated with certain genres had to be obeyed in order for something to be classified as belonging to a particular genre. Similar criticisms had been made earlier by Medvedev in challenging the dominance of the Formalist approach to literary analysis (in Titunik, 1986, p. 183).

While I do not subscribe to a 'straightjacket' approach to genre, what interests me about Derrida's remark is that he refers to genre as doing (or not doing) something. By saying 'do this' but not 'do that' it indicates what resources can be chosen and hence how meanings can be produced. This is how I want to think about genre. A genre does things. It has an effect. It 'manages' textual production according to the particular 'need' in hand. This is because, I argue, different genres have different affordances (Gibson, 1979, see below). In other words, just as Kress and Van Leeuwen (2001) show that modes and media are chosen for their particular affordances, I suggest that the same is true of genre. Genres are chosen because they frame a text in particular ways that both shape and are shaped by that frame and this is what identifies a particular genre. For instance, in the case of a haiku poem the limitation of syllable number and thematic constraints makes the poet, that is the producer of the text, do things which she would do differently were it a sonnet, or, indeed, were it a less closely related genre such as a letter. Whichever genre is chosen, a haiku, a sonnet or a letter, it has an effect in terms of the making of the text, design and production choices and the way in which that text is understood via interpersonal impacts. I exemplify this more fully below in relation to the choices made in the communication of certain information.

So far the terms of reference that I have used have relied on analogy for their clarification. In order to deal with this problem I use idea of *affordance*, which underpins my approach.

3.4.1 About Affordance

The term 'affordance' is one which is increasingly referred to in a range of disciplinary fields, as any internet search will demonstrate. The term was used by Gibson (1979, p. 127) in developing an ecological approach to visual perception which locates perception in the realm of the 'meaningful environment', as opposed to simply the 'physical environment'. For Gibson, the physical environment refers to things as they are – their material, their shape and so on – while the meaningful environment refers to how we perceive what things can do or provide. Moreover, the potentials we perceive depend also on our own particular circumstances, including physical conditions, such as size, temporary conditions, such as need for shelter from the rain, or personal conditions, such as purpose or interests. In other words, he suggests that things afford particular meanings as the result of the inter-action between their physical attributes and what we perceive those 'things' to mean. From a physical perspective, a tree, for instance, is just what it is – a tree with particular physical properties: leaves, branches, roots etc. However, a tree can be shelter, food, a play area, a vantage point, a hiding place, a landmark and so on, depending on how we perceive those physical properties in terms of what they mean to us at any given moment.

> [Objects] can all be said to have properties or qualities: color, texture, composition, size, shape and feature of shape, mass elasticity, rigidity, and mobility. Orthodox psychology asserts that *we perceive these objects insofar as we discriminate their properties or qualities*. Psychologists carry out elegant experiments in the laboratory to find out how and how well these qualities are discriminated. The psychologists assume that objects are *composed* of their qualities. But I now suggest that what we perceive when we look at objects are their affordances, not their qualities. We can discriminate the dimensions of difference if required to do so in an experiment, but what the object affords us is what we normally pay attention to. The special combination of qualities into which an object can be analyzed is ordinarily not noticed. (Gibson, 1979, p. 134)

Objects are, according to Gibson, perceived more by what they can do than by what they are composed of – in other words, their potentials. And importantly it is the perceived or observed or understood potential that is relevant rather than the inherent properties. The fact that a ball is round is not the point, rather that its roundness (among other things) allows it to do the things it is best able to do – roll, spin, bounce etc. Gibson describes this as the -ableness (or not-ableness) of things relative to the 'animal' that perceives them.

> If a terrestrial surface is nearly horizontal (instead of slanted), nearly flat (instead of convex or concave) and sufficiently extended (relative to the size of the animal) and its substance is rigid (relative to the weight of the animal) then the surface *affords* support ... It is therefore stand-on-able, permitting an upright posture for quadrupeds and bipeds. It is therefore walk-on-able. It is not sink-into-able like a surface of water ... (ibid, p. 127).

My argument is that genres can be understood in a similar way. Genres are chosen because they afford particular communicative possibilities for a given set of circumstances. Its specific communicative '-ableness' results from the semiotic resources that are available to the genre and the affordances of those resources themselves. We choose the genre because of what it does, or allows us to do, rather than what it consists of. However, just as with the tree or the ball examples above, what it consists of is precisely what lets us do the 'thing' we want to do. In other words, the relationship between genres and the resources it 'makes' us use (or not use) is one of affordance.

Affordance is a powerful conceptual tool in considering communication because it encapsulates possibility, not just in what can be done but also in what can be understood and experienced and how. It is a dynamic concept because it refers also to the interaction between environment, participants, intentions and available resources, as I explain in the next section.

3.4.2 A Multimodal Perspective

The first thing that might be asked is the question of why I use a multi-modal perspective when it is written work that I am discussing. The answer is quite simple. It is because the affordances of the genres my students chose in reproducing their essays meant that a different range of resources, that is different modes, different 'grammars', different organizational structures and so on, were available to them.

The term multimodal as understood by Kress and Van Leeuwen (2001) refers to the semiotic resources that are used in communicative activity. It is a development of the social semiotic framework that Halliday (1978) proposed and which was further developed in Hodge and Kress (1988). In this framework, semiotic resources are the elements which combine to make the communication. In my approach, these can be divided into four categories: *genres*, which establish the 'shape' of the communication as already discussed above and which can be considered as the contextual or framing resource; *modes*, which refer to the manner in which the communication is articulated (speech, writing, schema, gesture, etc.); *textual materials* (grammar, lexis, choreographic moves, etc.) with which the mode is articulated; and finally *media*, which are the channels used in the dissemination (distribution) of the text such as 'the internet', the submitted 'paper with writing on it' and the other things that occur around this process as I displayed in Figure 2.1 in Chapter 2.

From a social semiotic perspective, the process of communication, that is the exchange of meanings between participants, involves a process of transformation. This transformation is brought about by the interactions between the participants concerned in the communication, the resources with which they choose to articulate their meanings and the ways those 'meanings' are interpreted, or, as I suggest in Figure 2.1, redesigned.

Let me take as an example the communication of statistical information. One would need to take into account what kind of information it was (e.g. proportions, comparisons, fluctuations etc.) in choosing the most apt means with which to communicate the information. So, for the purposes of illustration, let us say that the statistical information concerns the proportion of males to females in a given situation – say teaching.

The information can be communicated in a variety of different ways using different semiotic resources: verbal, numerical, figurative, oral, visual, with objects or actions, and so on. These resources themselves draw on other resources which combine to produce particular effects. Verbal communication (speech and writing) uses syntactic structures (e.g. transitivity and mood, directness and indirectness), lexis (e.g. metaphor, connotation etc.), prosody (e.g. voice pitch, intonation, punctuation) and textual organization (e.g. foregrounding and backgrounding, sequencing etc.). Figurative (visual) communication might draw on colour, spatial arrangement or texture. The choice of which of these resources to use are determined by the genre which is determined by the circumstances of the moment.

A statistician could be writing a government report or an academic article and state that '60 per cent of teachers are women' (leaving the inference that 40 per cent are male). Or, in a pub argument, the same statistician could say 'sixty per cent of teachers ARE women', using her voice to stress the word 'are' to indicate disagreement. In a report or a lecture she could choose a diagram, a histogram for example, which employs a variety of representational modes (numbers, words, colours, graphics) arranged in a particular spatial order and which combined can produce a particular set of meanings.

In figure 3.1, for instance, the colours chosen intend to communicate special (cultural) meaning: pink (represented here as pale grey) for girls and blue (represented here as dark grey) for boys in certain cultural settings.

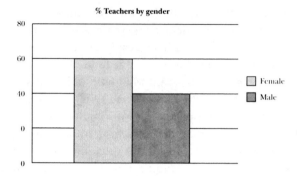

FIGURE 3.1

Or she could choose to reverse the colours to subvert the cultural meanings associated with them.

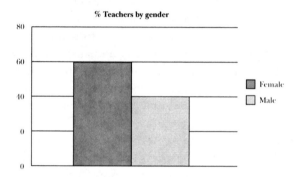

FIGURE 3.2

She might choose a different diagrammatic genre with a different spatial arrangement – say a pie chart without numerical representation. This is because the specific topological arrangement represents proportion more effectively in the pie chart than it does in the vertical arrangement of the histogram.

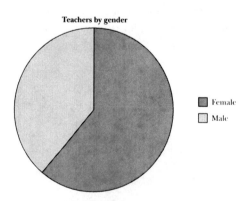

FIGURE 3.3

In each case different resources are used to communicate the same piece of information. However, in each case the choice of resources (genres, modes, textual materials and media) acts on the information itself and influences what it communicates and how. This corresponds to Kress and Van Leeuwen's (2001) concept of 'transduction', which refers to the semiotic transformations that occur when shifting from one mode to another.

Why the producer of the text chooses this or that genre or mode, these or those textual materials and this or that medium depends on what she considers to be most apt to the communicative event. This depends on the circumstances, including the purposes, the motivations and expectations of the participants as well as the availability of resources themselves. If the tools for inscription (pens, sticks, keyboards) are not available, then you do not produce pie charts of pieces of writing. If you have lost your voice, you can't have much of a conversation in the pub. Furthermore, those involved in the communication need to be 'ready' to understand the intended meaning. They need to know, for instance, that voice pitch or force indicates emphasis or that using blue to represent women is a subversion. These are not necessarily universally shared – different languages use tone for different purposes, different cultures value gender differently and may not use colour associatively in this way. An 'unready' participant may make different interpretations based on his own knowledge background (culture, history, environment, etc.).

In the final part of this section, I offer a view of communication which reflects this flow-like process. It combines the 'interactions' chart (Figure 2.1) that I introduced in Chapter 2 with the multimodal perspective I have provided here.

3.4.3 Communicative Flow

By using the term *communicative flow* I want to emphasize the way in which meanings are made and remade in the process of interaction. As discussed above, communication involves a particular circumstance or set of circumstances which lead to the need to communicate some kind of information (message) to someone for some reason or other. In order to do that the 'producer as designer' makes certain choices about what materials to use in the making of the message based on what she believes will express the intended meaning in the most appropriate or relevant way within the circumstances.

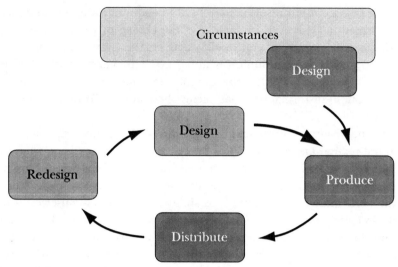

FIGURE 3.4

Figure 3.4 schematizes this process as a kind of cycle of making and remaking as follows. The process involves *design*, whereby the most apt (and available) resources are chosen for their affordances in *producing* the 'text'. The resources comprise the genres and the modes, media and textual materials afforded by the genre and the 'text' is whatever is produced with those resources. In face-to-face communication, production and distribution are simultaneous, but in 'remote' communicative activity, where the participants are separated by time, this aspect is delayed, as in writing or visual art. In this model, which emphasizes mutuality in communicative activity, the process of distribution involves interpretation, what I am calling *redesign*, and this depends on interactant's own expectations, interests and frames of reference. The process involves a constant round of making and remaking in a flow of social semiotic activity.

The interactions suggested in Figure 3.4 do not need to correspond in terms of resources selected one to the other. In the genre framing of a 'request', a spoken utterance can be responded to with an action which in turn could be responded to with another action or a gesture or a spoken utterance or nothing at all. Each of these choices carries meaning and is available for interpretive remaking by whoever is involved, whether co-present or not, in the communicative event.

3.5 Conclusion

This chapter has presented the theoretical perspectives which have informed how I have examined the students' work. The approach to genre that I am suggesting here, using the concept of affordance and the frames of reference provided by multimodal research, offers the chance to focus on what genres allow rather than what genres are allowed. In other words, it shifts the emphasis towards choice rather than obligation by considering the affordances of genres. As my data, the student work, reveals, the genre you choose has a profound effect on the whole process of text production, including on the producer, not to mention the 'readers' of those texts.

The next chapter explains the framework with which I analyse the texts. As the purpose is to understand the affordances of the genres used by the students, including the essays, I needed to develop a methodology that would enable me to unpack the data. For this I use the concept of *orientation*, which I referred to briefly earlier on in this chapter and which allows the possibility of separating out the different areas of change that emerged in both the social and the material dimensions.

Chapter 4

A Framework for Analysis

We do not know what we will find, and what we will be led to say by what we find. Although we need issues, assumptions, methods, hypotheses to drive our discovery process, we must be ready to accept the worlds revealed to us in our attempt to come to terms with what we discover. Otherwise, we may throw away our most promising stories. (Bazerman, 1988, p. 331)

4.1 Introduction

In his book *Shaping Written Knowledge*, from which I have taken the above extract, Bazerman encapsulates one of the core problems of writing about research. In the case of this book, as already mentioned, I did not set out to undertake a research study and therefore had no particular plan to investigate my students' work other than in the normal process of module assessment. However, being presented with such rich material, I felt that it deserved a much deeper analysis than routine assessment can provide. In fact, I was excited by what the students had done, realizing that the activity had enabled them to work with the disciplinary material in ways which not only showed the kind of 'mastery' that I referred to in Chapter 2, but something more interesting, something that brought the material closer to experience. In shifting genre, they had shifted from the 'academic' to the 'everyday', from the 'vertical' to the 'horizontal' (Bernstein, 2000), but without making it less academically valid.

This is borne out by the following comment from a lecturer whose assigned essay one of the students had regenred: '*it was both academically erudite and I think that it was simply entertaining*'. Clearly, recontextualizing the 'academic' into the 'everyday' had enabled the students to engage with their work in ways which did not diminish the intellectual quality of the ideas represented. Furthermore, the 'entertaining' dimension referred to raised other questions about how disciplinary knowledge is represented and how it is experienced in the process of that representation. In other words, how do the material dimensions (representation) interact with the social dimensions (agency and identity)? In order to do this I needed to develop a framework for analysis which would enable me to combine these aspects so as to explore what the regenring process revealed about knowledge, representation and learning.

The initial process with which I analysed the data involved interaction between my own reading of what the students wrote and their comments on what they had written, as discussed in Chapter 1. The interviews helped me particularly in exploring the new opportunities the regenring had given the students and the different experience they had in doing the work. Taking the interviews and my gradually developing analyses of the work together, certain themes began to emerge: who you are as a writer, what it is like being a student working with disciplinary material, how genres promote particular ways of telling the story, how they push you to follow certain paths and make you use particular 'types' of language.

This chapter, then, serves as a link between the theoretical considerations of the previous chapter and the analysis of the data itself in Chapters 5, 6 and 7. I introduce my analytical framework, using the concept of orientation as a means for identifying and talking about the different effects of genre choice in relation to both the essay and its regenred counterpart. I then explain the terms of reference used within the framework.

4.2 The Orientation of Genres

The usefulness of *orientation* as an analytical category emerged from my reading of Volosinov (1929/1986). As many people have pointed out (Hodge and Kress, 1988; Berkenkotter and Huckin, 1993; Lillis, 2001) the (re)discovery of Volosinov, Bakhtin and Medvedev revitalized linguistic debate because it offered interesting perspectives on many of the issues that were emerging out of social linguistics (as in Hymes) and social semiotics and functional linguistics (as in Halliday). Of particular relevance with regard to my understanding of orientation is their view that language (Volosinov) and genres (Medvedev and Bakhtin) need to be considered from a dual perspective, that is, the contextual and the thematic. This is because they believed that language is a social activity and not merely a system of structures, as was the dominant view of the day (e.g. Saussure).

The actual reality of language-speech is not the abstract system of linguistic forms, not the isolated monologic utterance, and not the psycho physiological act of its implementation, but the social event of verbal interaction implemented in an utterance or utterances. (Volosinov, 1929/1986, p. 94)

I have adopted the idea of orientation in relation to genres because, as I have already explained, genres mediate between the social and the material in the process of communication and in so doing 'orient' towards doing things in particular ways. However, I also want to introduce two further orientations: *discursive orientation*, which allows a focus on the issue of agency, and *semiotic orientation*, which considers representation. Figure 4.1 offers a schematic representation of the framework.

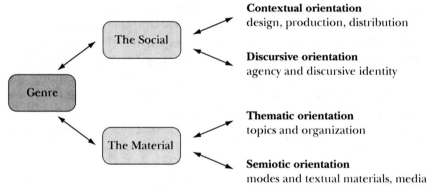

Contextual orientation
design, production, distribution

Discursive orientation
agency and discursive identity

Thematic orientation
topics and organization

Semiotic orientation
modes and textual materials, media

FIGURE 4.1

The Genre orients backwards and forwards between the social and the material, then the contextual and discursive and the thematic and semiotic. There is, in this framework, a reciprocal relationship between the different orientations.

4.2.1 Contextual Orientation

The theorization of 'language-speech' as 'social event' in Volosinov, above, is important because it identifies communication as intrinsically connected to what he calls 'concrete situations'.

The forms this connection takes are different and different factors in a situation may, in association with this or that form, take on different meanings ... Verbal communication can never be understood and explained outside of this connection with a concrete situation. (ibid, p. 95)

This relationship is fundamental to a social understanding of genre as it makes the crucial link between the text and the context for which it is produced, a view which has, of course, become common currency in much of the recent literature on genre, literacy and communication. It ties in strongly with the idea of contextual configuration (Halliday and Hasan, 1989) discussed in Chapter 3, where genres emerge in order to achieve specific social interactions. And because genres develop in response to particular contexts, they inevitably orient towards those contexts. For example, the genre 'joke' sets up a whole range of expectations based on what we understand a joke to be and do and how. Similarly, a student essay, as was seen in Chapter 2, orients us towards particular behaviours, interactions and experiences.

Kress (e.g. 1993) also refers to this, arguing that genres act as signifiers of social relations. In his approach he focuses 'not on the tasks being performed by or with the text but rather on the structural features of the specific social occasion in which the text has been produced' (p. 33). These social-cultural circumstances, or contexts, situate a communicative event within a particular environment or circumstance which, in turn, involves (or gives rise to) a particular set of interpersonal relationships. It refers to one side of the 'situatedness' that Barton et al. (2000) are concerned with and involves the activity in producing the text for which I use the multimodal terms of reference already discussed: *design, production* and *distribution*. However, I also want to refer to the other side, that is, the issue of agency, which emerged as a particularly strong aspect during the interviews.

4.2.2 Discursive Orientation

In the most simple way that I can, I want to suggest that genres configure the participants as being a particular kind of participant. In the case of the student essay genre, as discussed in Chapter 2, the student is oriented towards a particular discursive identity which derives from the way in which the institutional interactions frame the experience. Blommaert (2005) argues that 'identities are constructed in practices that *produce, enact*, or *perform* [sic] identity – identity is identification, an outcome of socially conditioned semiotic work' (p. 205). However, my point is that discursive identity with regard to genre, as a semiotic resource, is not so much an outcome but rather a condition. The genre, I suggest, orients one towards a particular *discursive identity*. This then links closely to the issue of *agency* in the discussion of student writing and is a theme I discuss specifically in Chapter 5 but which also features in all my analytical chapters.

4.2.3 Thematic Orientation

Thematic orientation, as proposed by Medvedev, concerns the elements that combine to associate a particular text with a particular genre. Pomorska (1978, p. 274) explains it as follows. 'The question posed now, regarding works of literature, was not "What is it about?" or "Why and how did it appear?" but "How is it made?"' Of course, here the focus is not on production in terms of semiotic resources as I am using that concept, but rather on narrative elements which typify a given literary genre. For instance, Propp (1978) writing in 1928, developed a system for analysing fairy tales which identified structural and compositional features that, he argued, typified this genre. These features were broken down into 'functions of the actors', of which he identified thirty-one in all, and 'constituents' or 'elements', of which he somewhat oddly suggested there were about one hundred and fifty. Examples of functions, according to Propp's approach, include things like 'dispatch', 'departure', meeting obstacles or overcoming adversity. Constituent examples include things like 'the hut in the woods', food and drink, a talisman and so on.

If we ignore the overly categorical and deterministic perspective that Propp offers with his attention to counting and regulation, this can be useful if by turning it away from description of what genres 'contain' to what genres do. As Martin (1993) points out, genres 'achieve their social purpose' (p. 121) by structuring information in the particular ways that have developed in expressing particular kinds of meaning. So in this case, there is a link between the thematic features and the purposes for which they came about in that particular way. This parallels Halliday and Hasan's (1989) discussion on contextual configuration whereby the thematic structure of a text identifies it as belong to a particular genre. Particular conversational gambits typify particular social encounters (or genres) which both reflect and promote the shape of the interaction.

Of course, this kind of approach is rightly criticized for its tendency towards a mechanical representation of genre as comprising a series of components assembled to produce a particular type of text. This was precisely the criticism that Medvedev directed at the Formalists (Titunik, 1986, p. 183) and is a criticism that can be made about genre as a pedagogical goal, particularly, as already discussed, when the idea of 'features' of a genre (i.e. what it looks like) is taken as the sole approach to the shaping of texts. Nevertheless, despite these reservations, there is much to be learned from considering the thematic features of genre particularly from the perspective of their semiotic affordances. In my own study, the thematic features of the genres used (essays, plays, radio phone-in, children's expository text) push the writers into constructing their meanings in certain ways, similarly to how the elements identified by Propp promote particular ways of meaning making in fairy tales.

For example, thematic features of an essay include 'introduction, development, conclusion' structure, which enforces a particular way of shaping the information being expressed. To achieve this kind of thematic development, it is necessary to provide paragraphs and sentences which further shape the meaning. There are particular 'functions', to use Propp's term, such as 'naming the topic', 'ascertaining the context and relevance', 'linking to evidence' and so on, and certain 'elements' such as references to other writers, use of particular terms, grammatical choices that typify the genre. Each phase has particular meaning potential within its generic frame and needs the participants to be familiar with those meanings if the genre is to succeed in being the most apt choice for the job in hand.

4.2.4 Semiotic Orientation

It may seem as if the previous orientations are all semiotic, and in fact, of course, they are if we understand genre itself to be a semiotic resource. However, I want to use the term here in order to highlight the materiality of genres. I will develop this idea in more detail below when discussing my terms of reference but for the moment I want to say that genres orient not only towards particular contexts or thematic organization or discursive identity but they also orient towards particular ways of meaning with particular materials, modes and media. Semiotic orientation concerns the material resources made available by genre itself; the materials with which the communication is produced; that is *resources* such as grammar and vocabulary (*textual materials*), or speech, writing and actions (*modes*), or paper, ink, vocal chords (*media*).

Media

This aspect of textual production has only a marginal relevance to the present study as the work I am examining is all produced with the same media: type print, paper, digital print, computer screen, vocal chords. From this it should be clear that I am adopting Kress and Van Leeuwen's definition of media as the 'equipments' used in the distribution of the work all of which have their own particular affordances and orient us towards particular kinds of production strategies. For instance, digital writing affords certain editorial strategies such as moving chunks of text around in ways that paper and pen media cannot achieve without the help of scissors, sellotape or glue. In my student productions, the work was produced on computers and then printed on to paper apart from one student who wrote his original essay by hand using pen and paper.

Mode

The simplest way of clarifying the category of mode is to use it to refer to what might be called the communicative channel. In other words, I want mode to refer to speech, writing, actions, gestures and so on in so far as they are used in communicating meaning. To clarify, it is helpful to return to the 'statistical information' I referred to in Chapter 3. In that case the genre (e.g. pub discussion, pie chart, formal report) insisted on certain modes of communication (spoken, visual, written) in its production. These modes in turn needed/allowed for certain textual materials (particular phonological elements, colours and shapes, grammatical selections).

Talking about mode is, as I have already mentioned, potentially problematic in my study because all the productions under analysis were produced with the single mode of writing. However, the different genres chosen by the students used modes other than writing as scripted speech and in some cases described gestures, facial expressions or props such as furniture or spatial layout as in places. I discuss this fully in Chapter 6. This importation into writing of other modes is a major focus of Volosinov (1929/1986) and Bakhtin (1986).

Bakhtin's framing of the issue as the 'problem' of speech genres relates directly to literary textual analysis, though of course much of his discussion revolves around the interactions involved in communication per se. In developing his argument, Bakhtin's use of the term 'genre' proposes, along with Volosinov's approach, that genres are concerned with the social purposes of what he calls 'the utterance' which is more or less equivalent to our notions of 'text' – the 'stuff' (Kress, 2003) of communication. Bakhtin distinguished between what he called 'secondary (complex) speech genres' and what he called 'primary (simple) genres'. The latter corresponds to Volosinov's 'behaviour genres', the everyday utterances of social interactions and routines, that is, spoken language, while the former could be considered to refer to written language as experienced through literature. For Bakhtin primary genres are the unmediated or direct (spoken) utterances that occur in everyday communication while secondary genres import these 'everyday' genres in order to create what he calls a complex of speech genres which are mediated by the producer into a unified (written) utterance.

> Secondary (complex) speech genres – novels, dramas, all kinds of scientific research, major genres of commentary, and so forth – arise in more complex and highly developed and organized cultural communication (primarily written) that is artistic, scientific, socio-political, and so on. During the process of their formation, they absorb and digest various primary (simple) genres that have taken from in unmediated speech communion. These primary genres are altered and assume a special character when they enter into complex ones. They lose their immediate relation to actual reality and to the real utterances of others. (1986, p. 62)

For Bakhtin the 'simple' versus 'complex' dichotomy is not one of 'linguistic' simplicity versus 'linguistic' complexity, but rather one of communicative immediacy (spokenness) versus communicative reflexivity (writtenness). In literature, as in other written genres, the utterance is produced by the author of the writing, at least one step removed from the 'everyday' utterances of social interaction.

> For example, rejoinders of everyday dialogue of letters found in a novel retain their form and their everyday significance only on the plane of the novel's content. They enter into actual reality only via the novel as a whole, that is, as a literary–artistic event and not as everyday life. The novel as a whole is an utterance just as rejoinders in everyday dialogue or private letters are (they do have a common nature), but unlike these, the novel is a secondary (complex) utterance. (Bakhtin, 1986, p. 62)

This is closely linked to Volosinov's discussions on what he calls 'reported speech' which has a particular resonance with my own discussions and corresponds to a large extent with Bakhtin's concept of monologic utterance, that of the author and objectified or represented utterance, that of the 'others'. By reported speech, Volosinov is talking about authorial representations of the 'speech' of others in literary and other 'authored' texts. 'Reported speech is speech within speech, utterance within utterance and at the same time also *speech about speech and utterance about utterance* [sic]' (Volosinov, 1929/1986, p. 115). He classifies his conception of reported speech into what he calls indirect or direct discourse with shades (quasi indirect and quasi direct) of reportedness. This conceptualization of 'discourse' differs, as I understand it, from both the linguistic use of the term (e.g. Brown and Yule, 1983) and the ideological use (e.g. Foucault, e.g. 1972). It corresponds more closely to how we today consider 'direct speech', the speech of others as uttered in its own right, versus 'indirect speech', the speech of others as synthesized, incorporated into the 'speech' of the author.

In literary texts Bakhtin's 'rejoinders' or 'letters', that is 'primary speech genres', and Volosinov's 'reported speech' form an intricate network that are combined by the author into the production of a (written) text or 'secondary speech genre' whereby both the author's speech and the reported speech

> take shape only in their interrelation, and not on their own, the one apart from the other. The reported speech and the reporting context are but the terms of a dynamic interrelationship. This dynamism reflects the dynamism of social interorientation in verbal ideological communication. (Volosinov, 1929/1986, p. 119)

I illustrate this below with an example from Assif's work. To remind you, Assif chose to regenre an economics essay as a radio debate and phone-in.

Extract 4.1 JMK = John Maynard Keynes, MF = Milton Friedman)

JMK: My alternative theory, and also more acceptable theory ...

MF: Acceptable? By who?

[MF jumps up]

JMK: By the majority!

[JMK looks sharply at MF]

Host: OK chaps, can we let JMK finish his presentation. You can debate your differences during the question and answer session with our listeners in part two of tonight's show.

This extract is an example of what Volosinov considers to be 'reported speech' in the sense that the 'speech' sits inside the author's context. The author has imported the 'speech of others' in the making of his own utterance, which is the production as a whole. In this example, the reported speech is represented as 'direct discourse', using Volosinov's term, in that it acts as if it were actually being spoken as part of a fully realized discussion. However, the 'other speakers' do not 'speak' on their own behalf, but in the service of the author who has created the dialogue in the first place. In the following extract, taken from the same student's original essay, the reported speech is presented as 'indirect discourse' where the 'speech' is presented as a synthesis within the author's speech.

Extract 4.2

Keynesian theory states that 'r' is determined by money demand and money supply, not thrift and productivity as in Classical theory ...

Both texts represent what Bakhtin (1978) explains here when he discusses the way in which an author uses the speech of others.

an author may utilize the speech of another in pursuit of his own aims and in such a way as to impose a new intention on the utterance, which nevertheless retains its own proper referential intention. (Bakhtin, 1978, p. 180)

Each of these two extracts is differently contextualized so differently shaped by the author. They represent different genres, the first being a *dramatized production* (a radio phone-in) or a kind of play, and the second being an *essay*. They also represent different 'behavioural' genres (Volosinov), the first being a *debate* (disagreement) and the second being part of a written *argument* (counterpoint or contradiction).

The terms of reference developed by the Russian circle could be considered confusing as they do not correspond to current conceptualizations of, for instance, genre or reported speech, and the use of the term 'discourse' here is also problematic, as already pointed out. However, the discussions and analyses that these writers produced have a fundamental relevance to conceptualizations of language as interaction contextualized in particular genre frames. The concepts of 'reported speech' and 'importation' are particularly helpful in overcoming the difficulty of discussing mode shift in my later analyses where the shift from writtenness to spokenness is all enacted through writing (i.e. essays to plays) and it allows me to treat the speech as 'reported' or 'primary' without falling foul of the fact that they are produced with writing. In relation to the idea of 'importation' I use the term '*scripted speech*' to refer to the dialogues in the regenred work as opposed to '*citations*' in the essays. I also use the terms *spokenness* with and *writtenness* in relation to the affordances of these modes and the textual materials they require. As Halliday (1989) has argued, 'speech and writing impose different grids on experience. There is a sense in which they create different realities' (p. 93).

By bringing a multimodal perspective into play, however, it is possible to also consider other modes because, in the same way that spokenness 'imposes a different grid on experience', so too do other semiotic modes. A gesture as greeting means differently to a verbal greeting. Each achieves a different communicative experience and each produces a different communicative effect as a result of their respective affordances.

Textual Materials

The final category to be considered in this section is the term textual materials. This aspect of the analysis concerns the different 'elements' that constitute the fabric of the communication. In Kress and Van Leeuwen's frame of reference, the term mode incorporates this category. However, in my analysis I am particularly interested in exploring the chain of affordances and this additional category facilitates a more closely focused discussion about the different affordances of 'spokenness' and 'writtenness' as represented in the students' work.

4.3 'Transgressing Genre Laws'

Writing in 1976, Todorov, in discussing the relevance of genre as a means to understanding institutionalized forms of social interaction, argues that

> through 'transgressing' genre 'laws' we can begin to see what those 'laws' are '… the norm becomes visible – comes into existence – owing only to its transgressions'.

In my work, the opportunity to compare the differently represented versions of what was essentially the same core material has allowed me to explore the effects of just such a transgression. It is precisely because I had the fortune to be able to analyse the two versions that I was able to reveal how the genres oriented the students towards making their texts in the ways they did. The affordances of each genre meant that they had to work differently with the materials, using different modes and different textual materials. The genres made them focus their texts differently, making different thematic choices. Furthermore, the different contexts for the work, both textual and in terms of the circumstances in which they did it, led to different emotional responses to the work. These different but interacting aspects are encompassed in the orientation framework that I have described here and to finish off this chapter I give a brief example to show how it works in principle.

4.3.1 A Working Example

The following extracts come from Andy's work, which used a politics essay as the source for the regenring. To recap briefly, the essay was a discussion about methods of classification of political systems and the regenred version was produced as a tabloid newspaper using the special layout formats and inserted images and captions typical of that genre as in Extract 4.3 below, which gives a flavour of the way in which he reworked the material.

Extract 4.3

The Daily Lie	Price 5 €uros	2nd January 2002

CLASSIFIED!

FREE INSIDE
Your pull-out guide
to the Top Ten
Political Systems

Greek philosopher provides model for political systems the world over

For the purposes of illustrating the analytical framework, however, I use two corresponding extracts. Extract 4.4 is from the essay and Extract 4.5 is from the 'newspaper'.

Extract 4.4

> Aristotle also gives too great a focus on the political elite when analysing the political system. As Sinclair points out in his introduction to *The Politics*, 'the privileges of citizenship were to him a matter of supreme importance' (Sinclair, 1962) mainly because he was not a 'citizen' himself . . .

Extract 4.5

> Malicious rumours have also been spreading about Aristotle that there is a hidden agenda behind his model, which clearly focuses on the political elite rather than the ordinary man in the forum. A senior source from the peripatetic school in Athens (at which Aristotle is a key teacher) has revealed that 'the privileges of citizenship [are] to him a matter of supreme importance'. *The Daily Lie* can today reveal that Aristotle is not in fact a citizen of Athens, but an asylum seeker from the Kingdom of Macedon. This being the case, there is only one question that is now on everybody's lips. We demand to know if Aristotle's book, praising as it does his own government, is merely an attempt to curry favour with the Athenian authorities?

Although each was a response to an assignment task within the institutional practice of university learning and demonstration of learning, the tabloid transgresses this relationship in that it suspends belief in the conventional social relations between the reader (me) and the writer (the student). Both versions present information drawn from the same source of disciplinary knowledge (Sinclair, 1962), which constitutes what can be considered a particular view on Aristotle's work. However, the difference in genre choice results in differences in how the texts can mean. Tabloid writing allows for, or rather demands, a different kind of explication of events and facts which Andy has made full use of in elaborating the underplayed comment regarding Aristotle's preoccupation with citizenship in the original essay.

In producing the two texts, Andy has drawn on different ranges of material resources (modes, media and textual materials). What is more, if we are socially and culturally familiar with the two genres (as produced within particular social and cultural contexts) then we as reader receive them differently. We have an expectation of how an essay will mean and we have an expectation of how a tabloid newspaper article will mean, and as such we (readers) adjust our interpretative perspective accordingly. Tabloids can make unattributed statements and express explicitly highly subjective opinions whereas essays are expected to attribute and moderate subjectivity.

Comparison of the versions also allows for consideration of how the material choices affect the social impact of the different texts, for instance discursive orientation, and this in turn facilitates discussion about what different genres do. The second extract, for example, 'violates' the conventional essay genre on several levels: use of certain textual materials (e.g. malicious rumours), the 'unnamed source', the use of the term 'asylum seeker' to undermine Aristotle and his arguments. In the essay, although this was alluded to, the terms of reference chosen promote a different kind of critique. Furthermore, the regenred version allows the writer to link the historical context to present-day attitudes, something which, arguably, adds a different angle on an understanding of Aristotle's work – the kind of 'originality' that the lecturers in Chapter 2 were so keen on.

Andy commented on how the process highlighted the way different genres express meaning. He had a sense that the tabloid genre demanded what he called 'pacey' writing whereas the essayist information he was dealing with had been produced with more 'technical' linguistic resources.

I was trying to make it as immediate as possible and in terms of the quotes it was often hard to find the right kind of quote because it was in such a different style of language, but yes, I just tried to make it sort of as pacey as possible ... I was trying to make it more accessible and make the language simpler. I mean, I attempted to do it a bit in the style of a tabloid newspaper and that was very hard 'cos looking at tabloid newspapers the articles are much shorter ... and the style of language was much more technical [in the essay] *so that was hard.*

His comment indicates his awareness of the kinds of change necessary in recontextualizing the disciplinary information with his reference to both the social and material aspects. He had to take into account who his readership was and how that meant he needed to make different lexical and syntactic choices in so doing.

4.4 Displaying Difference

For purposes of clarity and comparison, I use Tables 4.1 and 4.2 to display differences between the genres used in Chapters 5, 6 and 7. The tables represent the framework introduced above and provide an immediate overview of how the different genres orient the producers towards particular social positions and material choices. As already mentioned, I have excluded the category of media because it does not signify a significant aspect of the work under discussion here.

The Social		
	Genre 1	**Genre 2**
Contextual Orientation		
Design		
Production		
Distribution		
Discursive Orientation		
Purpose		
Process		
Identity		
Role		
Agency		

TABLE 4.1

The Material		
	Genre 1	**Genre 2**
Thematic Orientation		
Organization		
Topics		
Semiotic Orientation		
Modes		
Textual materials		

TABLE 4.2

Tabulated displays like these, of course, suggests direct correspondence between categories and versions and this is the case with regard to 'the social' aspects of comparison. However, in connection with 'the material' orientations, there is often no direct correspondence because the shift in thematic and semiotic orientations often leads to a fundamental shift in the resources used. Nevertheless, it is possible to identify points of comparison and demonstrate these with examples from the texts. As will be seen in the next chapters, the display summarizes the main effects of genre choice and serves as a reference point for the more detailed discussions that follow.

4.5 Conclusion

This chapter has presented the analytical framework that I use in discussing the effects of genre choice. It has clarified my terms of reference and explained why I have adopted a multimodal perspective in discussing these written texts. The next three chapters use this framework to analyse the students' work in detail.

Referring back to the quote with which I opened this chapter, in my effort to include 'my most promising stories', I have obviously omitted others. It has been extremely difficult to decide how to organize my own discussions particularly given the richness of the data and the breadth of field of the book's focus. I could, for instance, have used just one of the students' pieces of work as focus for analysis, but this might have given the impression of a 'one-off' experience and would have denied the presence of the other students who contributed so much to my thinking. However, in the end I decided on the following: Chapter 5 explores issues of agency and identity; Chapter 6 focuses on the resource implications of genre choice; whilst Chapter 7 investigates how recontextualizing disciplinary information enables new reflections on disciplinary materials and reflexivity on disciplinary practice.

One consequence of this organizational approach is that there is a tendency for what I have tried to separate out thematically in each of the chapters to overlap and merge. This is inevitable, given the interrelationship between the different orientations, so although I have tried to hold back from mixing my analyses up, there will be times when this has proved impossible. Equally, there might be the desire on the part of the reader, as there has been on my part, for me to mention things that are discussed in other chapters. This means that readers will need to hold back until they have finished Chapter 7 at least, by which point I hope the picture will have become clearer because it will be more complete. I realize that this is perhaps frustrating, and indeed it has been frustrating in the writing: however, it is the consequence of analysis.

Chapter 5

Repositioning the Writer

It wasn't so much having to reproduce facts and saying the right thing to get the marks, it was more of an exercise in doing it the way you wanted to. (Peter)

5.1 Introduction

In Chapter 2 I discussed the complicated interactions between students and lecturers particularly in connection with assignments. I argued that the complexity of these interactions results from the complexity of the many participants involved, both *immediately* present, as in 'the students' and 'the lecturers', and *implicitly* present, as represented by the disciplinary and pedagogical frames of knowledge and practice, not to mention the ideological principles that underlie and often drive the contexts in which the interactions occur. It is not, therefore, surprising that the kinds of frustration I discussed emerge and that both students and lecturers experience so many often conflicting emotions around essays and assessment. After all, the essay is the site where issues of identity and agency are foregrounded in the 'public' articulation of disciplinary learning and disciplinary knowledge. As Ivanic (2006, p. 26) points out, 'In educational contexts "learning" is not just an increase in knowledge, understanding and capability, but includes the discoursal reconstruction of identity too.' Learning is not a neutral process of acquisition of skills sets, as implied in skills discourses, but a transformative process in which our different identities and our different frames of knowledge intermingle.

In this chapter I develop these ideas in discussing the relationship between genre and agency, using the orientation framework that I introduced in the Chapter 4. I argue that the different genres used by the students oriented them towards different discursive identities. As a result, the interface between what they wrote (the content) and who they were as writers (discursive identity) led to a shift in their sense of agency.

For the purposes of this discussion, I want to represent agency as the 'ability' or 'freedom' to make choices. In other words, agency in this discussion is about ownership of the ideas (re)presented in the student work and ownership of the work itself. Peter's remark at the start of this chapter, referring to the regenring task, is a comment about agency. From a social semiotic perspective, as has been discussed in Kress and Hodge (1979), agency operates on both the material and the social planes, reflecting and reflected in the communicative activity. It is present in communicative interactions as discussed in Chapter 2 and it is realized in the texts that are produced with regard to what can be said, how and by whom. The greater the power distance between the participants the less flexible choice is likely to be. For example, in an interview between a detainee and the police, the power distance is always great and the power relationship always unequal. The suspect cannot say just what she wants in the way she wants to as the circumstances and the genre they give rise to, the police interview, ensures a particular set of textual materials and thematic moves which reflect the contextual and discursive framing within which the event occurs. The genre orients towards particular social constructions and particular material choices, as discussed in the previous chapter.

An aspect of agency is what is often termed 'voice', in this case the student writer's voice, in identifying 'self' in the text produced in relation to 'others' (e.g. Ivanic and Simpson, 1992; Lillis, 2001). This concerns the personal expression of agency. But for my purposes, like Scott (1999), I also want to think of agency as emerging out of the process of production using Kress's concept of the 'motivated sign' (Kress, 1993) where the means of production (choice of resources and their affordances) shows the producer's agency.

5.2 The Hand in the Work

In order to illustrate this further, I want to give an actual example involving the interactions between a carpenter and a client. In this example, the client, who is not an expert in matters of carpentry, wants some work done in a particular way and explains this to the carpenter in some detail. The work concerns the renovation of an old wooden floor in a house of the type the carpenter, who is very experienced and has a good reputation, is very familiar with. In the communication there is a misunderstanding, which neither party is aware of. This misunderstanding derives from how differently each party understands the design and consequently how different their expectations are. This corresponds to the chart I produced in Chapter 2, relating to the interactions between lecturers and students (Figure 2.1). The carpenter goes ahead with the work whilst the client is absent. On his return, the client sees immediately that the work undertaken is very different from the design he had in mind at the outset. The carpenter had done the work according to his own experience and expertise, using the resources that he knew to be appropriate based on his knowledge of the way that kind of job is done in those kinds of houses. This is displayed in Figure 5.1.

INTERACTIONS			
Design	**Re-design**	**Production**	**Distribution**
What the client envisages and why	How the carpenter (re)interprets and why	What the carpenter produces	How the production is received and what is done next.

FIGURE 5.1

The client now has a choice. Will he get angry and demand that the work be redone or does he accept the carpenter's new design? This all depends on a range of factors relating to the way in which the work has been completed (quality), the way in which the client views the carpenter (status), the acceptability of the product in terms of its appropriateness (relevance), the relationship between the participants (power) and the way in which each views themselves (identity). In other words, it depends on the agency of each party and of how, in this case, the client understood the carpenter's agency.

As discussed in Chapter 2, the question of how far the production is 'allowed' to stray from the 'blueprint' depends on the relationship between the participants and how they perceive themselves and each other. The more conventionalized the practice is, the greater the limitations are in production terms. Expectations of how a 'text' *will* be can become how it *should* be. In this story there was a happy ending with the client accepting the carpenter's work, recognizing his greater expertise and acknowledging the appropriateness of the new design even though it was not what had been originally anticipated. As far as the carpenter was concerned, there was no issue, as he was entirely confident in his own (re)design, not even recognizing it as such. And because he really was an expert and the quality of his work was excellent, the reinterpreted design and its outcome was acceptable. However, not all stories have such happy endings, as is well known and too often experienced, and in the design–redesign framework. If the client is not satisfied, the degree to which he might argue would depend on his own agency.

At university, in the case of student work, as already discussed in Chapter 2, agency is determined in part by the institutional positioning of the participants and in part by the degree of (perceived) expertise the parties hold, as the following comment from one of the lecturers bears out.

> *Because they are students we can't help but read their work more – perhaps even more – critically because it's not coming from an authoritative voice in a sense – so I think that – not necessarily by necessity, but effectively I think we land up reading our students' work expecting there to be problems with it.*

This view clearly situates the relationship as 'unequal' and reflects the experiences that students commented on in Chapters 1 and 2 with regard to their own feelings of powerlessness. However, despite the fact that the regenring assignment was going to be assessed just like their other work, they seemed able to divorce themselves from this eventuality, suspending belief and producing their new work within the fictional contexts that they created. This involved specifically 'constructed' readers or audiences such as children or radio listeners and this shift in contextual orientation, as the following conversation shows, changed the ways that the students felt about doing the work.

> Peter: *... you know when I did the Swahili one it was a proper essay – you know you felt you needed to be in the library surrounded by books whereas this one was more an exercise in just – it wasn't so much having to reproduce facts and saying the right thing to get the marks it was more of an exercise in doing it the way you wanted to.*

> Me: *So with the original one you were thinking of what 'they' wanted.*

> Peter: *Well the 'they' is different, you're not thinking about writing it* [an essay] *so that someone can understand, you know, like a child would, you're writing to fulfil requirements you know the whole academic way of writing, um, whereas re-writing was more being considerate to the audience as well as being more considerate to yourself. When you write an essay for the proper thing you sort of you're trying to think about the marks and not how best to maybe write what you want but how best to write what is required of you.*

What I want to show in the rest of this chapter is how regenring enabled the students to reposition themselves in relation to the disciplinary knowledge and the circumstances of assignments and assessment, and in so doing assert their own agency more strongly.

5.3 Shifting Identities

As I have already explained in earlier chapters, the work that I analyse in this and the next two chapters emerged from a first year module that offered the students the chance to write differently, using alternative genres to the conventional essay. This opportunity led to the students experiencing the work of writing about their disciplines in a very different way compared to their previous experiences, affecting not only what they could write about and how, but the way they felt about the work. It enabled them to reposition their identity as 'knowers' of the discipline, 'experts' rather than 'novices', as will be seen in this chapter.

The two students whose work I draw on in this chapter both exemplify a shift in agency, although each achieves this very differently. In both examples, the essay information has been reproduced for a younger audience, and both Sonia and Peter, who were doing the same BA, chose to regenre similar essays. The fact that both students were taking the same degree programme is incidental as is the fact that both of them chose to write about a similar topic. However, while Peter's original essay had been a competent piece of discursive writing, Sonia's was fragmented and marginally successful showing little evidence of confidence or engagement with the subject.

In choosing the work of these two students I do not want to give the impression that theirs were the only examples where a shift in agency occurred as a result of the regenring. In fact, this was a phenomenon in all the students' work. However, the work of these two students offers interesting opportunities to demonstrate this particular aspect of genre shift. Both of them choose a pedagogic frame in which to relocate the disciplinary information, thereby explicitly foregrounding a change in discursive identity from 'novice' to 'expert', but each of them achieves this in very different ways.

In the first example, Peter writes as the author of a children's 'information' book, adopting the discursive identity of a subject expert in communicating the information from the essay. In this case, he himself is the narrator of the text. Sonia, on the other hand, uses a fictional character to communicate the essay information, speaking not on her own behalf, but on behalf of the expertise that the information requires. Her new production involves a parent 'telling' his children about the subject, a device which enables her to characterize strong agency. However, in her case, the articulation of agency is rather different compared to Peter's approach. Rather than having a single discursive presence, she offers two: one as 'authority' and the other as a kind of resistance to that 'authority'. In this way, Sonia, offers a double reflection on agency and identity, including what it means to be a student, which is a theme I develop further in Chapter 7. For now, I want to focus on the issue of writer's experience and expression of agency and take each case in turn.

5.4 Peter's Work

Peter, as has been mentioned, was studying for a BA in African Language and Literature. He identified the Swahili essay as being an appropriate one to regenre as a children's (aged 11–13) text because he felt the topic lent itself to being rendered suitable for that age group. He also thought it would be interesting for them, learning about another language and about how languages borrowed words from each other. He also commented on how the module itself had developed his own language awareness and that it was something everyone should learn about, particularly in connection with other languages.

> *You know people use English as their own language but don't really think about things – I don't know, maybe it's learning about other languages that makes you think about your own.*

He also talked about his own interest in writing for children and how the combination of something he thought would be both interesting and useful encouraged him to choose the Swahili essay and the new didactic genre that typifies children's information books.

> *I knew I wanted to write it – I always used to, like, draw kiddy books and it was just picking one* [an essay] *that seemed to lend itself best ... I was trying to take one that would have been more useful, so I just picked that one.*

The choice of a younger readership meant a conscious repositioning of identity for Peter too, shifting from that of learner to that of teacher. This new role allowed him, as can be seen in Table 5.1 below, to be an informer rather than a performer, an authority instead of a novice and, following Bernstein (2000), a 'recontextualizer', using a pedagogized discourse, rather than a 'reproducer'. The new discursive identity, in fact, allowed him to position his own readers as novices, in much the same way that Hyland (2000) shows that textbook writers do. As is displayed in Figure 3.4, which schematizes the model of communication that I work with, Peter's choice of readership led to the choice of genre which, in turn, afforded particular ways of producing the text using the semiotic resources that were most apt for the purposes in hand.

The essay in question was his response to the assignment task: *From a set of Swahili loan words, establish the linguistic source of each word and suggest the probable period from when it was borrowed.* It is summarized in Chapter 1, along with the regenred work (1.7.1). The original essay is of about two thousand words and is a confident production which fulfils everything the task instruction demands. It is largely descriptive and provides, as expected, both historical and linguistic information. For the most part, the text is what can be called a *display* text, which, just like others I refer to in this book, provides a synthesis of information acquired from various sources and is presented here largely as a reproduction despite the wider framing that Peter introduces in the introduction, as I show below. There is nothing intrinsically 'wrong' with the essay itself or the way in which it 'makes' the student produce his knowledge. However, from Peter's perspective, it asked little more of him than to '*reproduce the facts, saying the right thing to get the marks*', a somewhat, perhaps understandably, pragmatic view of essay writing similar to those discussed in Read et al. (2001), but one which inevitably leads to the kinds of frustration that I discussed in Chapter 2. In writing the essay, Peter is responding to the design (the assignment task) established by the lecturer, not from the confident position of the expert, as the carpenter in the anecdote above, but from the uncertain position of the novice who is all too aware of the penalties if his work does not match the designer's expectations.

By contrast, writing the regenred version offered Peter a different kind of experience, '*doing it the way you wanted to*', whereby it is up to him how to articulate what is essentially the same information. This refers to the shift in agency that I have already mentioned and what I now want to show is how that shift reveals how agency is reflected in each of the two productions and hence, how they, in turn, reflect the writer's agency back to the reader.

5.4.1 The Orientations of Peter's Genres

Using the analytical framework that I introduced in Chapter 4, Tables 5.1 and 5.2 display how each of the genres Peter uses orients towards particular kinds of experience and how that experience is reflected in and by the texts themselves. Table 5.1 displays differences in how each version is experienced in the process of its production; that is the contextual and discursive orientations of the two genres used. Table 5.2 displays how this is represented in each – in other words, the thematic and semiotic orientations of the genres.

The Social		
	Essay	**Children's Information 'article'**
Contextual Orientation		
Design	Responding *to* client's design	Designing *for* client
Production	Essayist (student essay)	Expository (for young readers)
Distribution	For institutional assessment	For institutional assessment
	Normative practice, reproduction of …	*Alternative* practice, experiment, reconfiguration of …
	Evaluation against normative implicit disciplinary (and institutionalized) criteria and/or values	Interpretive effect – for assessment/evaluation against non-normative disciplinary criteria and/or values
Discursive Orientation		
Purpose	Display knowledge of client's design	Experiment with learning/writing
		Tell (teach) about disciplinary material
	Work with disciplinary material Display learning	'Infotainment'
Process	Acquire Reflect Synthesize Report Create	Reflect Synthesize Recontextualize Create Inform
Identity	Novice *as though* expert	Expert *as if* children's book writer
Role	Performer	Informer
Agency	Mediated Disguised/unidentifiable Intertextual	Unmediated Visible Interpersonal

TABLE 5.1

As discussed in Chapter 4, representing the effects of genres in this way offers an overview of how the genres oriented the writers and their texts towards particular kinds of experience. Of course, this is a generalized display and it does not claim to represent an exact account of the circumstances in which the students worked. In fact the table itself is designed to enable flexibility in the information that is displayed under each category and it depends on the research interest what and how much to include. In order to understand how the social and the material interact, it is necessary to consider both Tables 5.1 above and 5.2 below in conjunction with each other.

As far as Contextual Orientation is concerned, Peter's original essay was produced to the design of his lecturer and all the institutional, disciplinary and personal aspects that I discussed in Chapter 2. By contrast, the new version was produced according to his own design at someone else's request – mine. In this sense he was more like the carpenter above, designing for the client. This was similar for all for all the students. However, Peter's design is also for the imagined 'clients' who are his imagined readers – children. The design, then effects the production itself as the result of the semiotic choices made, as discussed in Chapter 3. The distributive dimension, in my approach, concerns the process of delivery and how it is received in accordance with the expectations of the participants. In the case of the regenred work, this is related to the 'suspension of belief' circumstances I have already referred to, even though it was part of the normal round of assessment within the university. In relation to the Discursive Orientation, there were, as can be seen, clear differences between the essays and the alternative genres under each of the categories. For this I have used a synthesis of textual analysis and the interviews in deciding on how to describe the experiences that are both reflected in and by the different productions.

Table 5.2 provides the other half of the picture in its representation of the material differences between the genres. It exemplifies the kinds of material resources that Peter used in each version, displaying them as a series of contrasts, although this is not the case with all the students' work. It is possible with Peter's work because both the essay and the new genre follow a similar thematic structure and the thematic content is quite closely matched. Even so, as will be seen in the discussion that follows, which clarifies the information in these tables, there are fundamental differences between the two versions.

The Material		
	Essay	**Children's information 'article'**
Thematic Orientation		
Organization	Essay management (introduction, 'body', conclusion i.e. sequence of information/ideas)	Organization (introduction, 'body' and conclusion)
	Discussion, descriptions, explanations, examples	Discussion, descriptions, explanations, examples
Topics	Disciplinary topics linguistic terms of reference	Disciplinary topics 'everyday' terms of reference
		Colonial history as background
	Swahili loan words, history of borrowing, etc.	English and Swahili as languages that each borrow words
Semiotic Orientation		
Modes	Writing	Writing
Textual Materials	Impersonal forms (e.g. 'it' fronted, passives, nominalizations)	Personal forms (e.g. subject fronted, addressivity)
	Density of expression/clause density Embedded/indirect questions	Looseness of expression/ clause intricacy
		Direct (rhetorical) questions
	Disciplinary terminology	'Everyday' terms
	Formal (writing-like) expression (e.g. full forms, subordination) Implicitness (assumed knowledge)	Colloquial (speaking-like) expression (e.g. contracted forms, co-ordinators in first position – so, and)
		Explicitness (assumed 'ignorance')
	12 point Palatino	14 point Palatino

TABLE 5.2

5.4.2 Comparing Extracts From Peter's Work

In comparing Peter's texts, I use three sets of paired extracts to exemplify the ways in which the orientations outlined in the tables interact on both the social and the material planes. As with the tables, it is not always possible to precisely map the essay on to the regenred work, or vice versa. This is because in the new work, the genre may 'push' in the information to be differently distributed through the text. Furthermore, the new genres may introduce different themes and discard others. It very much depends on the genres chosen. However, and in order to highlight the shifts that occur, I have attempted to select extracts where comparison is possible and in Peter's case, as already mentioned, this is easier than in others.

The first pair of extracts are the introductions to each text, starting with the essay followed by the regenred version. I have used the same layouts and fonts as were used in the student's original texts, particularly as this has a bearing on the semiotic orientation of each.

Extract 5.1

> It is not necessary to learn a foreign tongue to become aware that an individual language is far from immune to outside influence. The English with which we converse daily is littered with words and phrases borrowed from a host of other languages.

Extract 5.2

> 'Laissez-faire', 'Déjà vu' – and that's only a start. We all speak English every day, but do we realize how often we use foreign words and phrases? And this word stealing is not always as plain to see as the examples above. What country do you think of when you wash your hair? 'Silly question!' is what you are all thinking. But did you know that 'shampoo' is a Hindi word? That's the language that all the people in India speak. So if English can go around stealing words from other languages, then why can't other languages do the same?

The most immediate difference between Extracts 5.1 and 5.2 is the visual impact of each version. Font size may not be considered as particularly significant, but it is, nevertheless, a contributory factor in how the different texts can be read. Choice of font is a semiotic decision (Hillner, 2005) and the larger font size chosen for the children's text is intended to communicate readability and accessibility of content, and is more attractive to younger readers, as is shown by Owston and Wideman (1997). It could also be argued that in transgressing the institutional norms of the regulation 12-point fonts, issues of agency are also at play here.

However, the differences lie in considerably more than just visual impact, as Tables 5.1 and 5.2 indicate. They are mainly the result of the discursive orientation of the genres Peter chooses and the different identities with which he writes. This concerns the shift from performer to informer, from novice to expert, and hence from an agency where interpersonal interaction is mediated and disguised by its writtenness to an agency which is open, direct and unmediated at the interpersonal level. The regenred work uses a pedagogized discourse, available to those who are considered experts writing for novices, which is how Peter re-identifies in the new genre, whereas the essay, which promotes the hybrid 'novice-as-though-expert' identity, uses a display discourse that demonstrates what has been learned.

The most obvious example of pedagogized discourse in Peter's work is the use of rhetorical questions throughout Extract 2.1 (e.g. But do we realize how often we use foreign words and phrases? or What country do you think of when you wash your hair?). Interestingly, such use of rhetorical questions was not noted by Hyland (2000) in his analysis of textbook discourse. This may be because his work focuses on university textbooks, which identify more with their disciplinary knowledge than their pedagogical purpose. By contrast, rhetorical questions tend to be more prevalent in textbooks for younger readers as they indicate a more explicitly pedagogic relationship than 'adult' textbooks might wish to express. Rhetorical questions are also a resource often used in teaching, including at university, because they invite a kind of internal interaction, even if no actual uttered response is anticipated. Furthermore they enable a speaker to make the given information more salient by representing it as a question–answer (problem–solution) frame. In Extract 5.2 they are explicit demands for the reader to interact with the information, something which is possible only when 'authority' is with the writer. Using such textual resources in the essay would be unsuccessful because they would disrupt the power relationship, placing the lecturer in 'novice' position. Rhetorical questions imply that 'you' (the reader) may or may not have the answers, but 'I' (the writer) definitely have. In Extract 5.1, from the essay, however, the writer is obliged to present his ideas as assertions, which seems to give them factual authority even though, on closer inspection, the assertions offer a markedly different impression from the questions in Extract 5.2. Furthermore, the pedagogized discourse of the regenred work uses textual materials associated with speech, whereas the essay uses those associated with writing.

The main differences between speech and writing, as Halliday has pointed out, is that 'The complexity of the written language is static and dense. That of the spoken language is dynamic and intricate. Grammatical intricacy takes the place of lexical density' (1989, p. 87). As displayed in Table 5.2 above, the essay tends towards a more compact, lexical density while the children's version employs the kind of looser, clause intricacy more usually associated with speech. This can be seen in the grammatical and lexical choices Peter makes in each extract. For example, there is a shift from the *passive* 'the English with which we converse is littered with ...' in the essay, where the language is merely an objectified 'recipient' of all this borrowing, to the *active* 'if English can go around stealing words' in the children's version, which gives an impression of the language as a kind of brigand, actively robbing others of their words. The passivity of the former is further emphasized by the lexical choice 'littered with', compared with its regenred counterpart 'stealing'. Extract 5.2 also uses more colloquialisms, such as contracted forms ('that's only a start') as opposed to the fully expressed forms in Extract One ('it is not necessary'), further enhancing the 'spoken' quality of the regenred version and the 'written' quality of the original version.

A further interesting shift that occurs is between the way the two different extracts can be interpreted. Being introductions, they establish the general topic in this case, linguistic borrowing, although neither mentions Swahili as such. Instead the introduction is used in each case to promote the view that all linguistic borrowing is a normal practice as if pre-empting an anticipated, but unarticulated, contrary view about linguistic purity perhaps. This is an interesting point in itself as there is no expectation in the essay instruction for any kind of argument. On the contrary, it seems to invite a purely 'factual' descriptive account of the topic. Nevertheless, Peter chooses to start each version with a kind of polemic which is never revisited in the essay, but which provides a strong thematic thread in the regenred work.

However, if the regenred version did not exist, one might understand the original essay introduction quite differently from how it can be understood with the benefit of the regenred work. In the latter, the view of linguistic borrowing promoted is positive and upbeat with the questions and the other interpersonal resources such as personal pronouns (e.g. Did you know ... do we realize ...) which afford feelings of participation and involvement, not to mention the examples and additional pieces of information that he provides. However, in the essay extract a more negative view is communicated largely by Peter's choice of the two metaphors 'immune from' and 'littered with', both examples of what Fairclough (2001) calls the experiential value of lexical selection. This suggests a 'purist' attitude to languages which, from reading the regenred work, is a view Peter clearly does not hold.

The next pair of extracts, taken from later on in the discussion, use similar textual materials and further exemplify the effects of the two genres. With these two extracts, I focus on Peter's ideological stance towards a particular piece of historical information. I have used 'bold' to pick out the two ideological messages to be considered.

Extract 5.3

> Of all the languages to have influenced Swahili, English is perhaps the only one which continues to do so. Within the group of English loans there are many which I shall ignore here as they are used only by those engaged in a specific occupation and as a result cannot be said to be a true part of the Swahili vocabulary. **The British interest in Africa has been well documented. The colonization of large tracts of East Africa by the British, beginning in the 1800s,** introduced many new words to the Swahili vocabulary, many of them concerned with aspects of colonial government and many concerning the new machinery introduced in the dawn of the industrial age.

In both extracts Peter discusses the circumstances under which English words began to appear in Swahili and attributes this to British colonialism of the region. In the essay the information is represented as a matter of known fact (... *has been well documented*), known at least by his disciplinary readers. In fact, this reference to shared understanding could be seen as a note to the reader that Peter himself is a full member of those 'in the know'. He could also be using this as a strategy to avoid either digression from the main discussion or embroilment in a discussion that might be problematic, or both. Whatever the case, it is only when we read the second extract that a particular perspective on the 'facts' emerges.

Extract 5.4

So this leaves us with a chance to look at our own language: English. **The British became interested in Africa in the 1800s, a time when many European nations were trying to claim large parts of Africa for themselves. The British controlled huge areas of the continent, so much that you could walk from Cairo to Cape Town on British-controlled land. Like those who came before them, they ruled the area as if it were Britain itself,** and as a result a large number of English words were introduced to Swahili. The British brought with them a host of new machines that had only just begun to be used in Britain. It was called the industrial age and Britain was leading the way with many inventions such as steam power. Because of this many of the words which were borrowed are to do with these new machines and gadgets. They also introduced words to do with the new form of government.

In the new genre, because Peter cannot assume that his readers know about colonial history, unlike his disciplinary readers, he needs to provide the background that he merely alluded to in the essay. The elaboration of the historical background enables him to include a critique of colonialism – '*trying to claim* large parts of Africa *for themselves*' – which is not reflected in the essay. As he is now the 'expert' in writing about the topic, he does not need to worry about how his particular perspective will be received. His readers' reading purpose is not to evaluate his knowledge, as is the case with the readers of the essay, but rather to gain knowledge for themselves. This is something that he commented on:

> *There wasn't so much of a paranoia about it* [writing the second version]. *While I was writing this one* [version two] *there wasn't the thought of having someone telling me that I was wrong.*

Furthermore, as with the first set of extracts, reading the regenred version influences the way in which the original can be interpreted and phrases such as 'British interest in' or 'large tracts of land' acquire differently positioned meanings which could be construed as critical instead of merely neutral matter of fact.

The final extracts from Peter's work are his concluding remarks. In each case he uses them to provide a kind of 'valedictory' statement for the reader and, unlike the previous examples, the two extracts do not match in either content or in purpose.

Extract 5.5

> With the prospect of many African languages falling to the wayside in the new era of globalization it is good to see that Swahili continues to move with the times as it has always done.

Extract 5.5 stands out from the rest of the essay in that it is somewhat disconnected in terms of thematic development and offers a very strongly articulated opinion. However, it is not an academic opinion such as might be found in professional disciplinary writing, drawing on theoretical arguments: it is self-referencing opinion or rather an opinion given in relation to a different discussion to the one represented by the essay. The comment 'it is good to see that …' has a patronizing tone, which Peter is unlikely to have intended. One explanation for this strongly framed opinion could be that Peter, wanting to finish off the essay, drew on a strategy that is more typical of pre-university writing, as discussed in Mitchell (1994), than of university essay writing. In other words, he has shifted genre from student essay to secondary school composition. As such it serves more to detract from the overall essay, which is essentially descriptive and factual, than to add to it, and despite the strong agency reflected in the opinion, it reflects inexperience in using the essay genre rather than expertise.

Extract 5.6

> So next time you hear a strange word, try and find out where it has come from, and try and use it again some time!

Like the previous extract, Extract 5.5 produces a very strong sense of agency, but unlike the previous extract, it fits the 'children's information book' genre from both the social and the material perspectives. It continues to use the same range of textual materials (directness, personal forms, colloquialisms) which afford the kind of addressivity that typify pedagogical texts. Unlike in the essay above, the concluding section here is a genuine conclusion to the text as a whole. It reflects the content and focus of the introduction and ties up the thematic thread regarding the prevalence and benefits of lexical borrowing. The use of directives (try to find out … try to use it…) further reflect the pedagogical frame in which Peter has produced this text and promote a strong sense of writer's agency in its ownership, not only of the information used but in the authority with which Peter communicates it.

These examples of Peter's work illustrate the interrelationship between the 'social' and the 'material' in communication interactions, as displayed in Tables 5.1 and 5.2, and how the different genres he used afforded him different opportunities in representing his knowledge. What those opportunities are only become apparent when both genres are considered and it is only then that we can begin to see the extent of what Peter knows. In fact, without seeing the regenred work, which demonstrates the kinds of positive attributes that the lecturers in Chapter 2 mentioned, such as 'commitment' and 'interest', Peter's engagement with the subject might have remained hidden and his attitude to the issues being discussed might have been misunderstood. This point will be illustrated even more forcefully in the next section, when I discuss Sonia's work.

5.5 Sonia's Work

The second pair of productions were produced by Sonia who, as I have already indicated, was also following the African Language and Literature degree. She was unhappy with her chosen area of studies, despite having a personal interest in the region, and she subsequently dropped out of the degree programme. However, she returned a year and a half later to study for a different degree, which she successfully completed. Her work provides a vivid example of how regenring can offer new and different opportunities to a student, even one who was already beginning to feel disaffection towards her academic studies. She commented on this when talking about her reasons for choosing the regenring assignment.

Since I've started university I've felt myself struggling with the academic work and yearning to do something creative. This assignment seemed like a good opportunity.

Like Peter, Sonia incorporated a pedagogic dimension into her new work, but unlike him, she used a dramatic genre rather than an expository one which gave her different opportunities in working with the disciplinary material. Her essay task was *Give an account of the origin and present day function of one African lingua franca* and the essay she produced does exactly that, adopting a literal approach to the task. By contrast, the regenred work provides a completely different take on the topic and uses the disciplinary materials in an entirely new way.

The new version is produced as a dialogue, essentially a short play, with the aim of making the content of the essay accessible for a younger audience. Sonia felt that the topic leant itself to be 'told' rather than 'written', thereby reflecting what she considered to be the 'orality' of African narratives.

Considering that in Africa people rely on 'orature' rather than literature, it felt appropriate to the discussion.

It is an enactment of a parent telling a bedtime 'story' to his two children aged eight or nine and so the information becomes grounded in a 'real world' context where things need to be explained rather than presented. Her alternative title, *Culturally Confused*, indicates not only a different understanding of the topic compared to the original essay which 'gave an account of', but it also demonstrates her clear sense of ownership of the work.

5.5.1 The Orientations of Sonia's Genres

Table 5.3 displays the social orientations of the two genres Sonia used and Table 5.4 displays material orientations. As in Peter's case, each of the genres had different effects across these analytical categories.

The Social		
	Essay	**Dramatized Bedtime Story**
Contextual Orientation		
Design	Responding *to* client's design	Designing *for* client
Production	Essayist (student essay)	Dramatized didactic conversation

Distribution	For institutional assessment	For institutional assessment
	Normative practice – reproduction of …	*Alternative* practice, experiment, reconfiguration of …
	Evaluation against normative implicit disciplinary (and institutionalized) criteria and/or values	Interpretive effect – for assessment/evaluation against non-normative disciplinary criteria and/or values
Discursive Orientation		
Purpose	Display knowledge of client's design	Experiment with learning/writing
	Display learning	Tell (teach) about Inform Entertain
Process	Acquire Reflect Reproduce Replicate	Reflect (on disciplinary materials) Reflect (on experience) Synthesize Recontextualize Create Inform Contend/Evaluate
Identity	Novice *as though* expert	Expert *as if* parent (Unwilling) pupils (*as if*) young children
Role	Performer	Informer (parent) Dissenter (children)
Agency	Mediated Disguised/unidentifiable Intertextual	Unmediated Visible Interpersonal

TABLE 5.3

As in the case of my analysis of Peter's work, I do not claim to have covered every aspect in this table, and it may be that other readers might identify different aspects. However, it is clear that the two genres offered very different orientations across both categories. The contextual orientation is the same for Sonia as for Peter since they were both working under the same conditions for each piece of work. However, there are differences between them in the Discursive Orientation category. For example, under the category of 'process', Peter's essay involves 'synthesis' of the materials and therefore a degree of 'creativity', whereas Sonia's essay, as will be evident, tends much more strongly towards replication. Her regenred work also involves a much wider range of processes than Peter's and than her original essay because the new genre requires her to do very different things with the materials. In fact, compared to her essay, where she simply presents the material, in the play she has to work on it and with it. In so far as the category of 'identity' is concerned, she offers a dual reflection: one as expert (the father) and the other as novice (the two children) and with this device she is able to give a strongly reflexive dimension to the work, as will be seen in Chapter 7.

As far as the material aspects of the productions are concerned, there are inevitably substantial differences between them as a result of the wide gap between essayist writing and dramatic writing. The first major difference arises because the play employs dialogue; that is speech to articulate the information which, as Chapter 6 will show, affords very different kinds of meaning. Table 5.4 provides examples of material differences between the two versions and although I do not discuss these in detail in this chapter, they illustrate how the genres afforded very different design options.

The Material		
	Essay	**Dramatized Bedtime Story**
Thematic Orientation		
Organization	Essay management (introduction, 'body', conclusion i.e. sequence of information/ideas) Descriptions, examples	Narrative and stage management (sequence of events) Storytelling Interactions between characters, dialogues
Topics and specific characteristics	Disciplinary topics Linguistic terms of reference Swahili as a lingua franca examples of history and uses – presented as list	Disciplinary topics 'everyday' terms of reference Swahili as a lingua franca presented as political act, linked to discussion on linguistic terminology Didactic parent and argumentative, assertive children

Semiotic Orientation		
Modes	Writing (writtenness)	Written speech/scripted speech (spokenness)
		Characters, props, stage management
Textual Materials	Impersonal forms (e.g. 'it' fronted, nominalizations, passive constructions)	Personal forms – subject fronted, personal pronouns + impersonal forms where 'father' is 'recounting' the essayist information
	Density of expression/clause complexity	Clause intricacy + clause complexity during 'recount' sections
	Disciplinary terminology – unexplained	Disciplinary terminology explained + colloquial terms
	Formal (writing-like) expression (e.g. full forms, subordination)	Colloquial (speech) expression
	Topically organized with no explicit threading	Topically organized but strongly mediated by dialogic interactions (e.g. responses to questions, challenges, recapitulations)
	Absence of interpersonal resources (i.e. no cohesive directives, lack of attitudinal markers, no links between topics)	Frequent use of interpersonal resources, interruptions, agreements/disagreements
	Explicitness as asserted fact – encyclopaedic information (e.g. no hedges)	Explicitness – pedagogized information – didactic, directives (e.g. People need to learn …), approbation (e.g. That's a good question) hedges (e.g. perhaps it's to do with…)
	Single formatting	Mixed formatting

TABLE 5.4

A particular aspect of Sonia's regenred work is that she provides substantial 'notes' with the play. These include contextual notes, which explain why she designed the new version as she did, and stage management notes, which explain the physical and interpersonal contexts of the play. In this way Sonia uses both the physical environment, as discussed in Jewitt (2005), and the interpersonal histories of the participants as semiotic resources. The contextual notes demonstrate the strength of agency that Sonia has in relation to the new work and the confidence with which she can 'creatively' combine 'imagination' with 'intellect', something she feels unable to do in conventional academic work.

Extract 5.7

> *I propose to transform the essay into a bedtime story, being told by a parent to two children. In doing so I am able to simplify the ideas and slip into a world that allows room for the imagination as well as the intellect.*

She proceeds to a description of the characters involved in the play followed by a detailed description the set (Extract 5.8) and despite Sonia's claim that this is 'of no immediate significance' it actually very important. It establishes the relationships between the participants, which are fundamental in understanding the argument that Sonia provides, with reference to both the disciplinary content and the reflexivity that the play affords, both dimensions being entirely absent from the essay.

Extract 5.8

> *The set is not of immediate significance to the piece; it must be minimal and modern with two single beds and an armchair to the left. Perhaps the beds could have patched work quilts on them and the wooden floor a Moroccan rug. A giant world map can be stuck to the walls behind the beds, with pins, scribbles and highlighter indicating places they have been, want to go, or various important and trivial facts the children have learnt. Some of the visible toys should serve an education function and not be associated with popular culture. It is clearly a conscientious household striving to create a corner of individuality and safety in a contrary, consumer world. If there is the possibility of having a window, it should be to the right of the beds so that the parent can glance towards it in unconscious reference. Through the window should be a view of an intimidating grey city, harsh and cold against the bedroom warmth. The city serves as a contrast to the African world the parent talks about and represents the cruelness of reality against the fictitious world that is created with words.*

Such information has no place in an essay because essays tend to orient away from 'everyday' experienced knowledge towards academic 'articulated knowledge' (Laudrillard, 1993), as discussed in Chapter 1. However, these stage management notes do something that essays also do – provide authorial guidance. Successful essays do this by choosing specific textual materials such as discourse links or expressions of modality that indicate how the reader is supposed to understand the writer's intentions, as has been widely discussed (English, 2000; Hunston and Thompson, 2000; Charles, 2006). Writers of plays use stage management and Sonia has made good use of this resource in asserting this authorial control. The props communicate a particular kind of home environment (the annotated world map, the Moroccan rugs, the patchwork quilts) which has a semiotic importance in focus of the play; the contrast between the Africa of the imagination and the London of reality suggests, perhaps, Sonia's own longings.

5.5.2 Comparing Extracts From Sonia's Work

I now want to move on to compare Sonia's two productions to demonstrate how the regenring allowed for the kinds of shift in agency and discursive identity I have referred to above. I cannot provide paired comparisons in the way I could with Peter's work because the organizational structure of Sonia's two versions differs substantially and the mapping process is not as straightforward. However, I start with what could be considered a 'pair' and represent the point in each production at which the topic, Swahili, is introduced. Extract 5.9 is the opening paragraph of the essay. Extract 5.10 occurs a short way into the play script and is preceded by a series of exchanges between the father and the children which serve to establish that this kind of bedtime activity is the usual household practice.

Extract 5.9

> The word 'Swahili' is Arabic in origin and means coast. Swahili is spoken on the East coast of Africa by many as a first language and has spread into the interior as far as the Congo as a lingua franca. Though Swahili uses words adopted from Arabic, English and Portuguese, it has the definite structure of a Bantu language and is written in the Latin script.

The extract 'names' the topic, Swahili, simply by using the word itself and provides three thematically different bits of information. The first offers a translation of the word itself, the second is about its regional use and the third its linguistic typology. In fact, the introduction is a summary of the whole discussion that follows. The information is presented as unproblematic statements of fact, there is no given frame of reference and no interpersonal resources are used. In fact, as will be seen from later examples, this extract typifies the whole essay in its encyclopaedic rather than essayist style.

The regenred work, as might be anticipated from the notes in Extracts 5.7 and 5.8, offers a totally different experience for both writer and reader.

Extract 5.10

Parent: *[At this point seated in the armchair addressing the children.]* 'Can you remember what our bedtime story was about yesterday?'

Child 1: 'Yessssssssss! It was about ...' *[six more exchanges]*

Parent: OK, anyway, today I thought I could tell you the story about how Swahili came to be such an important language in East Africa. People always talk about the importance of English as a world language but they rarely consider that there exist many other important non-European languages all over the world. People need to learn one of these important languages so they can talk to people who have different first languages to themselves.

Child 1: 'Umm ... Why would they be speaking to people with a different language?'

Parent: 'That's a good question you bright little spark! Now in the situation of Africa there are two hundred thousand different languages spoken. It's not like in England. In Africa if you go from one village to the next you are likely to find a different language ...'

The demands of the genre, characterization and setting and the to-ing and fro-ing of dialogue between the children and the parent force Sonia to shape the information differently. Spoken communication involves instant feedback in its realization and it is this feedback that provides the motivation for maintaining the flow (Kress, 1994). The 'facts' of the essay are now represented as conversation, which means they are discussed rather than presented, argued over rather than accepted. Despite the factual exaggeration regarding the number of languages spoken in Africa, this version introduces new dimensions to the work, not least of which is 'critical perspective', that most elusive, but desired, aspect of student academic performance.

The next extract, which comes from the essay, follows on from the introduction in Extract 5.9 and Extract 5.12 is selected from further 'down' the essay. Both demonstrate the consistency of Sonia's encyclopaedic approach and emphasize the contrast between this and her play.

Extract 5.11

Swahili is presumed to have started its life in the region of the Tana River estuary and to have spread further when Arabs and Persians settled in the area due to trading, thus spreading the language along their trading roots. In 975 Ali Ben Sultan al Hassan Ben Ali bought the island of Kilwa in exchange for a few bails of textiles and it became an important trading centre encouraging the use of Swahili along the coast south of the Zambezi River ...

Extract 5.12

There are a very large number of Swahili dialects that have derived from specific social situations, some of which are dying out because of a change in social circumstances. Due to the function of some of these dialects, such as the mode of common communication in the army and work force, the dialect has undergone considerable simplification and lost much of its structure until it can only be called a pidgin ...

The assertiveness with which this information is provided might not seem to match with the uncertainty of the student as writer, but can, perhaps, be explained by its similarity to textbook discourse, which is undoubtedly the kind of source that Sonia is drawing on. As Latour and Woolgar (1986) point out in their discussion of 'statement types' (pp. 75–88), textbook discourse tends to present information as uncontroversial fact, using unhedged assertions in contrast to 'authentic' professional disciplinary debates and arguments. Myers (1992) suggests that because this kind of writing concerns the 'summation' of knowledge it tends towards a more strongly assertive impression. He suggests that students need to become aware of differences between textbook genres and other academic genres, something that Sonia did not realize in the essay. There is no commentary on the information presented, nor is there any explicit reference to the sources she uses apart from the bibliography she includes at the end of the essay. In fact, although it is obvious that Sonia has been able to identify relevant information and use certain linguistic terms of reference it is not clear whether she has 'mastered' the relevant body of knowledge or whether she has simply located it. I return to these themes in the next chapters, particularly because they are connected to the affordances of textual materials and the expression of personal involvement in disciplinary practice.

The conclusion to the essay (Extract 5.13) offers an evaluative comment about the difference between Swahili and English as lingua francas.

Extract 5.13

As well as English influences, Arabic continues to influence Swahili as a language and Swahili literary forms and songs. Although Swahili draws from other language sources it is seen as a nationalistic language and its success as a lingua franca in East Africa could be attributed to this and its strong association with the Africanism that evolved after gaining independence from colonial rule. **English's growing prestige as a dominant world language could be seen as a hindrance to Swahili's progression but it is difficult to imagine English ever performing the same functions of Swahili** in that Swahili has become a common medium for people of different vernaculars who otherwise [sic] would have no means of communicating.

The opinion, highlighted in bold in the extract, is strongly presented notwithstanding the hedged expression 'could be seen as'. It picks up earlier mention of the role of English in East Africa in certain domains such as education and law, but no hint was given as to this being an issue. In other words, like Peter above, she has saved the 'opinion' till the last, but unlike him, this was the only opinion identifiable as Sonia's in the essay. What is interesting, however, is that this opinion becomes much more strongly foregrounded in the regenred version than in the essay, representing one of the key themes, as can be seen in Extract 5.14.

Extract 5.14

Child 2: 'Why doesn't everyone just learn English?'

Parent: 'One of the main reasons why Swahili became important was because it is an African language. English was used in colonial times. Remember, we have talked about colonialism before. When Europeans took control of countries that never belonged to them. So you can imagine what native people think of English. Imagine if some country with a foreign culture took over England and made English people work for them, constantly asserting their power. You're probably not going to like their language because it will remind you of all the bad things they have done to your country. It was a bit like this in Tanzania. Swahili was seen as a nationalistic language, a way of retaining culture. If everyone spoke English, don't you think the world would be a boring place? A language isn't just about words – it's about who you are. People who study language are called linguists and they believe if you study a certain language you are able to learn about the way that the people who speak it think. If everyone just spoke English it would be like saying the English way is the only way to live your life!'

In this extract the 'opinion' is contextualized as a justifying explanation in response to a challenge. As in Peter's regenred work, because the 'audience' consists of children, prior knowledge is not assumed and so the 'parent' occupies the role of the expert who can say what he likes without fear of being challenged by a disciplinary expert. This is possible because of the ways in which Sonia has constructed her characters to reflect the particular identities that allow her to experiment with the topics in the essay by problematizing them instead of simply presenting them. The children, because they are children, are free to express strong unsupported opinions. The father, because of how she has created him, frees Sonia to interweave her own judgements and evaluations with the disciplinary information.

Other differences between the versions include how the content is managed. In the essay the organizational structure corresponds to the chronology anticipated by the assignment title giving it a list-like quality. This is avoided in the new version, being replaced by a structure which follows the flow of the dialogue. Furthermore, because of the changed frame, explaining to children, the need to make the topic relevant, interesting and accessible becomes paramount.

In comparing the two different versions it is difficult to remember that it is the same writer in each case with the same set of available sources of information. What is different, of course, is the difference in what each of the genres afford in terms of social and material orientation. The visibility of agency (the father's, the children's) in the regenred work allows for a much stronger sense of writer's involvement than does the essayist version. The writer of the dramatized 'bedtime story' reveals a strong sociocultural awareness and an emerging understanding of issues surrounding language and identity. By contrast, the essay writer remains an 'invisible' reporter of incontestable and uncontested facts compiled from an anonymous source or set of sources just as is the case with contributors to encyclopaedias. The sense of authoritative agency that results from the heavy reliance on assertion has no provenance to back it up because Sonia is not, in fact, a disciplinary expert but a disciplinary novice instead. Agency in the regenred work is everywhere made visible with the availability of resources and the different social frame afforded by the genre itself. In fact, the regenred version enacts the kind of disciplinary involvement that Latour and Woolgar refer to when contrasting the discourses of laboratory discussion with those of textbook writing.

Ultimately the new production moves away from giving an 'account of', as demanded by the original essay instruction, and into a discussion about the nature of language, of lingua francas and of the political agendas that might underlie them. In fact, in the play Sonia says much more *about* the topics than she managed to do in the essay whereas in the essay she refers to more topics but says very little about them.

5.6 Conclusion

The two examples I have discussed here demonstrate how regenring enabled the students to make their own agency more visible. In neither of the original essays was there much sense of who was producing the work; perhaps rather more so in Peter's case and substantially less so in Sonia's.

However, once they moved into their new design the choices that were available to them facilitated a different experience. Agency is facilitated through the new discursive identities that the writers create. This, I suggest, allows the writers themselves to work with the information more freely, unconstrained by their own lack of scholarly authority.

As the comment with which I began this chapter shows, the regenring allowed them to *'do it the way you wanted to'* instead of the implied 'the way *they* want you to' (... *having to reproduce facts and saying the right thing to get the marks*). And regardless of the rights or wrongs of Peter's comment, it is clear that the opportunity to write using these different genres was experienced positively among the group. What is more, it revealed aspects of their understanding that might have remained hidden from view.

In the next chapter I will look more closely at issues only touched on here concerning the affordances of the different modes that the genres demanded. In particular, I will consider how spokenness contrasts with writtenness in the making of knowledge and how the genre shift led to shifts, not only in agency and identity as discussed here, but in the knowledge that the students were able to produce and the new meanings that they were able to introduce.

Chapter 6

Reconfiguring Information

I think what was satisfying was allowing myself or being able to digress – go off at a tangent – and develop something and then realize that that could be used and that actually produces something that is useful and gives a new form to what I'm writing and takes it in other directions. (Anya)

6.1 Introduction

In the previous chapter I focused on the notion of a writer's discursive identity and the relationship between this and agency. I argued there that a shift in genre allowed a shift in agency because the new genres allowed students to adopt or create new discursive identities. This phenomenon was, in fact, evident in all the regenred work discussed in this book. In this chapter, however, I want to focus on how the regenring led to a reconfiguration of the essay *content*, that is, the information itself. What I want to show is how the new genres afforded different possibilities in responding to the original essay assignment tasks which, in turn, led to substantial shifts in how the disciplinary knowledge was configured. In using the new genres, as Anya's comment suggests, the students did different things with the information and in so doing, how that information could mean also changed, in the way that Kress's concept of 'transduction' explains the effects of mode shift. In my discussion I suggest that the process of shifting between genres is also one of transduction which also results in transformation, as I show in the rest of this chapter.

In exploring this phenomenon, I draw on mainly Anya's work because her regenred production (an eight-scene play) offers a good opportunity to compare two productions that were each very positively received by her disciplinary readers. Moreover, the characters she creates not only offer new discursive possibilities in the ways discussed in the previous chapter, but also embody the disciplinary issues presented in the essay. However, I also use another student, Assif's, work when focusing specifically on the differences between writtenness and spokenness. Like Anya, he incorporates the voices of the disciplinary experts used in the original essay as 'live' characters.

6.2 Anya's Work

I start of by discussing the different ways in which Anya and her readers responded to her work. This provides some insight into Anya's own experiences of doing each of the assignments and how she evaluated her work compared with the feedback that she got from her disciplinary readers. I then move on to discussing examples from each of her two versions.

The original essay, as has already been explained in Chapter 1, was from Anya's 'Voice and Place' module, which is where the lecturers talk about their own research practices and activities. In this case the topic revolves around 'anthropology of the built environment' and problematizes the role of anthropology in that context. The two titles, presented in Extract 6.1, offer an immediate impression of how the two genres afforded Anya the opportunity to think differently about the materials.

Extract 6.1

The essay: How might anthropological considerations of the built environment lead to better understandings of issues such as social status, identity construction and nationalism?

The play: Snails and Other Gastropods

The title of the essay typifies the 'discussion' essay with its seemingly tentative proposition (How might ...) disguising the strength of the disciplinary view that anthropological considerations do indeed lead to a better understanding of the built environment. If they did not, why have any such considerations in the first place? What the question is really asking the student to do is to identify the anthropological debates in relation to the topic. The title of the play encapsulates the 'essence' of the essay question in its subsuming of the topic (built environment) into the metaphor of the snail and the seeming simplicity in relation to the built environment that the snail represents. The metaphor of the snail also has a disciplinary resonance, as will be seen later, while the title itself, 'Snails and Other Gastropods', offers a non-disciplinary resonance in its evocation of Gerald Durrell's autobiography *My Family and Other Animals*. In this way the title points both outwards to a different contextual world and inwards towards the disciplinary one.

6.2.1 Attitudes and Perceptions

Anya had been quite dissatisfied with how she had done the essay. She felt that she had not done justice to the topic, which interested her, and despite the essay being 'too long' by the criteria laid down for assignment, she was unhappy with the breadth of her discussion. However, despite Anya's negative feelings about the original essay, it was highly valued by her official reader. She was awarded the highest grade (A) and the summary feedback comment was as follows:

> *Anya, this is an excellent essay, very clear and sophisticated, and you have a good writing style which combines ethnography and the theory excellently. The various conceptualizations of built space is also novel.*

This disjuncture between Anya's self-evaluation and that of her lecturer is not that surprising because what Anya did not recognize was the skill with which she had organized the essay and the elements of originality that she had introduced, which demonstrated her engagement with the topic. Inevitably, writing the play made her re-evaluate the work in the essay, which is something she remarked upon: '*It* [the rewrite] *made me realize what I knew already – what was wrong with the essay.*'

When talking about the difference in experience between writing essays and writing the play, Anya made some interesting observations on each.

> *It's harder* [the play] *– I found it harder. And then this question – was it a chore or fun. It was really fun at first but then I found it – well, with an essay if you've done the reading then I mean you don't really have – you can just write it in a really flat way because it's not really what you're going to be marked on, whereas with this, well because I was doing it in essay circumstances, then it was – I felt it was a real pressure and I felt oh I can't be funny anymore.*

The idea that essay writing can be 'flat' because 'that's not what you're going to be marked on' stands in marked contrast with the stylistic qualities

in essay writing that the lecturers in Chapter 2 looked for. Equally, the
pressure of the deadline for 'my' assignment had caused her to struggle to
finish on time, whilst maintaining the qualities that she wanted in the work.
In some ways this suggests that she had set her personal bar higher for the
regenring than she had for the essay. Writing it as a play meant that she had
to do more with the disciplinary material.

> *I think I also had much more, had to have much more of a take on it – a position
> that I could get away with – not really taking in the essay . . .*

Additionally, writing the play allowed Anya to approach the materials
very differently, connecting them to reality rather than the 'compilation'
approach she mentioned in relation to essay writing.

> *And I think it does – presenting those theories in that way – um, makes them much
> more concrete, much more . . .*

Anya was the only member of the group whose regenred work I was able
to show to someone directly involved in the module that the original essay
came from. I would have liked to do the same with all the work, but busy
schedules and people's availability made this impossible. However, the
feedback from Anya's lecturer, who happened to be the one whose lecture
had led to her initial choice of essay, offers a very positive response despite
his earlier reservations about transgressing disciplinary boundaries which I
cited at the beginning of Chapter 3.

> *It was evident that she had read widely and this is a perfect example really – of
> a student – incredibly in the first year – who was able to take these ideas and
> manipulate them in a very creative way – incredibly creative way – so it was both
> academically erudite and I think that it was simply entertaining . . .*

His specific reference to the dual impact of scholarliness and entertainment
is important as it offers a clear response to criticisms that 'everyday' or
'horizontal' discourses lie outside the domain of academia. He went on to
comment on the resources she had used in representing the various disciplinary topics and how the play drew in many more themes than would or
could have been expected from a student in the first term of her first year.

> *What's wonderful about this is that it gave Anya the possibility to explore these
> [themes] in a creative way but also attach the theory of the ideas to characters*

who interacted with each other and discussed or argued about certain issues, you know like – What is anthropology? What is nationalism? Um – What is a house and an identity? – I mean there's more than just my lecture in there – there's lots of lectures in this paper.

Indeed, a comparison of the two versions allows us to see what he means. Although each version was a response to the same assignment question, the shift from essay to play led to a fundamental change in how the disciplinary information could be used. The changes were on both a representational level (e.g. the shape, the textual resources, the modes) and on an affective level, by which I mean the meanings that were possible.

6.3 Themes, Topics and Management of Information

The thematic orientation of an essay inevitably differs from that of a play because of the organizational strategies and the range of topics included. For instance, in essays, at least in the British context, the writer can set out the core argument, the organizational structure and even the 'answer' right at the beginning in the introduction. This gives it a sense of having been 'properly worked through', providing a context against which to locate the rest of the essay. Other cultures employ different strategies, as has been shown in Hinds (1983), and more recently Lillis and Curry (2010). By contrast, plays use different organizational strategies, rarely revealing the whole until the end, as the denouement unfolds through a series of events. This section, then, analyses these particular aspects of genre choice.

Taking both versions together for the moment, there are some similarities in how the material is managed. Both deal with all of the topics suggested in the original task instruction and although they achieve this in markedly different ways, they nevertheless follow a similar overall structure moving from one topic to the next in the same sequential order. For ease of reference, I provide the essay question again as follows:

How might anthropological considerations of the built environment lead to better understandings of issues such as social status, identity construction and nationalism?

Both productions start off with one of the biggest anthropological issues, fieldwork ethnography, even though the original question makes no direct reference to this. Nevertheless, the issue itself will have figured strongly in the module from which the essay came (Voice and Place) as its particular focus concerned the different research interests of members of the anthropology department. In using this disciplinary preoccupation, Anya expresses an identification with the community and even though she is very much a peripheral member there is a sense that she could, if she so chose, become more closely integrated. In the essay, this 'insider' involvement serves only to 'top and tail' the essay whereas in the play it is the core narrative driver in a similar way to Peter's and Sonia's regenred work. I return to this in Chapter 7.

6.3.1 Focus on The Essay

As can be seen in Extract 6.2, the essay starts with a strongly assertive opening paragraph problematizing anthropological methodology. This is, as mentioned above, an example of a writer claiming disciplinary membership with its reference to past and present concerns and the authority with which Anya identifies each of her points. It also exemplifies the kind of assertiveness I referred to in the last chapter when discussing Sonia's work.

Extract 6.2

> Fieldwork methodology has undergone vehement inside and outside criticism over the past decades, and as a discipline, anthropology has been compelled to question and reappraise its approach. Consequently, there is an intensified concern amongst social scientists to submit rigorous, comprehensive research, by unfolding the many layers surrounding a specific aspect of culture.

This opening gambit is certainly of the kind that would soothe the reader because as one of the lecturers in Chapter 2 said '*I relax if the first paragraphs show a critical approach to the question.*' What this opening does is locate the essay at the centre of anthropological debate and even though she does not return to the particular issue of methodology until the final paragraph, this demonstrates to Anya's reader her disciplinary involvement. She continues by narrowing down to the anthropological area that she is writing about, the built environment, before moving on to map out the structure of the essay, as can be seen in Extract 6.3.

Extract 6.3

> Often we do not fully attend to our environments, 'we do not examine them but breathe them in' (Day, 1990, p. 10) – 'great monuments shout their presence and instil feelings of awe and wonder, yet a familiar environment is taken for granted' (Pearson and Richards, 1999, p. 3). An anthropological consideration of the built environment would pose a range of questions regarding how and why it was formed, what it represents and expresses and what its effects are on society.
>
> This study will approach these questions with the intention of gleaning some elucidation as to issues of social status, identity construction and nationalism. It will be initially concerned with the domestic and work spaces, to then reflect on the impact of architecture and urban planning within the wider environment. After examining its effects on social identity, the role of the built environment in terms of national identity construction will be considered.

On reaching the end of this introduction, the reader would be further reassured that Anya knows what she is doing and that what she is doing accords with what the essay question wants her to do. She has provided an 'answer' to the essay question, thereby showing that she is on the right tracks. In linking it, albeit rather awkwardly, to professional thinking through the citations, she shows that she can contextualize her ideas in the disciplinary literature. The introduction finishes off with a promissory statement that would be further reassuring. The themes she intends to cover closely match those listed in the question itself and correspond to the sequence in which she addresses each in the essay. Such mapping, provided it really does match the rest of the essay, conveys an impression that this going to be a well-organized discussion and that the writer has mastered the body of knowledge, because she has managed to select relevant bits of it. However, despite this bright start, as the work progresses, it moves into what Anya feels is little more than a series of quotes, representing the compilation approach that she describes here.

I may have had the thought and then I'll come across something that's very similar. But instead of just having a short paragraph paraphrasing that and then maybe quoting something at the end, I think, sometimes out of laziness or because I haven't left myself enough time, I just can't be bothered to think about how I can rephrase this. So I just quote and then add another quote by somebody else. But I think that sometimes I kind of shoot myself in the foot because it seems that I'm just compiling quotations but quite often that's not really what I'm doing, and maybe it's 'cos I think it's more convincing if I quote somebody famous.

Both at the time of writing essays and on later reflection, particularly following the regenring experience, this annoyed her because it made her feel she wasn't doing herself justice. She felt that she was missing the chance to show her knowledge and understandings or how these corresponded and complemented those of the professional anthropologists' work that she was reading. It is important to note that her comments were not criticisms of essays per se, but rather her own attitude and approach in producing them. The following extract, taken from about a third of the way into the essay, illustrates the kind of writing that she felt unhappy with.

Extract 6.4

> In many settings across the globe great significance is accorded to the type of structure one inhabits. As Sircar's 1987 study shows, 'the ranking of 'detached', 'semi-detached', 'terrace' and 'flat' in Britain indicates the amount of space, garden area and privacy which are indicators of social position (Pearson and Richards, 1999, p. 8). These authors go on to write that 'the match between social classes and house types may not be absolute, but the hierarchical classification of dwellings acts as a totemic system of moral and social taxonomies for the British class structure, both exemplifying it and reinforcing it' (1999, p. 8).

However, what Anya herself perhaps failed to recognize is that she does much more than merely compile. While it is true that information in this essay is presented as a collection of citations, it is also interwoven with reformulations which clarify and move the reader on to the next citation. She links the ideas with a commentary thread, making it her own 'individual mixture', as Elbow (1999, p. 154) puts it, and it is the combination of her selections, reformulations and organizational strategies that makes the essay hers. The above extract, for example, is linked to the next set of quotes with a summarizing comment highlighted in bold in Extract 6.5 below. This comment serves to synthesize not only what has just been said but locates that in what has been said previously. Furthermore, it acts as a signpost, to use a rather clichéd term in the study of academic writing, and one that is double directional, pointing backwards and forwards.

Extract 6.5

> **As the dwelling is a representation of the self, the status quo and the household as a collective entity, so is often its placement within a particular neighbourhood or landscape.**
>
> Andrew Turton's 2000 study of social identity in Thai states evokes, by its very title, the notions of 'civility' and 'savagery' with which the Thai people classify their environment … [followed by a series of quotes and paraphrases]

This kind of intertextual activity in academic texts has been studied in detail by, for instance, Hyland (2000), whose work analysed a substantial body of academic texts from a range of different disciplines. He suggests that 'The embedding of arguments in networks of references not only suggests an appropriate disciplinary orientation, but reminds us that statements are invariably a response to previous statements and are themselves available for further statements by others' (p. 21). His research demonstrates that this discursive practice is very strong in fields such as sociology and philosophy, to which anthropology is closely identified. Admittedly, Hyland was talking about published articles by professional academics, but as already discussed in earlier chapters, student writers often feel that they are shadowing the 'real thing'. In disciplines such as anthropology, most of the reading that the students do consists of published articles and monographs, making it unsurprising that at times they adopt the disciplinary voice of the expert and at others simply use it wholesale as citations. In the case of student writers, it is likely that they (and possibly their readers) would view referencing as 'suggesting an appropriate disciplinary orientation' rather than that their own statements 'are available for further statements by others', to reuse Hyland's comment above.

Anya's success in drawing together the citations in the way she has, along with her problematizing framing of the essay, is bound to have been appreciated by her 'official' reader and most probably explains the very positive feedback the essay attracted. Her essay indicates that she has managed to understand and synthesize her reading and that she can, moreover, use this type of synthesis in the development of a disciplinary argument. In other words, she is showing that she has 'mastered' the 'relevant body of knowledge' and presented it in her 'own terms' as articulated in the departmental guide referred to earlier on in the book.

6.3.2 Focus on the Play

As I have already indicated, the play follows the sequential structure that Anya set out in the introduction to her essay. However, unlike the essay, where the topics are presented as a series of linked informational blocks, in the play they are presented as a sequence of events as the plot unfolds. It is the narrative genre that the play uses, that of a quest, that guides the organizational structure, with the essay question providing the quest goal. We are not given the answer from the outset, as in the essay, but, if we are familiar with quests, we can infer the kind of structure that the play will entail. The promise of the play is that the 'problem' (identified in the essay question) will be resolved by the hero through the events that take place and the people he encounters in the course of his questing travels. This new organization means that additional topic elements, which maintain the narrative flow, need to be introduced. In some ways, these additional elements correspond to the linking resources that Anya uses in the essay, which also stitch the topics together. In the essay, this adds an impression of synthesis, even despite the heavy reliance on quotations from disciplinary sources. In the play, however, synthesis is complete and the disciplinary knowledge both embodies and is embodied in the thematic and semiotic resources the genre affords.

Although it is difficult to gain an overall impression of the play without reading the full script, Extract 6.6, which comes at the very beginning of the play, provides some contextual information. This will be helpful in understanding the longer extract (6.7) that I use to discuss the thematic organization of the play.

Extract 6.6

[Context: Boris, a 19-year-old male snail, has just left school. Undecided about which direction to slither in next, he makes a two o'clock appointment with Mr Austin Tatius at his local I.C.C.C. Bureau (Inter-Species Cryptic Careers Counselling)].

From this, one can gain an impression of the tone of the play and the humour that Anya uses as one of the thematic resources in providing the strong reflexive quality of the work which I discuss in Chapter 7. For the moment, I want to focus on how the organizational structure of the play is set out in relation to the essay. Extract 6.7, which comes near the beginning of Scene Two, demonstrates how the new genre allowed Anya to synthesize the information in her essay introduction as a plot driver using a very different semiotic configuration.

Extract 6.7

[Boris is being given a 'work placement' by careers advisor Austen Tatius.]

Boris: Urrrr ... I don't understand, Sir ...

Austin Tatius: Quite, quite! Well those are the kinds of issues the A.A. have been scratching their heads over for years ... and when I realized these two fellows were members of that very club, well! It all just seemed to slot beautifully into place!

Boris: How, Sir?! ...

Austin Tatius: Your first utterances, boy! Why, they are at the very crux of the A.A.'s raison d'être!

Boris : Oh Sir ... What's the A.A.?

Austin Tatius: Ah, yes! Well, you see, there is a club of humans called the A.A., Anthropologists Anonymous that is, and they've been schlepping around the world for a number of years, asking all those questions that you articulated as a mere infant. However, some people weren't too chuffed about the way they were doing things – some even said they should lay off anthropology and fieldwork altogether, give it up! – which made them very sad because they believe it can really help to understand their world. Presently, they are looking to recruit someone with a different approach, someone fresh, someone who will be more ... objective ... although there is

---

some disagreement about the latter. Well! I suppose you could try, at any rate! And I should imagine your indiscriminatory stance with regards to the infinite world of colours would stand you in good stead. All in all, I think that you, dear boy, would make the perfect candidate!

The parallels with the essay introduction discussed above are clear in so far as the disciplinary issue is concerned as it is a reworking of the essay's opening paragraph. However, because of the affordances of speech, which I discuss in the next section, it provides a rather different take on the original information. It is no longer presented as an insider's assertion but quite the contrary. Here it is an outsider's representation of the problem and as such there is no sense of identification as there was in the essay. What is more, the ironic tone in the play stands in marked contrast to the earnestness of the essay's representation of the issue. Extract 6.8, which follows on directly from the previous extract, is another example of this type of thematic twist. It stands in the position of the essay's promissory statement, but unlike the essay, which identifies the specifics of how the task is to be done, here it is the fact of the task itself which is introduced. Up until now, Boris, the hero, has no idea that there is a task or that he will be embarking on a quest. Furthermore, quest narratives do not give the whole game away at the outset, even though we are familiar with aspects of the genre. That would spoil the experience for all concerned.

Extract 6.8

Boris: I ... Do you really think I could do it, Sir? I mean, I've never ...

Austin Tatius: Of course you can! Rise to the challenge, my boy! You have brains in your head. You have feet in your shoes. You can steer yourself any direction you choose! And I think I've come across just the right research topic for you, although I cannot disclose its exact nature at present. I'm sure you'll understand that, like any club, the A.A. has its rules and regulations to abide by ... Anyway, there is a division of the A.A. at a place called S.O.A.S. (Save Our Anthropologists' Souls) in London, U.K. and that is where I'll be sending you to collect your assignment! I do hope this is all agreeable with you as I've taken the liberty of contacting some of the members on your behalf, and I managed to yield an unconditional offer for you! What do you say to that?

Other synergies in thematic content can be identified in comparing the two versions. For instance, all the topics that Anya names in her essay introduction are included in the play. But rather than dealing one by one in a series of sequences of fact, they are integrated into the narrative as linked

The Material		
	Essay	**Play**
Thematic Orientation		
Organization	Essay management (introduction, 'body', conclusion i.e. sequence of information/ideas) Topic driven Discussion, descriptions, explanations, examples	Unfolding narrative organized into scenes (Introduction, activity, resolution) Event driven Dialogues, movement in space and time, arguments, explanations (shown, spoken about, experienced etc.)
Topics (examples)	Disciplinary terms of reference The built environment Social status Identity The home The workplace Fieldwork methodology	Disciplinary terms of reference and 'everyday' clarifications Fieldwork methodology The home Identity The workplace Gender Friendship Building as a craft Careers Essays Events Journeys Adventures Meetings

TABLE 6.1

events that develop as the story unfolds. Furthermore, as already indicated, the problematic disciplinary issue of fieldwork methodology with which she framed her essay is used as the primary organizing theme. Scene Two itself finishes off with a wave and a goodbye, marking the transition from the introductory phase to the quest itself. In this respect both the introduction to the essay and the play act in similar ways, serving as a springboard into the rest of the text. Table 6.1 displays some of the differences between the two versions in relation to thematic orientation.

6.4 Meaning Differently: Transduction to Transformation

So far, I have considered how a shift in genre led to a substantial difference in terms of the content and organization with the need to develop the original themes and introduce new ones largely because of the organizational requirements of the play. I now move on to consider semiotic orientation.

As already argued in Chapter 3, how we choose to produce the thing that we wish to communicate is what makes the information *be* what it is. What I mean is that the means of production, the materials (genres, modes and media) from which the production is made as chosen by the producer, according to what she thinks will best represent her meaning in what circumstances and for what purposes, is inseparable from the production itself. Therefore it follows that if you take information that has been produced with one set of resources and re-present it using a different set of resources there will be a substantive shift in how that information means. The different expressions of the communication of the 'same' set of statistical information that I gave in Chapter 3 illustrate this point.

Kress (2003) proposes the terms *transformation* and *transduction* to explain the processes involved in communicating meaning, arguing that these concepts help us to understand better the relationship between the interactions and actions involved. This explanation challenges transmission models of communication, which tend to oversimplify communicative activity by describing it in terms of input, reception and output: 'transformation is a much better explanation of processes of apperception and of integration … than are notions such as acquisition' (p. 46). Acquisition implies a kind of direct correspondence between 'output' and 'input', to use technicist terms, between what the 'utterer' or producer 'says' and what the correspondent understands. By contrast, the concept of transformation allows for the effects brought about as soon as an 'idea' or 'thought' (text) is produced with the chosen resources. It relates to both the expression and the interpretation of the represented idea as represented in Figure 3.1 in Chapter 3.

Referring to a shift from written modes to visual modes in a science class, Kress suggests that this kind of shift 'is not a process of transformation' but rather one of reconfiguration 'according to the affordances of a quite different mode' (2003, p. 47). I want to add that transduction is always a part of the communicative process. The shift between 'idea', that is production as thought, which uses non-material (inner?) resources, and production as 'text', which uses material resources, can be considered as transduction. This section, then, considers the effects of the different modes used in each of the versions and the effects this had on the textual materials they use. I am particularly interested in the different configurations of the information that these shifts in mode and textual materials bring about.

Before discussing specific examples from Anya's work, I want to clarify my use of mode in relation to these texts. As I explained in Chapter 4, despite the fact that all the work was done with writing, it is possible to consider these texts as incorporating other modes. Anya's essay, for instance, uses imported characters, in the shape of her citations, to do much of the disciplinary display work. Her own character, that is she herself, does the topic selection and organizational work by choosing and linking the different citations. In the play, Anya uses a much wider range of characters, both fictional and imported. In this case, the workload is differently distributed, with Anya's own creations (the fictional characters rather than the imported real ones) doing both the thematic and the semiotic work. The imported characters act as a kind of disciplinary foil to the 'everyday' meanings represented by the fictional cast, as will be seen later, and provide disciplinary explanations for the events experienced in the course of the play.

So far I have mainly referred to verbal modality when discussing the essay and the play. However, a play can draw on non-verbal modes in representing meaning. Character is one of the few examples that appear in both the essay and the play, and much of the semiotic work that character does is verbal. However, character can also embody meaning. In academic writing this relates to the provenance that cited authors carry, communicating meanings of affiliation, for instance. In a play, however, the characters can embody many additional meanings through their own use of mode both verbal and non-verbal. Table 6.2, which compares the semiotic orientations of each version, displays examples of the modes and their associated textual materials used.

The Material		
	Essay	**Play**
Semiotic Orientation		
Modes (examples)	Writing (to be read)/ writtenness	Written speech (scripted dialogues)/spokenness
	Characters (writer, cited sources, reader)	Characters (fictional and 'real')
		Director's notes/stage management depictions (e.g. gestures, actions, voice pitch and tone)
		Props (e.g. household objects, plane tickets, costumes)
		Locations (e.g. park bench, internet café)
	Opinions and evaluations	Humour (irony, sarcasm)
	Length (size)	Length (size)
Textual materials (examples)	Clause complexity	Clause intricacy
	'it' fronted passives, nominalizations embeddedness intratextual links indirectness	Subject fronted structures, direct questions intertextual links directness
	'Formal' expression	Colloquialisms Exclamations
		Specific facial and gestural acts – 'melancholy glance',
		Ways of moving (Choreographic movements) – 'file in to'
	3,332 words	*10,474 words*

TABLE 6.2

Some of my inclusions may appear strange and open to debate. For example, I have included 'length' as a mode and the number of words as the textual material that comprises 'length'. Nevertheless difference in length adds a spatial as well as a social dimension, influencing the way in which things can be received, as the comment '*it is simply just too long*' indicates. Similarly, props or locations as mode may cause some disagreement. However, in Anya's play, these contribute in important ways to the representation of the disciplinary knowledge that she produces.

The following examples consist of an extract from a third of the way into the essay and its reconfigured counterpart in the play, represented by three extracts from Scene Five in the play. Extract 6.9 comes from the essay and represents the summing up argument on the issue of women's isolation in the domestic space. It is a paraphrased version of a direct quote that it sits next to and is an example of the compiling approach that Anya was unhappy about.

Extract 6.9

Research on the isolated and isolating nature of the housewife's role in Western society concludes that this seclusion is due to the privatized manner in which housework is performed.

In the play this theme is very differently handled. It uses a range of different semiotic resources in its articulation and the meaning unfolds in the course of a series of events and interactions. The 'core' meaning is represented by Extract 6.10, which appears in the play as a stage management note.

Extract 6.10

[At this, the woman they are sharing the table with lifts her melancholic glance from the depths of her mug of tea, and directs a steady but weary look at Boris. Hitherto silent, she suddenly interjects.]

Isolated from the rest of the action, it is difficult to understand the relevance of this extract and what it 'depicts' in relation to the strong assertion from the essay above. However, as part of the unfolding scene, the correspondence becomes clearer as Extract 6.11, which precedes the previous extract in the sequence of events in the play, shows.

Extract 6.11

> [They all file into the Someplace Else Café. It is lunchtime and very crowded, so they ask a woman sitting on her own if they may share the table with her, she acquiesces. They order a large pot of tea.]

'They' refers to what has now become 'the companions' in true questing style and consists of Boris, the hero, and two others that he has picked up on his journey. The identification of the location adds a layer of additional meaning, further developed by the conversation that follows, which is a heated discussion about the relationship between where you live or work and identity, some of the themes from the essay. Extract 6.12 is what prompts the actions described in Extract 6.10.

Extract 6.12

> Boris: Well, yeah … a bit … but the *class* thing … can't people change that? How are classes formed? How do people get *positioned*?

This additional context gives a new angle on the meaning of the woman with the melancholy glance and the weary look. The 'steady but weary look' she gives Boris now has a purpose and the meaning of the 'image' becomes even clearer when linked to the comment that the woman interjects.

Extract 6.13

> Woman: 'Household Service Work', pet! That's the way to climb the ladder! My name's Sudipta, by the way.

The combination of the companions' discussion, the location, the image of the woman and the comment in Extract 6.13 gradually move towards the meanings represented in Extract 6.9 from the essay. The meaning is further communicated as Sudipta's story is revealed (she is a South Asian woman with no children of her own, living by herself in a Western city). The final extract from this set confirms her narrative function as the embodiment of the point made in the essay.

Extract 6.14

> Sudipta: … I'm lonely, you see, so I come to Someplace Else to drink my tea … I like to look into my mug of chai, deep down at my reflection, it's sunny in there, it reminds me of home … and lots of people around me …

This may seem, of course, a very long-winded way of going about the business of communicating something that was achieved very economically in the essay. However, the semiotic resources that the play uses do not replicate the essayist information, but reconfigure, it and in so doing transform it from reported (reified) information to articulated (dynamic) experience. Each element of its representation (the stage directions, the conversation between the companions and the social and cultural background of the woman herself) all contribute to the meanings that Anya wants to communicate. Every choice that Anya makes in creating her characters, events and places is a semiotic opportunity. It is no accident that Sudipta is South Asian, for instance, just as it is no accident that Boris is a snail, and each choice she makes in reworking the essay offers her new ways of understanding the disciplinary material.

6.5 Spokenness versus Writtenness

In this part of the chapter I focus more closely on the differences between the writtenness of the essay and the spokenness of the play, the most immediate of which is that the play is much longer than the essay. This was noted by Anya's lecturer despite his great enjoyment of the play, as mentioned earlier.

> *I suppose first of all I think one of the problems with the text as a submission for coursework and being honest is that it's just too long.*

A simple word count, not to mention the physical thickness of the submitted versions, shows that the play is over five times longer than the essay. This can be attributed in part to the additional material that the play's narrative demands as discussed above, which forced Anya to '*have more of a take*' on the issues by having to develop the storyline. This enabled her to produce and incorporate her own meanings through resources such as characters, scenes, actions and so on, all of which had to be carried through and resolved alongside the original themes of the essay. This inevitably meant that the text would be longer or rather would take longer in enabling the meanings to unfold. However, the other main factor in this regard is difference between writtenness and spokenness.

Essentially, we use more words in saying something than we do in writing or rather we organize our meanings in a looser arrangement than we do in writing. This corresponds to what Halliday (1989) describes as the 'clause intricacy' of speech, which is characterized by 'lexical sparsity' (p. 79) and where meanings are more likely to be represented as 'whole configurations of processes related to each other in a number of different ways' (p. 86). This can easily be confirmed by transcribing even examples of formal spoken discourse such as a lecture. Equally, when written discourse such as an academic article or an essay is read out during a seminar presentation, it can appear dense and impenetrable because of its lexical density and clause complexity.

As I have already argued, communication is a collaborative phenomenon involving the negotiation of meaning between participants and the semiotic choices they make. In writing, there is, as Kress (1994) points out, a kind of explicitness which is necessary in order to cater for the absent reader. In other words, the writer has to imagine or anticipate the reader's interactions and respond to them within the frame of the written production. In speech, however, the 'other' is present and visible (unless on the telephone) and the speaker can adapt and modify the information depending on the observed feedback. The immediacy of the to-ing and fro-ing between the participants in the making and remaking that I describe in Chapter 3, in contrast to the delayed interactions in writing, means that the information may take longer in its 'saying'. On the other hand, as Kress (1994, p. 23) also points out, 'Spoken texts may leave information implicit because the speaker knows what the hearer knows and because he can assess as he speaks whether he has been correct in his assessment.' This means that speech can be more implicit and less elaborated than writing, which would suggest that things might take less time to say. Furthermore, the availability of other communicative modes such as gestures means that the information may not need 'saying' at all.

A play, of course, involves writing, but in writing a play, the writer uses the semiotic resources of 'live' interaction such as gesture, clothing, attitudes and opinions in combination with the thematic resources which define and drive the particular narrative. A play script is produced as speech and as in a 'real' conversation, every utterance in a play is a *response* to a previous utterance, framed by the circumstances in which it takes place. The writer of a play uses the direct utterances between characters to produce the meanings that she wishes to communicate. By contrast, the writer of an essay produces meanings as a network of indirect utterances involving absent participants (the reader[s] and the cited authors). This removes the negotiating options that are available in spoken communication, leaving the writer to work within a kind of communicative vacuum, which can be extremely challenging, as the discussion in Chapter 2 shows. Producing academic knowledge with a genre such as a play allows the writer to replace this communicative vacuum with 'direct' dialogue between the participants in an intricate configuration of utterances with which the meanings are negotiated.

6.5.1 The Living References

As the result of my stricture to the students involved in this study to incorporate the references they had used in their essays, some of them chose to achieve this through introducing those writers as characters 'speaking for themselves'. Sometimes the students reproduced the quotes from their readings in their original form, speaking, as it were, the written words.

> *And then because I wanted to add an extra dimension I allowed the scholars themselves to quote in their own words – um – just to make the whole thing come a little more to life.* (Dan)

In Dan's case, which I discuss in the next chapter, these referenced authors were introduced as holograms conjured up by a futuristic computer which was acting as a kind of library for a student engaged in research. In Assif's case, which I refer to in a moment, the living references are the economists whose theories his essay compares. In Anya's case, they were introduced as plotline characters speaking their words within the frame of a conversation which took place in the 'Someplace Else Café' mentioned earlier. The 'normality' of the social setting allows for the citations to be incorporated into a direct discussion as opposed to the reported nature of their incorporation in the essay.

Extract 6.15

[Unbeknown to Boris and his three key informants, the group at the adjacent table (three men and a woman) have been listening in on their conversation. One of the men leans towards them, addressing the whole group. Boris notices they are all wearing badges with 'A.A.' marked on them.]

Man: Hello there! Please forgive me, but I couldn't help overhearing you talking about Tailand, and Tai identity – I do hope you meant it without 'h' – it's more correct ... You see, this is my area of expertise, I've done lots of fieldwork there over the years ... Yes! ... I'm Andrew, by the way, let me introduce you to my friends: this is Constance, and these two fellows are Mike and Colin ...

[Boris, Holly, Michael and Sudipta all introduce themselves, exchange handshakes, and join the tables.]

Andrew: Yes ... You see, I introduced and edited a book very recently, and the very title, *Civility and Savagery*, refers to the way in which the Tai classify their environment ... There are two main binary oppositions: those of the 'tai: kha', and 'mŭang: pa'. And you see, by qualifying themselves as 'tai', the people of Tailand appropriate 'freedom-loving' values, and by contrast, they attribute a servile character to the non-tai: the 'ka'. Furthermore, 'mŭang', in which the Tai has historically asserted his identity, denotes the 'political domain' and social development, as opposed to 'pa', which is from the same root as the latin 'silva' – the forest – which denotes notions of the wilderness and *savagery*: the hill-people ... (1)

Boris: Right ... so they like think that all the goodies live in towns and the wild ones lurk in the forest? ...

Sudipta: Ha! Junglees!

Mike: Exactly ... the forest as a place of danger, or more positively as a place of refuge or purgation, was conceptually opposed to the security and order of the town and city ... (2)

Holly: Was? ...

Colin: Yes, things have shifted somewhat – today we invest the forest with attributes of retreat and tranquillity, in opposition to the social evils and stress of the city ...

[1.] Turton, Andrew (ed.) 2000 'Introduction' in *Civility and Savagery: Social Identity in Tai States.* Richmond, Surrey, Curzon Press
[2.] Pearson, M.P. and Richards, C.,1999 *Architecture and Order: Approaches to Social Space.* London, Routledge and Keegan Paul

In this extract, Anya presents a multilayered representation of the information that was expressed in the original essay. The contextualization of the citations and the dynamic nature of conversation lends a different set of meanings to the information compared with the essayist representation.

Extract 6.16

Michael Parker Pearson and Colin Richards write that 'the forest as a place of danger, or more positively as a place of refuge or purgation, was conceptually opposed to the security and order of the town and city. Yet today we invest the forest with attributes of retreat and tranquillity, in opposition to the social evils and stress of the city' (1999, p. 4).

The words of the cited authors are more or less the same but in the play they are integrated into an actual discussion, responding to articulated comments and questions. Because this is a spoken discussion there is a need to provide the kind of feedback that ensures conversational flow. The feedback itself needs to do something to facilitate the flow and that 'something' means something in its own right. In the case of this extract, they provide a synthesis of the information, but one which is firmly located in the 'lived' world of the companions as opposed to the 'intellectualized' world of the discipline. In others words, the interjections of the questing companions *mediate* the information provided by the cited authors and makes it palatable for the 'ordinary' 'person in the street', as represented by the companions.

It is also interesting to compare the two extracts in considering the effect of the speech-like elements that Anya adds to the quoted pieces. In the essay the Pearson and Richards quote follows on directly from the Andrew

Turton quote, presented in Extract 6.5 above. Unlike in that extract, where Anya provided an explicit, synthesizing comment as a linking device, in this case (Extract 6.16) she offers no explanation of how the two quotations relate to each other. Instead, the reader is left to infer relevance from the actual (physical) juxtapositioning of the quotes. This is something I return to later on in this chapter. Anya realized that she had tended to do this after revisiting the essay in preparation for our interview, attributing it to laziness.

> *I think sometimes out of laziness because I haven't left myself enough time or I just can't be bothered to think about how I can rephrase this I'll just quote and then add another quote by somebody else – and – you know, it's difficult to read.* (Anya)

The impact of such unmediated juxtapositioning is that the reader may or may not know how the writer means the information to be read. The lack of reflexivity that explicit mediation offers reinforces the sense that the essay is a compilation rather than a discussion that the students referred to in interview. The sequencing of the conversational gambits in the play, however, offers specific 'readings' of the information through the understandings and interpretations of the core characters – the companions. The reinterpretation of 'Andrew's' research-based information and the ensuing interchanges highlight the discursive quality of these views. 'Mike' picks up the two preceding comments with a strong confirmation of Boris's reinterpretation ('Exactly'), which serves not only as a cohesive spoken device but also to validate the way in which Boris has understood. It reflects the kind of approval that students writers desire, but which, when they are in the process of writing, are sometimes unsure of getting. Mike is, after all, an expert, and his approval must be worth having.

A different kind of interaction links the next two utterances. Holly's interrogation of the use of the past tense makes the transition between the two opposing realities – the forest as a fearful place versus the forest as a tranquil place – natural. The question requires a confirmation (or otherwise) and some kind of explanation so that the second half of the quote becomes linked not only to its other half but to Andrew's quote too. In other words, the information is now presented as a real dialogue between real people. They are a group of people (experts and lay) engaged in making the information. With different questions different answers might be given. If Holly had not noticed the use of past tense, perhaps Colin would not have mentioned the shift. Of course, before getting too carried away by thinking of this as a real-world conversation, it is important to remember that what I am talking about is a constructed product; a 'secondary genre', as Bakhtin might define it, in which Anya has contrived to bring about these 'conversations' in the pursuance of the task assigned to her – the exercise in regenring.

Assif also imported live references in his new version where he redesigned his original economics essay as a radio phone-in featuring John Maynard Keynes and Milton Friedman as guests. In this production, not only were the guests enabled to 'speak for themselves' in typical radio-style debate, but their presentations of theory were mediated by the radio host and the questions asked by the members of the public who phoned in with their questions. This allowed for the essay content to be developed and clarified within a context where these issues had a 'real world' currency rather than the more abstract account that the essay produced. Extract 6.17 is from the essay and Extract 6.18 is from the phone-in.

Extract 6.17

> If in a recession and investment doesn't respond through flexible interest rates, Classical theory states that prices and wages will also adjust to return the economy to full employment output.
>
> With a reduction in AD, prices fall (supply chasing fewer buyers). Purchasing power of money increases and AD returns to original level with full employment.

Extract 6.18 (PC = host, MN = member of public, MF = Milton Friedman)

> **PC**: Well, I hope that answered your question, Mr Bashir. Our second caller is a Mr Mike Need from Birmingham. Mr Need, your question please.
>
> **MN**: [Heavy Birmingham accent] Thanks. You just talked about flexible interest rates being able to get us out of a recession. My question to MF is, if in a recession and investments and savings do not respond through flexible interest rates, then what?
>
> **MF**: I'm glad that you asked that question. If flexible interest rates do not stimulate the economy, then the flexibility of prices and wages

would allow the economy to return to full employment. Listen. With a reduction in Aggregate Demand, prices would fall. This fall in prices means that our money that we hold has greater purchasing power. Since items are cheaper we can buy more. This would lead to greater spending, Aggregate Demand returns to its original level and the economy has full employment again.

The affordances of the question–response exchange that occurs helps to unpack the ideas presented in the essay. Furthermore, the spokenness of the dialogue leads to a shift from the heavily nominalized writtenness of the original version with a corresponding shift in agency. The 'looser' spoken version of the phone-in reflects what Halliday (1989, p. 93) refers to as 'grammatical metaphor', where the speech versus writing is expressed through different grammatical choices (e.g. 'Purchasing power of money increases' versus 'This fall in prices means that our money that we hold has greater purchasing power').

In fact, the essay did not actually refer to Friedman as such, but rather 'classical economics' as a theoretical field. The attachment of the theory to a real person is a necessary consequence of the genre which required an expert representative of the theory to oppose the 'real' Keynes in the debate-style structure of the programme. Having constructed a 'real' person, that person had also to have a point to prove, which led to the inclusion of 'I'm glad you asked that question' or 'Listen,' which further add a sense of agency, that these ideas really belong to the speaker, who needs to demonstrate his authority. There are, of course, other aspects of Assif's production that bear further consideration. For instance, what is the impact of knowing that the caller had a strong Birmingham accent? Perhaps it provides additional 'authenticity' in the representation of radio phone-ins. Maybe there is some connection to Birmingham and business. Other students also incorporated experts as live participants in their work. Andy, whose work I used in Chapter 4, produced his work as a newspaper report and included quotes and references to 'living' political theorists including Aristotle and Montesquieu alongside the modern-day commentators that he had been reading in full journalistic discourse. And Dan, as already mentioned, introduced holographic versions of the experts referenced in his original essay. This vitalization of the academic community as a lived and living thing will be picked up in the next chapter.

One major effect of the spokenness in all the students' work was the way in which the shift from written to spoken resources enabled the students to move away from the over-assertiveness that tends to characterize essays produced early on in the academic cycle, as discussed in Chapter 5. In the next section I explore this aspect of the work by comparing two paired extracts from Anya's work, the first from the essay and the second from the play.

6.6 From Assertions to Negotiations

In the two extracts I use in this section, anthropological considerations of 'the home' provide the thematic focus. This is one of the main themes in both the essay and the play, although in the play it is more centrally located as a plot-driving strand, embodied by Boris's own snail shell. As in all good quests, Boris does not travel alone. He acquires a band of fellow travellers, each of whom represents a particular issue identified in the essay: attachment to the 'home' is represented by Holly; the workplace and individual identity by Michael; and, as already shown, the issue of domestic isolation and gender by Sudipta. His companions provide Boris with help in achieving the quest's stated goal, that of writing the essay (see Extract 6.8), but, as is also typical of quests, is not what it originally seemed. In fact, Anya's play has some resonance with *The Wizard of Oz* in its focus on 'home', but unlike that story, which promotes the value of 'no place like home', this story promotes the opposite. The true goal of Boris's quest, as it turns out, is freedom from 'the home', emerging from his shell (also metaphorically significant) and literally leaving his home behind.

In my analysis of the each of the two extracts, I focus specifically on the observable textual materials such as grammatical structures, vocabulary and cohesive devices. As usual, I begin with the essay (Extract 6.19) before moving on to the play (Extract 6.20) in providing the analysis.

Extract 6.19

Most housing, across the globe, is made by people for themselves. 'Environments are thought before they are constructed' (Rappaport, 1980, p. 298) and 'man builds in order to think and act' (Preziosi, 1983). The 'immobile' home stands for a desire to fix a centre, it is a will to grasp orientation, order and identity. Thus, the dwelling can be interpreted as an elaborate metaphor for the concept of human identities. In Dovey's words, 'to be at home is to know where you are; it means to inhabit a secure centre and to be oriented in space' (1985, p. 36). The home can be perceived as a microcosm for the whole world, where human statuses and the central beliefs of a culture are represented through material design. Man strives to fix a centre, a 'focus' amongst the chaos. The organisation of domestic space is a cultural process that translates systems of classification. Dichotomies such as private: public, clean: dirty, front: back have cultural variations and are conformed to accordingly, in different settings, as shows R.J. Lawrence's comparative study of Australian and English domestic environments. 'Thus, the structuring of a home is not an unalloyed expression of "individuality" but is 'predicted by age, gender, class, ethnicity and other aspects of social context' (Pearson and Richards, 1999, p. 7).

This extract offers an elaborate definition of the home, but not one that would naturally come to mind. In this discussion, the home is not bricks and mortar, nor is it a place where a family lives. It is, instead, 'an elaborate metaphor for the concept of human identities', a 'microcosm for the whole world'. These are entirely disciplinary conceptualizations, matched by the other terms of reference used in the extract ('domestic environment', 'fix a centre'), all of which indicate strong disciplinary affiliation. Whether Anya really feels this connection or not is impossible to tell. However, the interweaving of her definitions with the quotations that frame the extract suggests that she can manage the discourses and concepts that she is writing about in a way that implies affiliation. This is further promoted by her use of binary categorization involving fundamental disciplinary dichotomies ('private: public, clean: dirty, front: back'), a strategy that also appears later on in the essay with other (anthropological) dichotomies ('permanent–temporary', 'inside–outside', 'intimate–impersonal'). This organizational strategy is a valuable resource in academic writing because it enables particular conceptualizations to be highlighted and encourages reflection on each part of the binary set through consideration of difference. It is a fundamental tool in the researcher's repertoire in whatever disciplinary field and Anya's use of it reflects her understanding of how anthropological arguments are made, thereby adding to the impression of community membership.

What is particularly striking about this extract is its impression of assertiveness. However, there is a sense that it feels too assertive and too authoritative. There is a certain awkwardness about it. This is, in part, associated with issues of discursive identity and the novice speaking as expert, dimension discussed in the last chapter, and is what Anya was referring to when she used the phrase 'shadow writing' in connection with the idea of borrowing the discourse of the professionals. The question is, what makes it seem assertive and why does it also seem awkward? The answer seems to lie in the textual materials she chooses, most notably the use of categorical statements organized as a series of uncontested and hence incontestable facts. Such resources, as has been discussed by Fairclough (2001), typify ideological discourses, such as political speeches, where ideological views are presented as 'common sense' truths. In this extract it is not only the number of categorical statements that are presented but the way in which they are organized that gives it its mixed impression, as I explain in the following.

Anya starts this paragraph with the very strong, though in reality questionable, assertion: '*Most housing, across the globe, is made by people for themselves.*' This sentence, despite its slight hedge (most), is, however, expressed as if it were an incontrovertible 'truth' only contestable by a direct challenge, as in 'No it's not!' This sentence is then followed by two equally assertive sentences, both of which are direct quotes ('Environments are thought before they are constructed' [Rappaport, 1980, p. 298] and 'man builds in order to think and act' [Preziosi, 1983]), presumably intended to support or clarify her original statement. However, there are two main problems here. Although, by association, these quotes identify Anya's initial assertion as a disciplinary conceptualization and not an everyday one, neither of them confirm its disciplinary validity or 'truth'. The second problem is that despite the textual juxtapositioning of the quotes, they are, in fact, neither textually nor semantically connected. These quotes come from two differently positioned arguments (we think in order to build versus we build in order to think) and their individual assertiveness comes from the arguments that have been developed in their own discussions. The next statement, Anya's own, ('*The "immobile" home stands for a desire to fix a centre, it is a will to grasp orientation, order and identity*') continues this strategy. By juxtaposing these different assertions sequentially in this way, there is the impression of the development of an argument even though the assertions themselves do not mutually interact. It is this that gives the extract its awkwardness. This is further compounded by the use of the connective 'thus' immediately following this sequence (*Thus, the dwelling can be interpreted as an elaborate metaphor for the concept of human identities*), which is used to indicate logical conclusion even though such a relationship has not really been demonstrated. This is not to say that they cannot be considered logically related points, but they have not been made to be so by the intervention of Anya's own evaluative voice. She has presented her commentary as assertion rather than evaluation and hence has almost erased herself from the text.

The use of 'thus' in the paragraph is interesting in its own right. It appears twice in the paragraph, once early on as discussed above and at the end. On the first occasion the 'thus' belongs to Anya. She introduces it to promote the strong, but not actually demonstrated, logical connectivity already problematized above. On the second occasion the 'thus' is not Anya's own, but belongs to somebody else, Pearson and Richards ('Thus, the structuring of a home is not an unalloyed expression of 'individuality' but is 'predicted by age, gender, class, ethnicity and other aspects of social context'). It is a quoted 'thus' and, as such, belongs in a different argument and not the current one. Therefore, the strong correspondence signalled by Pearson and Richards' 'thus' is to a different set of points than those it is being used to summarize in Anya's essay. However, despite this disjunction, the overall effect of this extract is one of categorical certainty, reinforced by the unassailability of the use of this connective and these definitions of 'the home' appear unchallenged and possibly unchallengeable.

A final observation is that the strongly affirmed agency implied in this paragraph, with its categorical statements and the use of 'thus', contrasts with the rather more hedged agency Anya shows in her reformulations and interpretations. For instance, her use of passive modality ('*Thus the dwelling can be interpreted as*...', '*The home can be perceived as*...') may well signal tentativeness despite, or because of, the strongly assertive context in which these forms appear. However, despite these two incidences, the whole remains strongly assertive. It is worth remembering, as I have already mentioned, this phenomenon is common in first year essays as students navigate their way through the disciplinary materials and discourses towards engagement, identification and participation. Anya's essay work is 'excellent', as her tutor remarked on the feedback, because she has demonstrated wide and relevant reading and has identified and understood the fundamental issues associated with her topic. That she presents this somewhat awkwardly is part of the process of learning.

As will be anticipated, the corresponding part of the play configures the information discussed above in a very different way. No longer are the arguments presented as disciplinary conceptualizations asserted as 'fact' but rather as personal experience told in conversation. Working with the play as the framing genre, Anya was enabled to draw on a much wider range of semiotic resources, as has already been seen. This allowed her to move from the essay's assertions to a more analysed and negotiated interpretation.

Extract 6.20 represents, in part, the content presented in the essay extract, though it is important to stress that the themes and issues expressed in the essay extract also appear at other points throughout the play as a consequence of the ongoing plotline and the relevance of the topic to the characters. This means that although this extract is most closely matched to the essay, the theme itself continues to be analysed and developed as the play progresses. This particular extract comes early on in Scene Three, shortly after Boris has been given his 'assignment', which is, of course, the essay question itself. It is a quite a long extract, which is a further example of the economy of writtenness in comparison to spokenness. But is illustrates how this different representation invites a different kind of interpretation of the disciplinary theme; one in which Anya can reconfigure it as familiar knowledge.

Extract 6.20

> [There is a young woman on the other end (of the park bench), bent double by the weight of her house. He can feel her looking at him out of the corner of her eye. Boris starts to feel self-conscious about the diminutive size of his shell. To mask his unease, he clumsily attempts to engage in conversation.]
>
> **Boris** (to the young woman): That's a big place you've got there! You must be proud to have so much! – (in petto): Durrrr! Why do I always have to come up with such crap?!
>
> **Young woman**: So much? I don't have anything, mate. They took it all ...
>
> **Boris**: Who took it? Who took what? ...
>
> **Young woman**: Oh god! I don't know how many times I've told this story ... Here we go: I got burgled a few days ago. The b******s took

everything, everything went out the window ... So here I am, minus everything about me, minus 'all the books and all the records of my lifetime'. My home is just a ... shell ... er, sorry, I mean, no offence of course ...

Boris: Yeah ... okay ... I mean, I'm sorry about what happened ... Umm, what's your name?

Young woman: I'm Holly, and you?

Boris: My name's Boris ... tell me some more about your shell ...

Holly: Well, yeah ... my home's a shell ... it's been, like, gutted ... Actually, I'm a shell, I feel like my insides have been scraped out. I had everything just the way I wanted it, you know. I felt so safe, so at home. I hate this expression, yeah, 'cos it denotes such an egocentric conception of the universe, but anyway, for want of a better one: it was soooo ME. D'you know what I mean? And now that's gone ... and – I don't mean to sound melodramatic – but my identity went with it ... They messed the house up so badly ... I'm such a mess. I've lost my centre, you know ... I'm, like, lost ... I don't really know where to go, so I sit in the park with the winos and, er ... snails ... It's such an invasion! ... All my notions of public:private have got mixed up ... Imagine if this happened to you, Boris ... if someone ripped off your shell and stamped on it ...

Boris: What's all this about being lost, though ...? Centres, and all that? Your, err ... notions ...?

Holly: Well, you know, to be at home is to know where you are; it means to inhabit a secure centre and to be oriented in space. If you take the home away – your reference point – you feel lost, you know, and exposed, nude ... you put so much of yourself into your home, people build homes out of their own essence, shells to shelter their personality.

Boris: Oh yeah ... I think I've heard about that before. But what about those notions ...?

Holly: You really do need everything to be explained to you, don't you? ... OK, my home was my canvas, yeah ... my arena for self-expression ... but everyone knows that we're culturally determined, so, like, I'm under no illusions, yeah, my way of organizing my space and its components pretty much cohered with everyone else's on this island, and differed from people's ways in other cultures, or from other backgrounds, or other age groups ... Get the picture? I mean, we classify things in terms of public:private, clean:dirty, and on and on, and that's all adhered to ... represented through people's domestic environments ... you know ...

Boris: Err ... Yeah. But Holly ... all this about losing your identity. I mean, I've just met you and I don't think you're empty, or lacking in personality ... you're alright, man. You still seem to be able to be yourself. Maybe you don't need that house as much as you think you do ...

Holly: Yeah, well, I'm adjusting, man. Reappraising, you know ...

As is evident from the extract, the encounter between the two characters in this scene provides the opportunity to express the essay content as an enacted dialogue. Anya, as author of the play, was able to create her characters so as to embody the essay themes in their experiences and attitudes. Holly's exposition of the essay content is reconfigured as the real world experience of having the 'security' of the home removed from her through the off-stage event of a burglary. The spokenness and the 'embodiedness' mean that other resources such as anger and regret enable the information to be enacted and talked over instead of being conceptualized, as in the essay. A comparison of Extract 6.21, from the essay, and Extract 6.22, from the play, demonstrates this.

Extract 6.21

The 'immobile' home stands for a desire to fix a centre, it is a will to grasp orientation, order and identity. Thus, the dwelling can be interpreted as an elaborate metaphor for the concept of human identities.

Extract 6.22

> It was soooo ME. D'you know what I mean? And now that's gone ...
> and – I don't mean to sound melodramatic – but my identity went
> with it ... They messed the house up so badly ... I'm such a mess.
> I've lost my centre, you know ... I'm, like, lost ... I don't really know
> where to go, so I sit in the park with the winos and, er ... snails ... It's
> such an invasion! ... All my notions of public:private have got mixed
> up ... Imagine if this happened to you, Boris ... if someone ripped
> off your shell and stamped on it ...

The implications of 'house', 'identity', 'possessions', 'security' are now no
longer generalized abstractions but instead have become particularized
experiences which the characters talk to each other about. Anya herself
remarked on this aspect of the regenring:

> *Because these characters – these snails and young women, whatever – were saying*
> *them, it connected it to the reality of what they were talking about because they*
> *were constantly subjectifying and talking about their lives, which doesn't happen*
> *with* [essays] ...

This results in one of the most significant shifts in terms of how the information is represented; that is from the asserted facts of the essay to the
negotiated understandings that this extract shows. Unlike the sequences
of propositional assertions organized into identified, themed phases with
paragraphs and sentences, in the play these 'facts' are expressed as
conversation. The assertiveness of the essay, which, as I said, presents the
information as unchallenged and unchallengeable, is here open to be
contested, as Extract 6.19 shows.

Extract 6.23

> **Boris**: Err ... Yeah. But Holly ... all this about losing your identity. I
> mean, I've just met you and I don't think you're empty, or lacking
> in personality ... you're alright, man. You still seem to be able to be
> yourself. Maybe you don't need that house as much as you think you
> do ...

What is also interesting about these examples is the way in which the essay information is problematized so that the conceptualization of 'the home' is no longer accepted in the ways that it was in the essay. Here it is represented as something of a burden ('There is a young woman on the other end, bent double by the weight of her house') and despite Holly's own claims that her house was her 'core', Boris challenges this idea, the disciplinary idea, as represented in Extract 6.21 above. What is more, the unassertive way in which he proposes this, characterized by lots of hedging ('Err ... Yeah ... But, I mean ... Maybe') comes across more persuasively than the categorical statements used in the essay.

There are many more examples of how Anya uses the resources afforded by the play to communicate both the essay information and her own reflections, for instance the appeals to shared knowledge, which is obviously not shared by the alien snail ('everyone knows'), the exasperation of having to explain everything ('you really do need to have everything explained), the irony of Boris's comment regarding shells, 'I think I've heard about that before ...' and so on. These aspects relate not to the essay or disciplinary materials but to the experience of 'being a student', which is something I discuss in the next chapter.

In fact, as the result of 'writing a play' Anya found herself paying attention to issues which emerged out of the plotline itself and could '*go off at a tangent and develop something ... that produces something useful and gives a new form to what I'm writing and takes it in other directions*'. Writing the play enabled her to explore, rather than present, all the anthropological issues that she so ambitiously listed in the essay introduction (identity, status etc.) in a way that, according to the lecturer quoted earlier, was '*incredible for a first year student*'.

6.7 Conclusion

The work discussed in this chapter demonstrates how working with different genres enables different configurations of the disciplinary materials. This was made visible by the comparing how the 'same' material was differently configured in the two genres discussed. The affordances of each, the essay and the play, gave Anya different opportunities in presenting the information, and particularly her own thinking in relation to it. In the essay the ideas were expressed as abstract thought organized around topics and presented as assertions of disciplinary 'truths' whereas in the play they were organized around events and expressed as activity and experience embodied in the characters created. The conceptualizations of the essay became lived experiences, as they were in the example from Assif's work, with consequences acted out through the ongoing plotline of the play. The essay was contextualized in disciplinary and academic communities in which the writer is positioned as a novice 'shadowing' the disciplinary discourse. By contrast, in the play Anya was able to position herself as a knower in her own right by choosing to contextualize the events in familiar domains. Ultimately, the reconfiguration involved a shift from what the 'domestic space' and other 'built environments' *are* in anthropological discourses, including her essay, to how they are experienced and what they *mean* in the play.

In the next chapter I move on to discuss how the regenring allowed the students to focus on aspects of academic work that are excluded from essay work. The discussion will refer specifically to what I want to call the visiblizing of practice through the reflexivity that the regenring offered the writers.

Chapter 7

From 'Read' Experience to 'Lived' Experience

You know, when I started writing it ... and I just felt like writing and I started on this play ... but I didn't have any clear plan to critique or to represent fieldwork or anything – so it was all quite subconscious I think. (Anya)

7.1 Introduction

In the previous chapter I discussed how the process of regenring led to a reconfiguration of the information presented in the original essays as a result of the affordances of the new genres. In this chapter I want to consider how regenring enabled the students to introduce a different kind of reflexivity to their work than had been possible in the essays. This was brought about by the different narrative opportunities offered by the new contexts in which they located the disciplinary materials.

There are two themes that I want to develop here. The first relates to how the regenring encouraged reflections on 'doing' the discipline; that is, the practice of disciplinary activity, a topic on which there has been a substantial amount of discussion, particularly in relation to scientific writing (Gilbert and Mulkay, 1984/2003; Bazerman, 1988; Bourdieu, 2004) and particularly with reference to not being able to show this aspect of the work. The physicist Feynman's complaint – 'There isn't any place to publish, in a dignified manner, what you actually did in order to do the work' (cited in Tobin, 1999) – is not so much a frustration with the scientific paper genre as such, but a desire for the chance for there to be an institutionally 'validated' context in which the 'real work' can be told. The second theme concerns the way in which some of the students used the affordances of their fictionalized genres to comment on what it means to be a student 'writing an essay like that', something that is never made visible in normal essayist work. In discussing both these themes the chapter shows how, working with the new genres, students were able to explore both their disciplines and their experiences in relation to their disciplines with a much higher degree of reflexivity than hitherto.

7.2 Writing as Reflection

All writing is reflexive. It is the inevitable consequence of the mode itself. As Ong (1982) has reminded us, writing is a technology involving the use of tools in its expression. He goes on to suggest that 'writing heightens consciousness' (p. 81) precisely because it involves transformation from what he considers the naturalness of speech into the artificiality of writing. Kress (2003) goes further than this in his discussions of transduction and transformation (see previous chapter) particularly in considering the different semiotic affordances of different modes. In this chapter, however, I am less concerned with the semiotic potentials of writing than I am with the potentials writing has in ensuring reflexivity. This, I suggest, is because there is a disconnection between thought and the action of writing: they are, essentially, different modes requiring different resources in their expression. Of course, thought is not actually expression, but the process from thought to writing or any other mode implies a shift in thematic and semiotic orientation. Getting thoughts 'down on paper' is not a process of transfer but rather one of transformation. Furthermore, writing involves reading as the writer checks back over her work and it is the combination of these activities that leads to a process of continual appraisal and reappraisal of the thoughts as written down.

7.2.1 Essay Writing

The kinds of reflexivity that an essay affords are those that result from selecting from a 'relevant body of knowledge', as was stated in the departmental guide to essay writing presented in Chapter 2, and organizing these selections into a particular kind of narrative sequence, which, as Andrews (2003) suggests, derives more from Greek rhetoric than the informal and highly personalized 'essaies' of Montaigne, for instance. Indeed, it is likely that Montaigne would have failed dismally had he been writing under the assessment conditions that exist for university students. The reflexivity of the conventional student essay is a 'rationalist' type of reflection. Gee (1996), for instance, argues that essayist literacy is

> founded on the idea ... of people transcending their social and cultural differences to communicate 'logically', 'rationally' and 'dispassionately' to each other as 'strangers' ... in a thoroughly explicit and decontextualized way. (p. 156)

Although his representation of logical and dispassionate communication typifies the (apparent) norm associated with essayist literacy, I disagree with the notion that it is 'decontextualized'. It is, perhaps, the student who is decontextualized rather than the essay and it is the student's job to try to connect with the disciplinary material 'at second hand', as Bourdieu and Passeron (1994, p. 14) pointed out. The student essay, in fact, involves the recontextualizing of information 'gleaned' or 'culled' or 'researched' from other sources such as lectures, books and articles. In other words, it invites a kind of 'read' experience where events are reified and participants are turned into thoughts and ideas. Wood (1999) argues that essays are designed to reflect a 'truth oriented knowledge' based on 'monastic' conceptions of knowledge which is 'text based and serves to validated and to fortify belief' of existing thoughts and ideas. He argues that this genre 'appears to emphasize the self-justifying and rhetorical aspects of writing, rather than their auto-didactic and reflective capabilities in the context of other practices' (p. 1). He contrasts this to what he calls 'crafts-guilds result oriented knowledge' which is 'task based knowledge that facilitates situated actions and judgements' (p. 2). However, despite his concern that essayist literacy may not be the best way to encourage reflections on practice and experience, he acknowledges, as does Andrews (2003), that the essay provides a familiar and what has come to be considered in the context of assessment rigorous genre in which students manipulate their course learning.

> We should also admit that it has provided a well-established structure, and therefore formal criteria, by which the academy can apply rigorous academic evaluation. The idea of rigour is a helpful benchmark for discussing consensus within the bureaucracy of assessment but we tend to use it carelessly to discuss symptomatic gestures rather than embodied attitudes. (Wood, 1999, p. 3)

The student essay is a self-referencing activity which exists, as already discussed in earlier chapters, only in the context of formal school and university learning. Its affordances are limited to manipulation of information within whatever frame has been established by the question asked. The qualities that make it successful, or otherwise, rely on the student's ability to make the 'right' choices according to the precepts laid down by the original question itself. Its thematic orientation, particularly in relation to the organizational structure with its specific phases (introduction – body – conclusion), leads to a particular kind of discussion based on the establishment of a premise, generally problematic, which is to be 'resolved' in the course of the essay. Furthermore, the discussion must be valid in relation to the discipline itself and this is achieved by selecting the 'right' disciplinary materials to justify any claims that are made in the essay. The essay offers a closed context in which a student writer can reflect on the meanings ('truth' or otherwise) of certain (relevant) selections from the 'body of knowledge'.

This is not to say that essays are a 'bad' pedagogy. On the contrary, they are a highly valuable pedagogical resource precisely because of their affordances. They insist that students work within a particular frame and, provided the essay question has been well designed, that frame facilitates students' own disciplinary learning. The kind of reflexivity they afford is one of reflection on knowledge as 'thing', characterized by the phrase *body* of knowledge. This contrasts with the affordances of the new genres that the students in this study chose, where knowledge is represented as *process* characterized by actions, experiences and embodied attitudes and opinions and which therefore produced a very different kind of reflection.

7.2.2 Writing with Different Genres

As discussed in earlier chapters, the new genres oriented the writers towards different thematic and semiotic material, as shown in Chapters 5 and 6, and as a result, led to them 'saying' or being able to 'say' different kinds of things to the things they 'said' in the original essays. Anya's comment at the beginning of this chapter is a case in point. She found herself writing about things that she hadn't 'meant' to because the genre she chose took her that way and what had been referred to only in passing in the essay (fieldwork methodology) became the core of the play. It took her along pathways of discussion that were, of course, already in her thoughts, as they form a fundamental part of her studies, but were either absent or at the very most heavily disguised in her original essay. The world that she created in the play was one in which she was able to represent, through informed imagination, the activity of fieldwork methodology, of ethnographic research. It allowed her to explore the practices involved in 'being a field researcher' or 'being a disciplinary professional' based on, as she put it, *'what I understood of what an anthropologist might do in the field'*.

This is similar to Andy, referred to in Chapter 4, whose imagined conference of time travelling political theorists and commentators was based on his own experiences of attending political conferences (he was a 'party' activist). The decision to produce the essay as a newspaper article meant that he had to do, as he put it, some '*person-based research*', which would '*give some background detail as to where that particular person was coming from ... and it did give you a different way of analysing somebody's writing*'. The process had clearly encouraged him to view the essay material through a very different lens.

Of course, the fact that the regenring was also revisiting information that these students had already worked with meant that the students were already in a position to encourage reflection on their original materials. However, it was more than the kind of reflection that editing and revising enables – it was also the effect of having to do something different with it.

Yeah it was different, just different. Not just having the information but trying to juggle with it so that it would fit into whatever, I mean I didn't have a clear kind of plan as you do with an essay. I mean, I did as I went along, had the plan – well, how can I bring this in? (Anya)

This 'juggling' served to refocus the students' conceptualizations of the things they had produced in the essays. Dan, whose new version took the form of a kind of Socratic dialogue, makes this point below, associating new understandings with the mode shifts that his own regenred work entailed.

To be able to put it in that format [a spoken 'dialogue'] *to re-express those ideas in a form of interaction between two and sometimes three characters certainly gave more vitality to the whole theme and it clarified a lot of the issues for me also. And to reword some of the ideas, to go over those, some of the things I'd written first of all, and to modify them, edit them and express them in a new way which refined more particularly the way in which I wanted to express those ideas – that was a big help. And only the format of dialogue and character allowed that to happen.* (Dan)

Jordan (2001) discusses the impact of writing differently in connection with her own foreign language students. She is referring to their 'year abroad' projects, which she wanted them to write as ethnographies instead of the more familiar essayist genre.

Suddenly everything to do with writing must be thought through afresh, and there is a new level on which they are being asked to make strange, to un-learn what they thought they already knew, to question what they had assumed to be unquestionable. (Jordan, 2001, p. 44)

I want to suggest that a similar kind of process occurred with my own students, despite the fact that what they were writing were not 'ethnographies' based on actual experience. What they were doing, instead, was constructing imagined realities, replications if you like, which allowed them to develop the kind of 'critical' reflexivity that Jordan attributes to her students. Writing differently led my students to think differently about the ideas and information represented in their original work. Using the genres they chose meant that the thematic organization could change, as discussed in the last chapter, so that what had been organized as 'topics' in the essays became organized around 'events' in many of the new genres. What was presented as 'facts' became represented as discussions and arguments. In other words, there was a shift from information to activity.

7.3 Doing the Discipline: Visiblizing Practice

Meaning does not come … from the contemplation of things or analysis of occurrences, but in practical and active acquaintance with relevant situations. (Malinowski, 1923)

In this section I want to consider how the regenring process enabled students to develop a more 'active acquaintance' with their discipline through their imagined enactments of the discipline at work. More importantly, I want to illustrate ways in which 'active acquaintance', albeit imagined, allowed them to develop the kind of reflexivity that emerges as the result of engaging in practice at first hand, of having expertise in the doing of the research itself, in other words 'lived' experience rather than reporting other people's research: 'read' experience.

Read et al. (2001) point out that essay writing is 'a daunting task for the student who has to argue from a position of authority that he/she does not actually possess' (p. 389), referring to Bartholomae's (1985) observation that students are required to mimic the style of the professional academic. These are issues that I discussed in Chapter 2. Authority comes partly from having experience of the things that you are writing about, partly from the reading that you have done, partly from the conversations that you have had and partly from having these 'validated' through institutional channels, as discussed in Bourdieu (1991). Through reconstructing the kinds of experience that 'professional academics' have or might have, some of the students in my study were able to offer the kinds of reflections on practice that normally only results from primary engagement. The reflections on practice and theory that were communicated in these dramatic productions acquired an authenticity that was missing from their essays.

In these new genres the underlying preoccupations of the disciplines, which in the essays were presented as objectified abstraction, became realized as preoccupations and concerns that arise out of practice. The problems associated with how we get information and how we negotiate ideas which were only available in the essays as the actions and experiences of absent others, the professionals, became realized as the actions and experiences of 'people' who were present, including the students themselves. In the new productions, the students had the opportunity to shift from second- or even third-hand reporting to first-hand experience. Assif's radio phone-in *performs* interactions between opposing theorists, rather than reporting their 'written' ideas. Anya's play *enacts* the doing of fieldwork and describes the field researcher's experiences as *own* and *lived* experience rather than *other* and *read* experience.

The two examples, one from Anya and the other from Assif that I consider below, demonstrate ways in which the regenring exercise allowed students to show what really happens in the process of doing the disciplinary work.

7.3.1 Anya

The first example exemplifies the different opportunity regenring gave to Anya in her representation of the disciplinary preoccupation, fieldwork methodology, with which she framed her original essay. The essay *describes* fieldwork as a problematic methodology by adopting the concerned voice of nameless but presumably qualified others. By contrast, the play *enacts* the concerns expressed in the essay by representing the methodology in and as practice.

Extract 7.1 below is the first paragraph of the essay initially discussed in the previous chapter from the perspective of the problem as read experience. Now I want to consider it from the perspective of the problem as lived experience.

Extract 7.1

> Fieldwork methodology has undergone vehement inside and outside criticism over the past decades, and as a discipline, anthropology has been compelled to question and reappraise its approach. Consequently, there is an intensified concern amongst social scientists to submit rigorous, comprehensive research, by unfolding the many layers surrounding a specific aspect of culture.

As the opening paragraph, this extract serves to establish the discursive tone for the rest of the essay. Already discussed in Chapter 6, it is an appropriate opening given the institutional context of her course, although there is no specific reference to this theme in the assignment question itself. By recognizing this key disciplinary preoccupation, Anya indicates that she has engaged with the subject and has taken on board important underlying considerations. It was awarded an approving tick in the margin and may well have contributed to her receiving the positive comment that her essay was successful in '*combining ethnography and the theory excellently*' from her official anthropology reader. This opening is certainly a clear indicator that the writer is adopting the 'insider' concerns of anthropology. She is 'being an expert' despite her actual (student) status as 'novice'.

However, as has been seen, despite this strongly assertive opening, the rest of the essay is an almost entirely unproblematized presentation of the work of several ethnographers working in this particular field of anthropology. A question that comes to mind is: why is this so? The answer is, perhaps, simple. To have taken this theme and developed it through her overall discussion would have required the knowledge and experience that could only be derived from being a practitioner in the disciplinary field instead of being a student ('*being a first year undergraduate and having a question like that*'). What the extract shows is Anya's awareness that underneath much anthropological discussion is the concern about ethnographic work. She recognizes how this frames much of the discussion, particularly in the module the essay is associated with. However, having declared her recognition of the issue and indicated a critical perspective, it is only when we get to the end of the essay (Extract 7.2) that we remember that any specific reference was made to it at all.

Extract 7.2

> Thus, it seems that anthropology has much to contribute to a better understanding of society in general, but it must further strive to develop better means of applying this knowledge.

The strongly articulated 'thus' here serves as a reminder that the main discussion is supposed to be read as a critical evaluation of fieldwork methodology, even though it is not written as one. As a first year student, Anya has neither the disciplinary background nor the fieldwork research expertise to maintain this critical strand throughout the essay and so she relies on the rhetorical power of this 'thus' to do the work instead. Furthermore, the seemingly added-on final comment stands somewhat outside the 'normal' practice of the student essay, moving, as it does, into a different communicative function. Expressed as a piece of advice, it is somehow misplaced. Student essays are not (usually) the place for giving explicit advice, although it is possible, as discussed in Chapter 5, that the influence of pedagogical genres might explain this. Agency here is certainly strongly represented, that is agency as someone who 'has the right' to 'advise' professional field workers, hence a borrowed agency.

In the end, perhaps this final paragraph was simply the quickest means with which Anya could finish off; an attempt to balance the positive (anthropology has much to contribute) with the negative (vehement criticism) anticipated by the opening paragraph. Or perhaps, after all, it is the real Anya commenting herself on what she thinks should happen with anthropology. In interview Anya said that she was '*only referring to it* [fieldwork methodology] *en passant – it wasn't really part of the essay*', though, as I have already indicated, it clearly demonstrates an affiliation to disciplinary concerns.

In the previous chapter, I showed how this theme was integrated early on in the play, presented in conjunction with Austen Tatius handing out the quest task of 'doing the essay'. Here, however, I want to look at how Anya handled the 'problem' of ethnographic methodology in the play, not as something explained, but as something enacted. Because she had set up her narrative as a quest based around the essay question Boris (the hero) had to research, she, Anya, had to reflect on what it would be like actually to do fieldwork so that she could write it into the play. This meant that she had to set up a scene in which Boris did the fieldwork, using the research tools that ethnographers (reportedly) use, and create something, or rather someone, for him to observe. The problematic of doing ethnographic fieldwork to research the issues discussed in the essay (the home, identity etc.) becomes a 'real world' experienced problem acted out in the play instead of simply being reported as 'a problem', as in the essay. In the play the 'unfolding the many layers surrounding a specific aspect of culture' stated in the essay becomes the work that Boris has to carry out so that it can be 'rigorous and comprehensive'.

The combination of Anya's creative imagination and the affordances of plays give her plenty of opportunities to reflect on fieldwork methodology. For instance, making the protagonist an alien from another planet allows her to represent the concepts of both 'otherness' and 'othering' from a dual perspective. Boris is 'the other' from the perspective of the encountered informants and they in turn are 'the other' from his. In this way Anya is able to represent the anthropologists' dilemma around the problem of cultural subjectivity, the 'gaze' of the ethnographer (Clifford, 1992). Furthermore, she constructs an 'insider' joke regarding the physiology of this alien field researcher by creating him as a snail from a planet which is populated by snails. This trope is itself a manifestation of a quote in the original essay ('Like some strange race of gastropods, people build homes out of their own essence' Csikszentmihalyi and Rochberg-Halton, 1981). Boris serves as both the embodiment of the essay topic (the built environment) and the practitioner engaged in research on the topic. The fact that he is an intergalactic alien allows Anya to develop her arguments about fieldwork methodology around everyday experiences in familiar settings, at least to her, but which are 'exotic' and other to Boris.

Extract 7.3 is a good example of this opportunity to vitalize the 'read' knowledge. The immediate narrative context is that Boris has started out on his research and meets Holly, who has recently been burgled and is sitting in the park, despondent. They have been talking for a while about what happened to Holly (Extract 6.20) when she notices that Boris has started taking notes.

Extract 7.3

> **Holly**: Hey!! Why are you taking notes, man?! You weirdo park-prowling freak boy!
>
> **Boris**: Err … well, I've got to do a study on *humans* and the built environment, for the A.A. … so I need to take *fieldnotes*.

Holly: Oh yeah?

Boris: Yeah … and what you've been telling me seems pretty relevant … but I've got to try and be *objective*, so, you know, about my shell … don't like ask me to *subjectify*, ok? … But I can, err, *empathize*!

Holly: Oh, cheers …

The device allows for a double reflection on ethnographic methodology, that of the researcher and that of the informant. The 'vehement inside and outside criticism' that Anya obliquely refers to in the essay becomes, in the play, realized through the interactions of these two characters in the constructed context of a real person being 'used' as 'subject' (or informant) for a 'real' piece of ethnographic study. Until this point Holly had considered herself to be having a genuine conversation about her predicament and thought that Boris had been genuinely concerned. The enacted shock of realization that she is now the subject of research, along with the embarrassment that Boris displays in having to explain himself, is a manifestation of the problem of fieldwork methodology and the response Boris gives, with Anya's italicizing of the problematic terms – 'humans', 'fieldnotes', 'objective', 'subjectify' and 'empathize' – play out the awkwardness that an ethnographer might experience having been 'caught out'. The italics removes these words from the norm and places them in some kind of parenthetical space where they attract a different kind of reading, a disciplinary one which doesn't really belong to the 'real world' chatting of two 'ordinary' people. This separating out offers an ironic reflection also on the student using these words self-consciously, an example of the 'being a student' that I look at in more detail below.

What is important here, though, is the way in which the meaning of 'vehement criticism' expressed in the essay is transformed into the experience of both being criticized (Boris by Holly) and being the 'victim' of the methodology itself (Holly by Boris). This is not reported criticism, but 'real world' criticism through 'real world' experience of the act. Moreover, because it is an imaginable experience, the evaluation of fieldwork methodology appears more authentic than the objectified 'vehement inside and outside criticism' of the essay. We can imagine how we'd feel if we were Holly and we can imagine how we'd feel if we were

Boris. In short, the play articulates the criticism through acting it out as opposed to the essay, which merely identifies it.

7.3.2 Assif

In the next example, which comes from Assif's work also discussed in the previous chapter, I want to illustrate the activity of disagreement which is typically represented in essays with an 'argument–counter argument' organizational structure. This conventional organizational strategy is constructed by a writer who, through specific organizational and grammatical or lexical choices, provides an essayist logic to the construction of an argument. In Assif's essay, the argument–counter argument revolves around two opposing economic theories: classical and Keynesian. I have already explained that in the regenred production Assif 'brought the theories to life' by creating 'living' proponents of those theories (Keynes himself and Milton Friedman). The point I particularly wish to illustrate here concerns the sorts of things that actually happen around disagreement, that is the interactions around arguing in person (face to face) as opposed to arguing in solitude (in front of the computer).

Assif's essay starts 'cold' with no discursive framing, unlike Anya's above. Instead he moves straight into descriptive account first of 'classical' theory (in relation to interest rates) followed by an account of Keynesian theory, which he sets in contrast to the parameters already established in the first part of the essay. The overall effect is one of logical and measured written discussion realized through the sequential organization of argument (classical) followed by counter argument (Keynsian), an arrangement that is often used to indicate preference, though in this case it could equally reflect the historical sequence of events. The juxtapositionings of the opposing theoretical stances in relation to the specifics of the question and the use of verbal expressions of difference and evaluation contribute to the coherence of the essay and its thematic structure. Extract 7.4 exemplifies this.

Extract 7.4

Keynes's view of investment <u>also differed from</u> the classical view. The classical theory suggests that investment is also primarily a function of the interest rate. <u>Keynes didn't accept this</u>. First, Keynes suggested that during a recession or depression the interest rate may already be so low that it cannot go any lower. Interest rates are not flexible during economic downturns. Consequently, you don't get the needed stimulus to I and AD that a drop in the real interest rate might give you. Second, Keynes believed that even if the interest rate was able to decline significantly, investment would not be responsive. For example, during a recession or depression when demand has fallen, firms would not invest in new production equipment when its existing equipment was underutilized.

Disagreement here is presented strongly ('Keynes didn't accept this') but dispassionately with reference to concepts in general (e.g. recession or depression). However, in the regenred production the 'real work' of disagreement is vitalized in the familiar genre of the radio phone-in, through the imagined characterization of Keynes on the one hand, and Friedman, representing classical economics, on the other. Because the new genre enacts the disagreement, third-person ideas are recontextualized as first-person dialogue. The new genre affords Assif the opportunity to convey the subjective and dynamic nature of theory making, the cut and thrust of argument between people rather than the seemingly objective representations that essay writing promotes. The extract offers us a different take on scholarly discourse – one which reflects the 'everyday utterance' of human communication. It represents theorists 'doing' the discipline. The extract follows the guests' presentation of their respective theories and precedes the calls from the general public.

Extract 7.5

[Show goes off-air. PC (host), MF, JMK remove their headphones. Adverts play on-air.]

PC: So, what do you think of the show so far?

JMK: I must admit, I was nervous at first, but it all happened so quickly. The talk went through just like that.

MF: So, JMK, you're still stuck up with your views about 'r', heh?

What was it that you said, 'more acceptable view'? What was all that about???

JMK: You know very well. Your allegiance to Classical economics, that school's as good as dead. After you couldn't explain the effects of the Great Depression in the 1930s, I would have thought that you would have given up that sinking ship by now!

MF: What, and your Keynesian theories could explain the Great Depression?

PC: Listen, this isn't the time or the place for this.

[PC points at clock, then headphones.]

[All put on headphones]

Because Assif chose a radio phone-in for the essayist information, he was able to provide this momentary glimpse within the overall frame of the genre. Radio phone-ins, if they are on commercial radio stations, have advertisement breaks during which something hidden from the public happens. The revelation of 'what happens' allows Assif to offer a reflection on the practice of doing academic work rather than the results of the academic work, as is the case in the essay.

This interlude in the radio programme provides a 'fly-on-the-wall' view of these two theorists, the hidden world of academic debate, to which novices (first year students) and outsiders are rarely privy. Just as in the case of Anya above with her representations of disciplinary preoccupation, Assif reconfigures theoretical positioning as experienced interaction, doing disagreement. This reconfiguration allows Assif to normalize the ideas through turning these 'gurus' of economic thought into ordinary people who argue just like anybody else. The disagreement is no longer objectified as it is in the essay but is, instead, subjectified through first-person speech. The kind of disagreement here is made with speech with all its own affordances of tone of voice and attitude represented visually in the text with multiple question marks, exclamation marks or inverted commas. We can almost visualize the raised eyebrows. Furthermore, the generalized '*during a recession or depression*' in the essay becomes the specific '*the effects of the Great Depression in the 1930s*', a much more evocative and emotive example because it is real and hence imaginable. Those involved in disagreement seek hard evidence because it is more immediate in the fast movement of spoken communication. Writing, by contrast, moves at a very different pace where there is 'time' to develop the meanings contained in abstraction.

Both examples illustrate ways in which the new genres allowed for a reflection of disciplinary practices that was not available to the students in their original essays. The chance to remove the practices and ideas from the abstractions of academia and relocate them in imagined real world contexts allowed these students to normalize them in the way that usually only first-hand practical experience affords.

7.4 Being a Student: Asserting Identity

At the beginning of this chapter, I said that the opportunity to write about the experience of being a student in relation to writing an essay is not usually available in the formal learning and teaching portfolio. The student essay is certainly not the place for writing about what it is like to be a student doing the work, nor should it be. Essays, as has already been discussed, have quite a different purpose. Of course there have been attempts, particularly with the incorporation of the 'learning journal' into the assessment portfolio, to 'give' students the chance to reflect on their learning as a process of development. However, as Crème (2005) has pointed out, these are problematic, particularly where assessment is concerned, as the issue of writing purpose becomes confused. Furthermore, as personal observation has shown, the advantage of this approach can be lost as students quickly learn to write the sorts of things in the sorts of ways that are 'expected' of the genre, especially when, as is sometimes the case, students are running journals for several of their modules. Nevertheless, the evidence of the regenring work in this study suggests that some students at least appreciate the chance to reflect on their own experience, and what is more, doing so enabled them to both imagine and re-imagine the work.

Of the six students in the study, three of them, Dan, Sonia and Anya, incorporated reflections on being a student. This was not necessarily part of their initial plans, but something that emerged as they began to think through their new versions and the characters and plotlines that they would use to rework the original material. By having fictionalized characters to represent 'the student' they were able to create a bit of space between their 'real' selves and their 'dramatic' representatives. This enabled them to present a less self-conscious and self-oriented reflection on experience than journals tend to encourage. Furthermore, it gave them the opportunity to use humour as a reflexive resources, perhaps as self protection, but certainly to great effect, as will be seen. In all three cases, the student characters were represented as active in the process of 'doing the work'. For instance, Dan, whose regenred work involved a dramatized account of a student of the future involved in a kind of library (talking computer) research for the assignment topic, realized that the narrative device he had designed meant that his new production was essentially framed, not by the question of the original essay itself, but by the experience of being the student gathering the information in response to the question. It was about what you *do* when you read and undertake library research, your thinking and your responses to the information, more than the information itself.

> *It was almost, not a paradox, but one of those things where it is representative of the situation in which I wrote the first essay – there was me the student, you know, taking information from these resources – these books – formulating my own ideas and perceptions of them ... and then taking that position, which I was inside in the first instance, and then applying it to another situation in which I became the outsider – but almost telling the story or how I received that knowledge and formulated my own ideas.* (Dan)

Anya's plotline, as has already been discussed, also focused on the process of 'collecting' the disciplinary information, although in her case the process itself was also part of the information. In contrast to Dan, her version of 'getting' the information relates more to doing the discipline, as discussed above, than to being a student. In fact, her reflections on being a student focused more on the difficulties inherent in the experience, issues of agency, identity and positioning.

> *Well, I think I did want to communicate through Boris the awkwardness of being a first year undergraduate and having a question like that ... and, I guess, mixing what I understood of what an anthropologist might do in the field – with someone just not having a clue what he's doing.* (Anya)

Sonia's reflections were different again and far less explicitly represented. In her case, they were represented by character attitudes and behaviours rather than by articulated observations, as in Anya's case, or plot framing, as in Dan's.

Each of these three writers, then, offered a different take on the experience but in their own ways each offered insights into their own sense of agency or otherwise. Each foregrounds the process of 'getting' information but each develops the idea very differently, highlighting different aspects of the student experience. Each reflects very different experiences of 'being a student' which, in turn, reflect the real experiences and attitudes of the students concerned, as my own observations, supported by informal conversation with the students, have suggested. Dan's protagonist is very much in the apprentice mould, engaged in a kind of Socratic dialogue. His 'Socrates', however, is a computer, which means that the power relationship where 'the dice are weighted toward Socrates', as suggested by Andrews (2003, p. 122), is rebalanced more favourably towards the student. His 'student' is ready and fully prepared to undertake the essay, as indicated in Dan's prelude to his play.

Extract 7.6

> Joshua is young and restless, but duty beckons. His education, in the formal mould, has entered its concluding phase …

By contrast, Anya's 'student' character description portrays someone who is uncertain, inexperienced but looking for direction.

Extract 7.7

> [Context : Boris, a 19-year-old male snail, has just left school. Undecided about which direction to slither in next, he makes a two o'clock appointment with Mr Austin Tatius at his local I.C.C.C. Bureau (Inter-Species Cryptic Careers Counselling)].

Sonia's is different again, represented as the young children of a well-meaning but somewhat overly didactic parent. Her 'student' is somewhat disconnected from the actual content of the discipline.

Extract 7.8

> The children are ... 'little adults' tucked up in bed, who watch their
> parent with awe, wonder and often bemusement. It should not be
> completely clear as to whether they are mentally absorbing what is
> being said or are simply enjoying the rise and fall of their parent's
> voice ...

With these characterizations, each of the writers was able to promote a
strong sense of their own identity, which was nevertheless presented with
the distance afforded by the fictionalized dramatic personae, something
that both Dan and Anya specifically commented on.

*And so Joshua was me in a sense and he was reacting in the way I would have
reacted ... so it was a kind of reflection – a futuristic reflective response to my own
situation of writing the first essay.* (Dan)

*And you know Boris is me in that sense – not particularly in the detail of the
character – but in his position.* (Anya)

To demonstrate how these characterizations enabled the students to offer
the kind of reflexivity on experience I have been talking about, I discuss
examples from each of the three students' work. Unlike the previous
discussions, I do not provide paired extracts for this aspect of my analysis.
This is because the essays do not include these kinds of reflections, at
least explicitly articulated, although they may well be implicit in the
quality, and confidence, of the essayist discussion as referred to particularly in Chapter 5, when I discussed issues of agency as represented in the
different versions.

7.4.1 Sonia

I start off with an extract from Sonia's work which concerns, as explained
earlier, a discussion on Swahili as an example of an African lingua franca.
As I have already indicated, her regenred production does not have
a character explicitly identified as 'the student', as do Dan and Anya.
Instead, that role is given to what might be considered the unready and to
some extent unwilling 'recipients' portrayed by the children. Throughout
the production, their role is to both guide, through questioning, and

subvert, through challenge and distraction, the parent's 'lecture'. Their interventions are intended to shift the discussion away from what *he* (the parent) wants to talk about to what *they* want to talk about.

Extract 7.9

> **Parent**: OK, anyway, today I thought I could tell you the story about how Swahili came to be such an important language in East Africa. People always talk about English as a world language but they rarely consider that there exist many other important non-European languages all over the world. People need to learn one of these important languages so they can talk to people who have different first languages from themselves.
>
> **Child 1**: Umm … Why would they be speaking to people with a different language?
>
> **Parent**: That's a good question … People often refer to the people in different social groups as different tribes, but it is best not to use this word as it has negative associations.
>
> **Child 1**: So it's a bad word, like 'SHIT' or 'FUCK'!
>
> **Child 2**: Ha ha! YOU LITTLE *TRIBE*! I HAD A *TRIBE* OF A DAY! *TRIBE* YOU!
>
> **Parent**: Yes, ok now! I think you both know it is not a swear word! …

However, as the parent's contributions become longer and longer, adopting more of a lecture mode than a discussion mode, there is a gradual shift from initial enthusiasm on the part of the children towards a growing boredom which echoes, it is tempting, and probably true to say, Sonia's own experiences at the time.

Extract 7.10

> **Parent**: [after a lengthy phase of expounding on the topic of Swahili] Sorry, I can see you're getting bored now – but I just want to tell you one more thing! It was only late in the eighteen hundreds that Swahili became a written language. Africa is not like England. Here we write about everything we think is important, whereas in Africa people pass on information by telling each other stories. Story telling is important, it is only Western influence which brought about the idea of recording information in writing.
>
> **Child 2**: If you lived in Africa people would put sellotape over your mouth or everyone would always be asleep!

This exchange, coming as it does towards the end of the play, provides observational reflection on what, for Sonia, had been the somewhat negative experience of being a student on the receiving end, as she portrays it, of the disciplinary information. This disengagement is also reflected in how she represents the material in her original essay, as discussed in Chapter 5. The opportunity to give voice to such feelings would be difficult in the formal, public and power conditioned arena of the lecture, let alone the essay, though it is sometimes visually performed in the real world context through the drooping or glazed over eyes that can sometimes meet the lecturer's gaze! However, here, in the regenred work, it is made possible by the construction of the plot and the characters who 'perform' it. In fact, the humour of the child's remark in Extract 7.10 reflects an attitude not of despair but rather of exasperation, an attitude confirmed by Sonia's eventual re-engagement with academia.

7.4.2 Dan

While Sonia's 'students' are not 'students' in the sense that they are being expected to fulfil a task, both Dan's and Anya's 'students' are explicitly engaged in student work. In both cases the protagonist is acting in response to the requirement to do an assignment – the essay itself. It is quite interesting (and telling) that in neither of the productions does the 'student' actually end up *writing* the essay. The narratives concern the getting of information rather than the writing of it. As Dan said, he was telling the story of how he acquired that knowledge and how he formulated his own ideas. However, unlike Anya's production, Dan's does not reflect on experience as experienced but almost entirely on experience as process. In fact, what he produces is an idealization of the experience of being a student, one that he would, perhaps, have preferred to the one he actually had. In this production he is enabled, through the enacted dialogue, to articulate his own questions and his own responses to the information that he is confronted with.

The original essay question, as already mentioned, concerns an evaluation of the advantages and disadvantages of phenomenology, a key approach to the study of religions. In the dialogue below, 'J' stands for Joshua, the name allocated to the 'student' and 'V' is for Viddy, the talking computer. The computer is retrieving information and references from its database and giving out the information in response to Joshua's questions. It is worth pointing out that the computer, as will be seen from the extract below, is not without personality itself and offers reflection on doing library research.

Extract 7.11

V: ... Of the religious phenomena to be understood, 'it moves within the framework of the given context of meaning ... (blah blah) ... and neither in the sphere of empirical nor within that of ultimate realities'. That's on page 408.

J: That's a little 'heady' for me. What are the practical applications? I want 'ether to earth'.

V: OK, just wait. There's a section on 'Perspectives of a phenomenological study of religion'. Here we go: Pettazoni, 1954, pages 639 to 642. He pleads for a closer relationship between phenomenology and history of religion, as two forms of a singular science.

J: Sounds sensible.

V: He asserts that a deeper understanding and meaning of events can only be asked from phenomenology. It separates out the different structures from the multiplicity of religious phenomena.

Such structures prompt 'meaning', independent of time, space and cultural environment.

J: You mean the arrival at a universality, which necessarily escapes a history of religion?

V: But his insight is that 'religious phenomena do not cease to be realities historically conditioned merely because they are grouped under this or that structure'. The risks of phenomenological judgement may only be escaped by applying constantly to history. Phenomenology 'hangs' on history: its own conclusions privy to revision in view of historical research.

J: So a kind of fake autonomy?

This extract is typical of Dan's production in that it visiblizes the 'student's' thinking as he processes the information being imparted. The too-ing and fro-ing of the dialogue, articulated 'out loud', allows us to see and recognize the kinds of practices that students and indeed professionals engage in when reading. It visiblizes the hidden 'voice' of the reader almost as a running commentary or perhaps as the notes that we might make in the margin of a text.

There is also reflection on the process of reading scholarly texts articulated by the 'blah blah' in Viddy's speech, which indicates the impatience that scholarly texts can sometimes evoke, particularly when reading for an assignment. The 'blah blah' articulates the usually silent thoughts while skimming for what is relevant to the job in hand and in so doing expresses impatience with what might be considered unnecessary detail. The practice of academic reading is here made visible through the thinking out loud of the talking computer.

There is, of course, another dimension to what this dialogue achieves and that concerns the way in which Dan reflects his own engagement with the literature, or rather his re-engagement with it. As he says above, regenring clarified and refined the issues for him, partly because it was a revisiting of the ideas and partly because, as discussed in Chapter 6 in relation to Anya's and Assif's work, it was reconfigured as dialogue ('*And only the format of dialogue and character allowed that to happen*'). The kind of visiblized reflections ('That's a bit "heady",' 'Sounds sensible') suggest a more 'sophisticated' engagement with the literature than is often the case with first year students at the beginning of their courses, where 'textbook' information can tend to be taken as matter of fact (see e.g. Mitchell, 1994 regarding the transition from school to university study). The enacted dialogue articulates the kind of critical engagement with the literature that universities educators, for instance those cited in Chapter 2, so desire from their students. Through Dan's representation of the process of 'getting' disciplinary information we can see (or hear) him pondering over the issues, trying to make sense of them. We can 'hear' him engaging in the process of integrating the new knowledge with his own existing knowledge frames.

What is also interesting about this extract is that once we move from the 'ether to earth', that is the practical applications, the student, Joshua, engages in a very different way. There is a shift from the rejecting attitude of 'it's too heady' to a different kind interaction with the information. Perhaps this can be seen as a shift in agency from unempowered (lost in the ether) to empowered (in the world of experience). Now instead of standing off from the information he remakes it through reformulation ('You mean ...?', 'So a kind of ...?'). The articulation of his thinking visiblizes the process of making sense of the ideas. This kind of reformulation is, of course, typical also of essay writing. In the previous chapter I showed how Anya did this type of reformulation in her original essay, the reformulation of quotes as part of the process of organizing the information. However, what is different here is that the new genre allows Dan not only to reformulate with 'everyday' meanings, but to reconfigure the original monologic essay into the dynamic of a dialogue. This allows for the 'student' to get instant feedback on his understanding from his 'guide', the 'computer companion', as he puts it in his prelude. What is more, because the dialogic partner is a computer, there is a sense in which his corroboration is authoritative. This is further enhanced through the evocation of holographic representations of some of the key theorists who 'speak' for themselves. The result of all this is that the regenred work recreates the experience of *doing* the essay and by enacting it, Dan recontextualizes it as an exchange of ideas, a collaboration between the student, the library (represented by the computer) and the disciplinary sources themselves.

7.4.3 Anya

Anya's production differs from the other two in the way in which she develops her 'student' character. Boris is not like the children in Sonia's play, resistant recipients of the disciplinary information, nor is he like Dan's character, Joshua, who is both willing and dutiful in relation to the work. Boris is a much more self-conscious creation, not in the sense of offering a self-conscious impression of Anya's own reflections but self-conscious as a fictional character, something that owes much to the disciplinary discussion in hand. The awkwardness of Boris offers a double reflection on both the disciplinary issue of fieldwork methodology as discussed in the previous chapter and on '*being a first year undergraduate and having a question like that*'. Throughout her play, but most particularly in the earlier phases, this 'awkwardness' is realized through the activity of the protagonist. This is expressed initially in the description of his character. 'He has just left school' so he is young and inexperienced, and he is 'undecided about which direction to slither in next, so is open to suggestions'. He is also the embodiment of the 'outsider', doubly reflected in this production, with Boris the alien snail doing ethnography on the 'other', and Boris the student, the disciplinary outsider, as Extract 7.12 shows.

Extract 7.12

> **Boris**: Well, Sir … I liked the bit about me having brains in my head and err … feet in my shoes … but I'm a bit confused by all those akra…akro-whatsits …
>
> **Austin Tatius**: Acronyms? Ah! The world's full of them, boy! A nifty way of keeping things exclusive, but you'll soon get the hang of it! Deconstruction is the key! It'll open many a door lining your anthropological path … That is all you need to remember!

The topic of acronyms is well observed in this extract because they are a classic example of exclusion, particularly poignant for students, but something that everyone experiences throughout their lives. Acronyms are always associated with insider–outsider knowledge and Anya's reference to them in this extract is a reflection on both knowledge positions: the current outsider ('I'm a bit confused by all those akra … akro-whatsits …')

and the potential insider ('you'll soon get the hang of it ... It'll open many a door lining your anthropological path ...').

The next extract (Extract 7.13) offers a different perspective on 'being a student'. In this case it is not about exclusion but the experience of being confronted with a challenging assignment.

Extract 7.13

SCENE THREE

[Three days later, Boris is sitting on the steps outside the (college) building. He has just collected his assignment: HOW MIGHT AN ANTHROPOLOGICAL CONSIDERATION OF THE BUILT ENVIRONMENT LEAD TO BETTER UNDERSTANDINGS OF ISSUES SUCH AS SOCIAL STATUS, IDENTITY CONSTRUCTION AND NATIONALISM? Bewildered, he scratches his head, as that is the only thing he can recall Mr Austin Tatius telling him about *anthropological considerations* ... When the chosen scratch-patch is quite sore, not knowing what to do with himself – or his project – he decides to take himself off on a little exploration of the city.

This description of experience (bewilderment), further expressed through activity (he scratches his head), serves to reinforce the sense of the enormity of the task expected of the student *'having a question like that'*. The 'size' of the task is further emphasized by the capitalization of the essay question itself. We can visualize Boris's demeanour. We can imagine being him and feeling his bewilderment.

Having established her protagonist as 'undecided' and 'bewildered' but with a clear task to undertake, Anya is able to develop Boris as a character both in disciplinary awareness, as exemplified in Extract 7.14, which comes about a quarter of the way into the play, and in his increasing familiarity with human activity, that is his ethnographic learning.

Extract 7.14

Boris: Yeah ... and what you've been telling me seems pretty relevant ... but I've got to try and be *objective*, so, you know, about my shell ... don't like ask me to *subjectify*, ok? ... But I can, err, *empathize!*

As with the capitalization of the essay question above, here Anya uses italics to highlight the self-conscious use of the newly learned disciplinary terms, reflecting the testing out of newly learned disciplinary terms of reference. By the end of the play, after the many adventures he and his companions have experienced, Boris has gone through a major process of change. However, the things he achieves are not necessarily the things he initially set out to achieve. He still has to write the essay, for instance. Nevertheless, he has successfully undertaken an ethnographic study, he has researched the disciplinary material, but most importantly, true to all good quests, he has confronted his own fears and become confident, decisive and, above all, free, as represented by the metaphor of liberating himself from his shell, even though it means changing his identity, as in Extract 7.15.

Extract 7.15

Holly: You mean that you're ready to *detach* yourself from your shell? ... Wow! You're sure, yeah? Not a *spur of the moment* thing? I don't want to be blamed for ...

Boris: Course it's *spur of the moment*, Holly!! Well, I mean ... I *have* been thinking about on and off since we met ... but it's the whole slug thing I can't get my head round ...

Holly: I know what you think ... but you're right in that no French people would waste their time making fancy sauces for you if they thought you were a slug, I mean they wouldn't eat *slugs* ... You'd be free, Boris!

Boris: Yeah, Holly ... So do it *NOW*! Take it *off* ... gently! Hurry though, he's coming to ...!

[Holly starts the process of liberation: she gently detaches Boris's brown, beige and white patterned shell and puts it in her pocket. The Chef, livid and clenching his jaw, approaches them.]

Chef: *Mon Petit Escargot*! Where are iou, leettle one?! Whaaat av ioo done wis im, ein?!

Holly: Oh, that snail? You just missed him …

[The chef looks around the room. He spots the *new* Boris.]

Chef: Errrgh! You disgusting girl! Don't ioo pepple av any *stondarrrdz?* Get that *SLERG* owt of my keetchen … As soon as *NOW*!!! *Allez!* Pfit-Pfit! Get owt! Get owt! Dirty, dirty *SLERG*!!

[Boris and Holly willingly comply and make a hasty exit.]

It is impossible to say whether the issue of identity and freedom has anything much to do with 'being a student', as do the other extracts I have used to exemplify this phenomenon. It is more connected to the original theme of the built environment and particularly Anya's interpretation of literature that represents the home as associated with possessions and with identity. Nevertheless, what Extract 7.15 does demonstrate is the progression of the 'student' character through the process of learning. In fact, it is ultimately an upbeat representation of the student experience reflecting a resolution both to the essayist problem and to the 'problem' of being a student.

7.5 Conclusion

The two themes discussed in this chapter, the 'visiblizing' of disciplinary practices and the reflections on being a student, are both connected to the same generic effect. The enactments of experience that are afforded by a play or a radio phone-in foreground practices and experiences that are not the province of essay genres, least of all the student essay. The opportunity to show what you did to do the work, to paraphrase Feynman, cited earlier, enabled the students to experience their own disciplines from the perspective of practitioners. However, it also gave them the opportunity to represent their own reflections as part of the new narrative that they produced through the regenring. The recontextualizing of the original materials in 'real world' exchanges and interactions brought the disciplinary debates to life as real and realized discussion in which they, the students, could also engage.

The students I discussed here took the opportunity to be playful not only with the disciplinary materials but also with their own perceptions and their own experiences as students. This introduced a subjectivity that was largely missing from the original essays, produced as they were under the delusion that academic writing is an entirely objective affair. In fact, the enactment of disciplinary debate, as in, for instance Assif's production, promotes an awareness that academic arguments are produced not discovered readymade. What is more, by mediating the disciplinary materials, whether by creating a kind of student representative, as did Dan, Sonia and Anya, or other interventionist characters, as did Assif, Andy and even Peter as reteller of the disciplinary material, the students could clarify the issues by re-examining them in contexts that existed outside of the essayist domain. To some extent, the essay is intended to exclude experiences of the kind discussed here. It is meant to encourage students to 'communicate logically, rationally and dispassionately', as Gee (1996), cited above, put it. This is not to say that that is a 'bad' thing. It is just a different thing from the things I have discussed here. The kind of reflexivity that the regenring in this study promoted allowed the students to assert their own identities as legitimate outsiders or peripheral insiders, to borrow from Lave and Wenger (2002). Regenring, as this chapter has shown, offers students the chance to think differently about their disciplines, to see them as activity and not just information and to be able to explore how they themselves are or can be involved in that activity.

In Chapter 8 I consider the implications of my research from two main perspectives, each of which reflects the parallel strands of the discussion. On the one hand I discuss what this work contributes to genre studies and academic literacies and on the other I consider its relevance to higher education pedagogy.

Chapter 8

Genre as a Pedagogical Resource: Conclusions and Implications

The advantage of having taught at [this university] *for so many years and read so many essays is that in fact you have a positive inclination towards something that's different. So rather than bringing existing criteria to bear we're in a state of hunger for excitement in something that's different.* (Maurice)

8.1 Introduction

This book has been about transformation. It has been about the transformations that occur as the result of shifting information from one genre to a different genre and the knock-on effects that such a shift entails. It has been about transforming the ways in which we can think about academic knowledge. It has been about transforming the experiences of students as academic writers and learners. And because the discussion in this book emerged out of the context of my own teaching it has also been about a transformation in how I think about disciplinary learning and teaching.

The work that I have presented in this book, the students' work and my own, has led me to (re)consider the ways in which students are expected, and expect, to represent their disciplinary learning. It has helped me to see how important is the relationship between disciplinary knowledge, learning and the kinds of production that our students are expected to work on. And despite the contradictions inherent in assignments for learning and assignments for assessment, the requirement for students to do something with the disciplinary materials that comprise their courses of study is crucial. Recontextualizing is key to learning because it engenders reflection in the remaking of the material. However, what this discussion has also shown is how strongly the genres that typify higher education orient towards 'replicational' work, as in the student essay (shadow writing), and how overreliance on those genres, despite their importance as pedagogical resources, means that student disciplinary learning remains in a kind of self-referencing loop. The regenring task, which revealed as much about the pedagogical value of essays as it did about the new genres, demonstrated that working with disciplinary materials in unconventional ways can enhance not only disciplinary understanding but its epistemological relevance, as the following comment confirms.

> *Well, I think it brought it all to life – and made this whole thing of personal identity the shell, the house um ... made me have to link it to projected people's experience. You know sometimes things like that just make you think, because it's so familiar – and this is the point of anthropology really ... and I think it was, er, possibly a realization that anthropology was quite important and quite relevant.* (Anya)

Furthermore, it offers the students the chance to say 'Listen to me, I have something to tell you,' as Elbow (1995, p. 82) wanted them to feel able to say, rather than always be positioned as 'replicators' of what is already known.

So what are the implications of this work? Is there a place for this kind of activity in higher education and if so how would it be received by both students and lecturers alike? Would it retain the freshness of the work and the experience in this study or would it instead become yet another genre in the academic production canon? In responding to these, I will review the themes that I have discussed in the book. Firstly, I will reflect on the context in which I located my work and the way in which that has shaped the direction I have taken. Secondly, I will review the approach that I developed in analysing the work and finally I will reflect on what this study suggests about the means of production and assessment within higher education. How do the kinds of activities that students are engaged in through their university studies shape the way in which they learn? How far does what is considered valid within the academic and disciplinary environment extend or limit ways of knowing? What do the kinds of tasks we ask students to engage in allow them to do and who do they let them be?

8.2 Revisiting the Context

Because the study discussed in this book evolved out of my normal everyday practice, my work as a teacher in a university, it has absorbed a wide range of issues associated with that particular lived experience. This has made it difficult to control the topics that I have considered here, so perhaps it is worth reminding myself and my readers why I embarked on this particular path. As I pointed out in Chapter 1, I wanted to do something with the work that my students produced because I felt that it was too exciting and potentially too important simply to archive away. I wanted to share my own excitement with a wider audience, but more importantly, I realized that if I were to be able to say anything useful about the work, I needed to develop a way to talk about it that would explain that excitement. It became clear from talking to the students involved that the experience of producing the new work had differed from writing the original essay. This was attributed to a variety of reasons ranging from the creative opportunities the regenring offered them to the fact that they were revisiting, and hence reviewing, already researched topics. However, of greater interest was how the regenring allowed the students to transform the information represented in the essay into something quite different. The difficulty was to find out what that *something different* was and, by default, what the *something* in the original was. This translated, for me, into the idea of the affordances of genres, building on the concepts emerging from research in multimodality (Kress and Van Leeuwen, 2001).

As I began my investigations, two main areas of difference began to emerge: the difference in the material impact of the genres and the difference in how the students seemed to relate to the disciplinary information, what they could say about it and how they could say it. In other words, there was not only a shift in ways of meaning, but there was also a shift in ways of being. This last raised questions about how students and lecturers are both positioned within the university, questions which became a real and very personal concern due to a change in my own circumstances. I myself shifted, literally, from one institution to another. But more fundamentally, I shifted from one identity to another. Instead of being in the position of an impartial participant, a kind of academic 'confidante' seen as offering a 'safe haven' where the high stakes environment of summative assessment plays little part, I became highly partial, a 'subject' lecturer with the 'power' to pass or fail students. I had crossed over, or so it seemed, and that crossing over, which was difficult to adjust to, allowed me to gain new understandings of the sometimes conflicting expectations and desires of both students and academic staff alike that I discussed in Chapter 2.

8.3 Reviewing the Frames of Reference

The epistemological framing of my own practice is strongly aligned to academic literacies thinking, which Lillis and Scott (2007) have usefully overviewed and which is represented in, for example, Jones et al. (1999). My theoretical approach in relation to the social and material aspects of communication is obviously strongly informed by social semiotics (Halliday, 1978, 1989; Halliday and Hasan, 1989; Hodge and Kress, 1988) and multimodality (Kress, 2003, 2010). One of the most valuable conceptualizations in my approach, that of the *semiotic resource*, derives from these theoretical contexts and, in fact, it was from the work of Kress and Hodge (1979) that I first encountered the idea of 'choice' and 'meaning potential' in relation to language. Their discussions on 'what the language is doing, and how a linguistic analysis bears on an understanding of social and psychological processes' (p. 14) made an enduring impression on my approach to language and my subsequent interests in the kind of social, cultural and linguistic interactions that I have discussed here. Using this theoretical lens in combination with multimodal frames of reference, I used genre as a semiotic resource rather than a linguistic and/or functional form, as is more typical of language and literacy studies, and this then enabled the theorization in Chapter 3 and the analytic framework in Chapter 4 to emerge. In this approach, genre acts as an enabling resource, a kind of interface between the utterance and the social context in which a communicative event occurs. Genres gives 'shape' to the utterance, as Kress (2003) suggests, or, as Bahktin (1986) argues, they 'organize our speech'.

> The speaker's speech will is manifested primarily in the *choice of a particular speech genre* [sic]. This choice is determined by the specific nature of the given sphere of speech communication, semantic (thematic) considerations, the concrete situation of the speech communication, the personal composition of its participants and so on. And when the speaker's speech plan, with all its individuality and subjectivity, is applied and adapted to a chosen genre, it is shaped and developed within a certain generic form. (p. 78)

The utterance, then, is shaped by the genre which is itself already a response to a given circumstance or set of circumstances. This ties in with social semiotic theory 'context of situation' (Halliday, 1989), and locates my own conceptualization of genre within this theoretical frame. The transformations that occurred during the trans-genre shift were both textual (material) and contextual (social).

My decision to use multimodal concepts in my analysis was because I felt these offered the kind of flexibility I needed, despite the obvious fact that the materials I was analysing were all written. Nevertheless, as I explain in Chapter 3, the implicit shifts in mode (e.g. writtenness to spokenness) that typified it warranted this kind of framework. However, it is, perhaps, helpful to re-emphasize the points I made in Chapter 3 regarding my use of the category *mode*. In my discussion, mode is taken to refer to the 'channels' for communicative activity (e.g. speech, writing, gesture, visualized depictions, stage management), the 'mode' of communication, to use a more commonsense term. To this category, I have added a further one, that of *textual materials*, which refers to the 'grammar', lexis and organizational aspects of the production. This concerns, as Halliday (1989, p. 26) says, 'the role assigned to language', for want of a better word, expressing textual (ideational, interpersonal and textual) meanings and corresponds to the 'modality markers' discussed by Kress and Van Leeuwen (1996, p. 159). This terminological distinction between mode and textual material, which differs from Kress and Van Leeuwen (2001), was helpful in unpacking the different aspects that I needed to consider in discussing the student productions. These descriptive categories (genre, mode, textual materials, media) allowed me to consider the interactions between the various semiotic resources used in the productions and the knock-on effect from one to the next, as illustrated by my examples in Chapter 3 of the communication of statistical data (pp. 94–5). Moreover, the terms of reference (design, production and distribution) developed by Kress and Van Leeuwen (2001) were very useful in explaining communication as social, interactive and, more importantly, co-productive involving semiotic choices in a process of 'textual' making and remaking.

This brings me to the final theoretical conceptualization that frames my analysis, that of 'affordance' (Gibson, 1979). This does not specifically concern what a thing looks like (its properties) but what it can be perceived as making possible – in other words, in semiotic terms, its meaning potential. This concept allowed me to think about what the different genres used by the students allowed to happen. In other words, what were the affordances of the essay and what were the affordances of the alternative genres? This led to a consideration of how the new genres made available different sets of mode and textual resources, compared to the essays, and equally importantly, how the respective genres 'insisted on' these particular sets of resources. This, in part, led to the analytical framing of 'orientation', which I discuss below, and formed the basis for Chapters 5, 6 and 7, where I considered how the genre shift brought about a repositioning of authorial (or discursive) identity, a reconfiguring of the information through the process of transduction (Kress, 2003), and, through the process of recontextualizing the original work, a new and more personally reflexive understanding of the issues under discussion.

8.4 Implications for Genre Studies

It is inevitably difficult to anticipate how this research might contribute to discussions on genre as the approach I have discussed here is differently conceived when compared to other genre approaches. As discussed in Chapter 3, genre studies have tended to focus on what genres look like (structural approaches) or what they are used for (functional approaches) whereas in my study I have tried to focus on what genres let us do. I have considered genre as a semiotic resource which both shapes and is shaped by the social context and the material resources available to it. In other words, I have considered genre from the perspective of its *affordances*; what it allows to happen (or what it insists on happening) in textual production.

I have proposed the concept of *orientation*, drawing on Volosinov (1929/1986) and Medvedev, in considering how genres shape texts and their producers and I have suggested four interlinked orientations of genres: contextual orientation and discursive orientation, which concern social framing, and thematic orientation and semiotic orientation, which concern material framing. These orientations, in combination with multimodal terms of reference, offer a comprehensive framework for talking about the effects of genre choice from both the social and material perspectives.

The approach to genre, described in this book, offers a different way of thinking about the category in that it moves the focus away from what a genre looks like, which can easily be reinterpreted as what a genre *should* look like. It also means that instead of focusing on genre appropriacy, as in what genre should be used in what situation, towards genre affordances – that is, what happens if you use this or that genre. This is not to say that those other approaches are not useful or relevant, but rather that they foreground different things and, in connection with pedagogy, have very different purposes. My work suggests that genre can be used as a resource to explore knowledge rather than as a frame into which knowledge is fitted. In other words, instead of being a pedagogical goal, where the teaching focus is on language and literacy development, my approach uses genre as a pedagogical resource where the focus is on disciplinary development.

8.5 Implications for Learning and Teaching

As my discussions in Chapters 1 and 2 show, higher education pedagogy is the site of much debate and disagreement (e.g. Bernstein [2000] and Barnett [2000]). These debates are inevitably played out in the context of learning and teaching and specifically in the work that students produce. Andrews (2003) suggests that alternative forms of assessment are desirable not only because this would give students different opportunities to learn but also different ways of being judged on their learning. He argues for new forms of written assessment, not because the essay is ineffective, but because it limits students to one kind of knowledge making. He argues that:

> Abreactions or alternatives to the essay … can be seen as true alternatives to the default genre, or they can be seen as alternative versions of or routes toward the essay, keeping it alive … Refreshing a genre like this, or indeed challenging more vigorously its dominance as the default genre is what keeps the most important qualities alive: clear thinking, exchange of views, reasoned commitment and lively expression. (p. 126)

Parker (2003) proposes a 'transformational curriculum' where student activity (or 'engagement' as she prefers) is negotiable. She suggests engagements such as 'writing in various voices including pastiche, parody and other genres' alongside the conventional forms of assessment in order to make space for the students to do what they 'actually want to do with this (disciplinary) knowledge' (p. 541). This evokes Wood's (1999) discussion, where he argues for a more contextualized approach to writing which gives, in his case, design students the chance to situate their writing within the design task in hand. This, he suggests, will 'encourage a more "embodied" form of learning' (p. 12) that would allow students to make connections between theory and practice more effectively than the conventional essay genre allows. As my own research shows, the regenring had precisely this effect.

Another major issue that emerges in much of the literature on student writing concerns the validity and authority of students' own opinions and experiences (Ivanic, 1998; Lillis, 2001), as I discussed in Chapter 2. This point was also evident from my own discussions with students, both informal and as part of the present study. They do not feel they have the authority to express the interpretations that they themselves have towards the 'body of knowledge' that they are having to handle, and when they do attempt to do so, their 'opinions' may be rejected, as happened to Peter in this study. This is particularly the case with first year students who often display the conflicting attitudes of either being too opinionated or too uncertain, and often both. Elbow (1995) remarks on this when discussing what he calls the two 'sins' of 'arrogance' and 'naiveté'.

> Admittedly, first year students often suffer from a closely related [to arrogance] sin: naiveté. For being naive and taking oneself too seriously can look alike and can take the same propositional form: implying simultaneously, 'Everyone else is just like me' and 'No one else in the universe has ever thought my thoughts or felt my feelings.' But when we see a paper with these problematic assumptions, we should ask ourselves: Is this really a problem of the writer taking herself too seriously and being too committed and self-invested in her writing? Or is it a problem of the writer, though perhaps glib, being essentially timid and tapping only a small part of her thinking and feeling? (p. 80)

First year students are too new to the disciplinary material and disciplinary frames of reference to be able to engage in the discourses of their disciplines with the confidence of a real shared understanding. The essays they produce, as I have indicated, invite them to 'act' as if they were confident even though they are not. Lea (1999) considers this problem in her challenge to Laurillard's (1993) argument that academic knowledge is a 'second order' phenomenon removed from 'everyday' experience. Her discussions with students indicated that they found it helpful to use their 'real world' experiences to make sense of the disciplinary content. Referring to one particular student, Lea points out that 'Her reading of the course materials was mediated by the understandings that she brought to the reading from her own familiar cultural contexts within which she was reading for and writing for' (1999, p. 119). And as my own work has shown, using the 'everyday' to recontextualize the disciplinary can have a profound effect on a student's understanding.

To be able to link disciplinary to their previous and current experience gives students the chance to explore disciplinary knowledge from a position of power (they are experts in their own experience) as opposed to a position of powerlessness. This does not mean that they will not notice the difference between academic genres (essays and articles) and other genres (personal narratives, plays and letters). On the contrary, this kind of work highlights the different ways in which genres shape our texts and can help students move towards a more explicit understanding of how academic knowledge, and more pertinently disciplinary knowledge, is made. By asking students to write differently we are also asking them to notice different written genres and hence the resources (modes and textual materials) that different genres use and what these resources can do. Developing genre awareness in this way encourages students to see language rather than to 'see past language' (Carter and Nash, 1990, p. 24) and this in turn encourages a more critical relationship to their academic learning and beyond, something Andy commented on.

I mean, even when I'm reading newspaper articles I focus in much more on what the author's message is about.

8.6 Back into Practice

Since working with material discussed in this book and having shifted my own professional position, as discussed above, I have begun to place the experimental work I did with the students in this study into the context of my current teaching. I felt should move towards taking forward what I have been writing about here into the normal hurly burly of disciplinary teaching. In other words, I thought I had better 'put my money where my mouth is'. I have, therefore, introduced a different kind of writing into one of my modules, which is part of an MA in TESOL and Applied Linguistics. It involves students from all over the world who bring very different experiences of both teaching and learning. For the main assignment, instead of asking students to produce a conventional essay on a particular topic, I ask them to write an auto-ethnography based around their experiences of their new circumstances, as students instead of teachers, in a new culture (disciplinary, regional, etc.) and in the multicultural and multilingual community represented by the course and its participants. I discuss ethnographic writing with them and give them examples to read. I explain that the purpose of this assignment is to give them the chance to 'just write' and not worry about whether it is 'academic' or not. However, as with the regenring work, I want the students to work with the literature associated with the module to see whether and where it relates to their own experiences. As with the regenring assignment, I want the students to explore their learning through a different frame than that offered by the essay. I want to give them the chance to reflect on their own lived experiences in relation to what they have been reading and to do so on their own terms and in their own (often negotiated) ways.

The first time I introduced this assignment I was met with two basic responses from the group of around fifty students. Half the group were delighted with the chance to write differently while the other half were appalled because they felt they were being denied the 'academic' experience they had expected. The following extract from one of these assignments reflects this view very strongly.

Extract 8.1

> I have been wondering why I did not receive the task well other than its seeming ambiguity, and I think that it may have to do with the fact that I felt as if I was being cheated out of what I should get from an MA in the UK.

The writer's feelings towards the work derived from her own perceptions of what academic writing is and what constitutes academic study and reflect Andrews' (2003) remarks about student conservatism when it comes to assignments.

> Students seem reluctant to abandon the essay as their preferred form for submitting coursework. Another reason for their timidity might be that they would rather the devil you know than the devil you don't know. (p. 121)

However, what this extract also shows is that despite her initial outrage, and it was expressed loud and clear when I introduced the assignment, this student was using the new writing opportunity to reflect on the situation she was in. Extract 8.2 appears a little further into the work and continues the reflexive thinking that this kind of writing affords.

Extract 8.2

> This one [task] defied any prior structures I have because I am faced with the challenge of writing a seemingly non-academic assignment for an academic purpose.

In fact, her struggle with wanting to do good work (she was an intellectual high flyer) and her resistance to it is played out in this assignment as she moves gradually and inexorably to the conclusion in Extract 8.3, which is, obviously, a teacher's dream.

Extract 8.3

> My earlier misgivings about the assignment and its relevance have been unfounded because the writing of it has proved revealing although quite tasking, both in the effort to remember meaning making events and to properly relate them to the MA. I am not completely sure if the things I have chosen to speak about are right for the purpose of this work and if I have been able to bring them into the discussion properly but I have at least begun to realize how much I have learnt about the things I thought I knew. I have realized from this writing that in writing down some things I am able to relive them again and in reliving them, I am able to put them into proper perspective, to categorize them and interpret them in totally new ways.

While not everybody moved through the assignment with such dramatic effect, working against their own initial preconceptions, as the above student did, most have taken advantage of the chance to write differently within the context of module assessment. Since the initial foray discussed above, students have chosen many different genres with which to write their auto-ethnographies. One student wrote it as a letter to me, arguing that this genre allowed her to write more freely. The shift in discursive identity that a letter entailed gave her a frame with which to address me (the reader) more directly and more personally precisely because it positioned her differently as a writer when compared to a conventional essay. Others have produced quasi-narratives, drawing on literary resources such as *Alice in Wonderland* with which to align their own experiences;

some have constructed interviews with themselves. More recently there has been a blog reconstructed from the student's own personal blog, charting phases in her experience and including hyperlinks to other sites that are significant to her reflections.

Not all of this work has been outstanding or produced the kind of reflexivity that I might hope for and is shown in the extracts above. For instance, the success of an interview depends on the kinds of questions that are asked. If the student using that genre does not ask probing questions of himself, then the result will not be, as has happened on a couple of occasions, as thoughtful as it might be. However, writing differently has enabled all the students, at the very least, to recognize that disciplinary knowledge can connect to everyday experience and that learning involves recontextualizing, not (merely) reproducing. What is more, of all the assignments this is the one that we, the course team, enjoy reading the most because each one is a surprise, is new and tells us something we did not know before. Stepping outside of the conventional academic writing frame encourages this to happen.

8.7 Reflections on Doing the Work

I realize that I have attempted to cover a lot of ground in this study. This is the result of my own substantial experience of working across and with all the things I have talked about and reflects the difficulties of compressing these many years of work into a book! Of course, I could have chosen to focus on a much narrower range of issues, perhaps ignoring the socio-political context in which this work occurs, or I could have decided to analyse the productions from a less socially situated perspective. However, this proved impossible for me, as every time I attempted to stick to one thing, the other things kept on pushing their way through. In the end I decided to show as much of what I found out as possible and to contextualize it in the real, lived experience of my students and of myself.

However, this meant that certain areas of analysis were not covered in as much depth as they might have been. For instance, I could have provided a much more comprehensive discussion on the material transformations that I discussed in Chapter 6 had I decided to take a narrower approach. For example, I could have chosen the work of only one student or focused on only the reconfiguration aspect of the genre shift. This might have provided a more detailed analysis of the material resources selected following the more linguistically oriented approach of writers such as Hunston (2000) or Martin (2000), whose close analyses also explore linguistic choices in the descriptions of how we do certain things with texts, in those cases, how we express appraisal or evaluation. Conversely, I could have focused more specifically on institutional practices, prioritizing the student experience over their production, as in Lillis (2001). I could also have taken a more obviously pedagogic stance, as in Burke and Hermerschmidt (2005). However, I preferred to adopt a hybrid approach because I wanted to bring all these different elements together.

This interweaving of issues (the material, the experiential and the pedagogical) reflects the kinds of interactions that constitute the university learning and teaching communication cycle and, in combining them in this way, I have been able to explore issues that might otherwise have been overlooked. This is particularly true in relation to the interviews with the students and lecturers who participated in this work. Their commentaries on the different themes that I have investigated provided insights that could only have come from their reflections on the different activities in which they were involved; being students doing their things or being lecturers and doing their things. This has undoubtedly enriched the discussion.

8.8 Final Comments

My approach throughout this work has been, and continues to be, based firmly in the experience of my own practice and the insights and understandings I get from this. It is itself an enactment of how the everyday and the disciplinary can merge. In this sense, perhaps, my present study was a reflection on practice or more accurately a series of practices over time, a process of theorized reflection. The core material represents an important moment of realization for me which led to the theoretical and practical discussion that I have offered in this book.

In the end, the ideas presented here suggest that there are many different genres with which academic knowledge can be expressed and developed. The essay, with its insistence on a specific kind of organizational structure and its demands for explicitness in expressing information, is a valuable and valued resource within the university teaching and learning repertoire. However, what my work suggests is that it may be risking the chance for other forms of learning and of knowledge representation if we put all our eggs into one basket. Variation in genre allows for different kinds of responses and different ways of relating to the academic knowledge as my study has shown. It allows students to interact with the information in different ways, linking it to experience and to other kinds of contexts. It embeds the concepts better, deepens understanding and allows for new perspectives on old knowledge that one of my lecturers in Chapter 2 longed for. Furthermore, it brought about a shift in how the students themselves thought about their own work. As one of them remarked, '*I think I try to make my essays a bit more interesting since writing this.*' Surely that is something to be appreciated.

Of course, as has been argued (e.g. Kress, 1993, 2003; Bhatia, 1997; Hyland, 2000), it is only the powerful who can challenge genre convention. However, in the learning and teaching context, particularly in universities where lecturers (still) have power over what they teach and how they teach it, there is the opportunity to break the rules. If we, as course designers, module leaders and curriculum developers, incorporate alternatives to the essayist canon then we legitimize them as part of the repertoire of student activity. In this respect, I hope that this book will contribute to such a challenge. After all, if we are to educate people in ways that are 'adequate to a situation of supercomplexity' (Barnett, 2009, p. 439), then we need to offer them the chance to explore their disciplines in ways that enable them to link their knowledge to both lived and read experience and in so doing foreground and value both.

References

Andrews, R. (2003), 'The end of the essay?'. *Teaching in Higher Education*, 8, (1), 117–28.

Bakhtin, M. (1978), 'Discourse typology in prose', in L. Matejka and K. Pomorska (eds), *Readings in Russian Poetics*. Ann Arbor, MI: Slavic, pp. 176–96.

——(1986), *Speech Genres and Other Late Essays*. Austin: University of Texas Press.

Barnes, D. (1976), *From Curriculum to Communication*. London: Penguin.

Barnett, R. (1997), *Towards a Higher Education for a New Century*. London: Institute of Education.

——(2000), 'Supercomplexity and the curriculum'. *Studies in Higher Education*, 25, (3), pp. 255–65.

——(2009), 'Knowing and becoming in the higher education curriculum', *Studies in Higher Education*, 34, (4), 429–440.

Barthes, R. (1977), *Image Music Text* (trans Stephen Heath). London: Fontana.

Bartholomae, D. (1985), 'Inventing the university', in M. Rose (ed.), *When a Writer Can't Write*. New York: Guildford Press.

Barton, D., (1994), *Literacy: An Introduction to the Ecology of Written Language*. Oxford: Blackwell.

Barton, D., Hamilton, M. and Ivanic, R. (2000), *Situated Literacies: Reading and Writing in Context*. London: Routledge.

Bazerman, C. (1988), *Shaping Written Knowledge*. Madison: University of Wisconsin Press.

Beard, R. (2000), 'The National Literacy Strategy: review of research and related evidence'. Department for Education and Skills, available at: www.standards.dfes.gov.uk/primary/publications/literacy/63541/919945 (accessed 31/01/07).

Berger, J. (1972), *Ways of Seeing*. London: Penguin

Berkenkotter, C. (2001), 'Genre systems at work'. *Written Communication*, 18, (3), 326–49.

Berkenkotter, C. and Huckin, T. (1993), 'Rethinking genre from a sociocognitive perspective. *Written Communication*, 10, (4), 475–509.

Bernstein, B. (2000), *Pedagogy, Symbolic Control and Identity* (revised edn). Oxford: Rowman and Littlefield.

Bhatia, V. K. (1993), *Analysing Genre*. Harlow: Longman.

——(1997), 'The power and politics of genre'. *World Englishes*, 16, (3), 359–72.

Biber, D., Conrad S., Reppen R., Byrd P. and Helt, M. (2002), 'Speaking and writing in the university: a multidimensional comparison'. *TESOL Quarterly*, 36, (1), 9–48.

Bizzel, P. and Herzberg, B. (eds) (1990), *The Rhetorical Tradition*. Boston: Bedford.

Blommaert, J. (2005), *Discourse*. Cambridge: Cambridge University Press.

Bourdieu, P. (1990), *The Logic of Practice*. Cambridge: Polity Press.

——(1991), *Language and Symbolic Power* (trans Gino Raymond and Matthew Adamson). Cambridge: Polity Press.

——(2004), *Science of Science and Reflexivity* (trans Richard Nice). Cambridge: Polity Press.

Bourdieu, P. and Passeron, J. (1994), 'Introduction: language and relationship to language in the teaching situation (trans Richard Teene), in P. Bourdieu, J. Passeron and M. de Saint Martin (eds), *Academic Discourse*. Cambridge: Polity Press.

Brown, G. and Yule, G. (1983), *Discourse Analysis*. Cambridge: Cambridge University Press.

Brown, S., Race, P. and Smith, B. (1996), *An Assessment Manifesto*. London: Kogan Page, accessed from www.londonmet.ac.uk/deliberations/assessment/manifesto.cfm (24/01/06).

Burke, P. J. and Hemerschmidt, M. (2005), 'Deconstructing academic practices through self-reflexive pedagogies', in B. V. Street (ed.), *Literacies Across Educational Contexts: Mediating Learning and Teaching*. Philadelphia: Caslon Press, pp. 346–65.

Candlin, C. and Plum, G. (1999), 'Engaging with the challenges of interdiscursivity in academic writing: researchers, students, tutors', in C. N. Candlin and K. Hyland, *Writing: Texts Processes and Practices*. Harlow: Longman, pp.193–217.

Carter, R. (ed.) (1990), *Knowledge about Language and the Curriculum: The LINC Reader*. London: Hodder & Stoughton.

Carter, R. and Nash, W. (1990), *Seeing Through Language*. Oxford: Blackwell.

Castells, M. (1996), *The Rise of the Network Society*. Oxford: Blackwell.

Charles, M. (2006), 'Revealing and obscuring writers' identity', in R. Keily, P. Rea-Dickens, H. Woodfield and G. Clibban (eds), *Language Culture and Identity in Applied Linguistics*. London: BAAL/Equinox. pp. 147–61.

Clifford, J. (1992), 'Travelling cultures', in L. Grossberg, C. Nelson and P. Treichler (eds), *Cultural Studies*. London and New York: Routledge, pp. 96–116.

Cope, B. and Kalantzis, M. (1993), 'Introduction: how a genre approach to literacy can transform the way writing is taught', in B. Cope and M. Kalantizis (eds), *The Powers of Literacy*. London: Falmer Press, pp. 1–21.

Crème, P. (2005), 'Should student learning journals be assessed?'. *Assessment and Evaluation in Higher Education*, 30, (3), 287–96.

Csikszentmihalyi, M. and Rochberg-Halton, E. (1981), *The Meaning of Things: Domestic Symbols and the Self*. Cambridge: Cambridge University Press.

Davidson, C. and Tomic, A. (1999), 'Inventing academic literacy: an American perspective', in C. Jones, J. Turner and B. Street (eds), *Student Writing in Higher Education*. Amsterdam: Benjamins, pp. 161–169.

Derrida, J. (1980), 'The law of genre' (trans A. Ronell), *Critical Inquiry*, 7, (1), 55–81.

DES/Welsh Office (1988), *A Report into the Committee of Inquiry into the Teaching of English (The Kingman Report)*. London: HMSO.

Devitt, A. J. (2004), *Writing Genres*. Carbondale: Southern Illinois University Press.

Dudley-Evans, T. (1990), *The Language of Economics*. London: Macmillan Education.

Elbow, P. (1995), 'Being a writer vs. being an academic: a conflict in goals'. *College Composition and Communication*, 46, (1), 72–82.

——(1999), 'In defense of private writing'. *Written Communication*, 16, (2), 139–170.

Elton, L. (2000), 'The UK Research Assessment Exercise: unintended consequences'. *Higher Education Quarterly*, 54, (3), 274–83.

Engeström, Y. (1999), 'Communication, discourse and activity'. *Communication Review*, 3, (1–2), 165–85.

English, F. (1999), 'What do students really say?', in C. Jones, J. Turner and B. Street (eds), *Student Writing in Higher Education*. Amsterdam: Benjamins, pp. 17–36.

——(2000), 'Moving between cultures', in H. Wong, S. Nair-Venugopal, N. Maarof, Z. Yahya and J. V. D'Cruz (eds), *Language and Globalisation*. Kuala Lumpur: Longman, pp. 50–64.

English, F. and Fusari, M. (2002), 'The internet and academic rigour: a question of expertise', proceedings from Knowledge and Discourse 2, University of Hong Kong, http://ec.hku.hk/kd2proc/proceedings/fullpaper/Theme2FullPapers/EnglishFiona.pdf.

Fairclough, N. (2001), *Language and Power* (second edn). Harlow: Longman.

Foucault, M. (1972), *The Archaeology of Knowledge*. London: Tavistock/Routledge.

Gee, J. P. (1996), *Social Linguistics and Literacies: Ideology in Discourses* (second edn). London: Taylor and Francis.

——(1999), *An Introduction to Discourse Analysis: Theory and Method*. London and New York: Routledge.

Geertz, C. (1973), *The Interpretation of Cultures*. New York: Basic.

——1985, *Local Knowledge: Further Essays in Interpretive Anthropology*. New York: Basic.

Gibson, J. J. (1979), *The Ecological Approach to Visual Perception*. Hilldale, NJ: Lawrence Erlbaum.

Gilbert, N. G. and Mulkay, M. (1984/2003), *Opening Pandora's Box: A Sociological Analysis of Scientists' Discourse*. Cambridge: Cambridge University Press (1984); University of Surrey (2003) at: www.soc.surrey.ac.uk/Books/OPB/prelim.htm.

Gorman, T. P. (1986), *The Framework For The Assessment Of Language*. London: Department for Education and Science.

Gorman, T. P., White, J., Brooks, G. and English, F. (1990), *Language for Learning*. Schools Examinations and Assessments Council, London: Department for Education and Science.

Griffin, L. (2006), 'Who or what is the students' audience? The discoursal construction of audience identity in undergraduate assignments', in R. Keily, P. Rea-Dickens, H. Woodfield and G. Clibban (eds), *Language Culture and Identity in Applied Linguistics*. London: BAAL/Equinox, pp. 133–45.

Haggis, T. (2004), 'Meaning, identity and "motivation": expanding what matters in understanding learning in higher education', *Studies in Higher Education*, 29, (3), 335–52.

Halliday, M. A. K. (1978), *Language as a Social Semiotic: The Social Interpretation of Language and Meaning*. London: Edward Arnold.

——(1985), *An Introduction to Functional Grammar*. London: Edward Arnold.

——(1989), *Spoken and Written Language*, Oxford: Oxford University Press

Halliday, M. A. K. and Hasan, R. (1976), *Cohesion in English*. Harlow: Longman.

——(1989) *Language, Context and Text: Aspects of Language in a Social-Semiotic Perspective* (second edn). Oxford: Oxford University Press.

Halliday, M. A. K., McIntosh, A. and Strevens, P. (1964), *The Linguistic Sciences and Language Teaching*, Harlow: Longman.

Hammersley, M. (2006), 'Ethnography: problems and prospects'. *Ethnography and Education*, 1, (1), 3–14.

Hart, R. P. (1986), 'Of genre, computers and the Reagan inaugural', in H. W. Simons and A. A. Aghazarian (eds), *Form, Genre and the Study of Political Discourse*. Columbia: University of South Carolina Press, pp. 278–98.

Hattie, J. and Marsh, H. (2004), 'One Journey to Unravel the Relationship Between Research and Teaching'. Research and Teaching: Closing the Divide. International Colloquim, Winchester.

Herrington, M. and Kendall, A. (eds) (2005), *Insights From Research and Practice*. Leicester: NIACE.

Hillner, M. (2005), 'Text in (e)motion', in *Visual Communication*, 4, (2), 165–71.

Hinds, J. (1983), 'Linguistic and written discourse in English and Japanese', in R. Kaplan (ed.), *Annual Review of Applied Linguistics III*. Rowley, MA: Newbury House, pp. 78–84.

Hodge, R. and Kress, G. (1988), *Social Semiotics*. Cambridge: Polity Press.

Hodginson, L. (1996), *Changing the Higher Education Curriculum Towards a Systematic Approach to Skills Development*. Milton Keynes: Open University Vocational Qualifications Centre.

Houston, R. A. (1988), *Literacy in Early Modern Europe*. Harlow: Longman.

Hunston, S. (2000), 'Evaluation and the planes of discourse: status and value in persuasive texts', in S. Hunston and G. Thompson (eds), *Evaluation in Text: Authorial Stance and the Construction of Discourse*. Oxford: Oxford University Press, pp. 176–207.

Hunston, S. and Thompson, G. (eds) (2000), *Evaluation in Text: Authorial Stance and the Construction of Discourse*. Oxford: Oxford University Press.

Hyland, K. (2000), *Disciplinary Discourses: Social Interactions in Academic Writing*. Harlow: Longman.

——(2004), *Genre and Second Language Writing*. Ann Arbor, MI: University of Michigan Press.

——(2006), *English for Academic Purposes: An Advanced Coursebook*. London: Routledge.

Hymes, D. (1974), *Foundations in Sociolinguistics: An Ethnographic Approach*. Philadelphia: The University of Pennsylvania Press.

Ivanic, R. (1998), *Writing and Identity: The Discoursal Construction of Identity in Academic Writing*. Amsterdam: John Benjamins.

——(2006), 'Language learning and identification', in R. Keily, P. Rea-Dickens, H. Woodfield and G. Clibban (eds), *Language Culture and Identity in Applied Linguistics*. London: BAAL/Equinox, pp. 7–29.

Ivanic, R. and Simpson, J. (1992), 'Who's who in academic writing?' in N. Fairclough, *Critical Language Awareness*. Harlow: Longman, pp. 141–79.

Jewitt, C. (2005), 'Classrooms and the design of pedagogic discourse: a multimodal approach'. *Culture and Psychology*, 11, (3), 309–20.

Jones, C., Turner, J. and Street, B. (eds) (1999), *Students Writing in Higher Education*. Amsterdam: Benjamins.

Jones, K. (2003), 'What is affordance?'. *Ecological Psychology*, 15, (2), 107–114.

Jordan, R. R. (1997), *English for Academic Purposes*. Cambridge: Cambridge Language Teaching Library.

Jordan, S. A. (2001), 'Writing the other, writing the self: transforming consciousness through ethnographic writing'. *Language and Intercultural Communication*, 1, (1), 40–56.

Karlsson, A. (2004), 'How to build a house from reading a drawing: professional and popular mediations of construction'. *Visual Communication*, 3, (3), 251–79.

Kress, G. (1982), *Learning to Write*, London: Routledge & Keegan Paul.

——(1989), *Linguistic Processes in Sociocultural Practices*. Oxford: Oxford University Press.

——(1993), 'Genre as social process', in B. Cope and M. Kalantizis (eds), *The Powers of Literacy*. London: Falmer Press. pp. 22–37.

——(1994), *Learning to Write* (second edn). London: Routledge.

——(2003), *Literacy in the New Media Age*. London: Routledge.

——(2010), *Multimodality: A Social Semiotic Approach to Contemporary Communication*. London and New York: Routledge.

Kress, G. and Hodge, R. (1979), *Language as Ideology*. London: Routledge.

Kress, G. and Van Leeuwen, T. (1996), *Reading Images: The Grammar of Visual Design*. London: Routledge.

——(2001), *Multimodal Discourse*. London: Edward Arnold.

Kress, G., Jewitt, C., Ogborn, J. and Tsatsarelis, C. (2001), *Multimodal Teaching and Learning: The Rhetorics of the Science Classroom*. London: Continuum.

Language in the National Curriculum (LINC) (1992), *Language in the National Curriculum: Materials for Professional Development*. Nottingham: Department of English Studies, University of Nottingham.

Latour, B. and Woolgar, S. (1986), *Laboratory Life: The Social Construction of Scientific Facts* (second edn). Princeton, NJ: Princetown University Press.

Laudrillard, D. (1993), *Rethinking University Teaching: A Framework for the Effective Use of Educational Technology*. London: Routledge.

Lave, J. and Wenger, E. (1991), *Situated Learning: Legitimate Peripheral Participation*. Cambridge: Cambridge University Press.

——(2002), 'Legitimate peripheral participation in communities of practice', in M. Lea and K. Nicoll (eds), *Distributed Learning*. London: Routledge, pp. 56–63.

Lea, M. (1999), 'Academic literacies and learning in higher education', in C. Jones, J. Turner and B. Street (eds), *Students Writing in Higher Education*. Amsterdam: Benjamins, pp. 103–24.

Lea, M. and Nicholl, K. (eds) (2002), *Distributed Learning*. London: Routledge.

Lea, M. and Street, B. (1998), 'Student writing and faculty feedback in higher education: an academic literacies approach'. *Studies in Higher Education*, 23, (2), 157–72.

——(1999), 'Writing as academic literacies: understanding textual practices in higher education' in C. N. Candlin and Hyland, K. (eds) *Writing: Texts, Processes and Practices*, London & New York: Longman, pp. 62–81

——(2000), 'Student writing and staff feedback in higher education: an academic literacies approach', in M. Lea and B Stierer (eds), *Student Writing in Higher*

Education: New Contexts. Milton Keynes and Philadelphia: Open University Press/ Society for Research into Higher Education, pp. 32–46.

Lea, M. and Stierer, B. (eds) (2000), *Student Writing in Higher Education: New Contexts.* Milton Keynes and Philadelphia: Open University Press/Society for Research into Higher Education.

Lewin, K. (1948), *Resolving Social Conflicts: Selected Papers on Group Dynamics*, G. W. Lewin (ed.). New York: Harper and Row.

Lillis, T. M. (1999), 'Whose common sense? Essayist literacy and the institutional practice of mystery', in C. Jones, J. Turner and B. Street (eds), *Students Writing in Higher Education.* Amsterdam: Benjamins. pp. 128–47.

——(2001), *Student Writing: Access, Regulation, Desire.* London: Routledge.

Lillis, T. and Curry, M. (2010), *Academic Writing in a Global Context: The Politics and Practices of Publishing in English.* London and New York: Routledge.

Lillis, T. and Scott, M. (2007), 'Introduction: new directions in academic literacies research'. *Journal of Applied Linguistics*, 4, (1) 5–32.

Malinowski, B. (1923), 'The problem of meaning in primitive languages', in C. K. Ogden and I. A. Richards (eds), *The Meaning of Meaning.* London: Routledge and Kegan Paul, pp. 146–52.

Marchand, T. (2000). 'The lore of the master builder: working with local materials and local knowledge in Sana'a', Yemen'. *IASTE Working Papers Series*, 137.

Martin, J. R. (1993), 'A contextual theory of language', in B. Cope and M. Kalantizis (eds), *The Powers of Literacy.* London: Falmer Press. pp. 116–36.

——(2000), 'Beyond exchange: APPRAISAL systems in English', in S. Hunston and G. Thompson (eds), *Evaluation in Text: Authorial Stance and the Construction of Discourse.* Oxford: Oxford University Press. pp. 142–75.

Martin, J. R. and Rothery, (1993), 'Grammar: making meaning in writing', in B. Cope and M. Kalantizis (eds), *The Powers of Literacy.* London: Falmer Press. pp.137–153

McNoleg, O. (1996), 'The integration of GIS, remote survey expert systems and adaptive co-krigging for environmental habitat modeling of the highland haggis using object-oriented fuzzy logic and neural network techniques'. *Computers and Geosciences*, 22, (5), 585–8.

Miller, C. (1984), 'Genre as social action'. *Quarterly Journal of Speech*, 70, 151–67.

Mitchell, S. (1994), *The Teaching and Learning of Argument in Sixth Forms and Higher Education.* Hull: University of Hull.

Mitchell, S. and Evison, A. (nd), *Writing in the Disciplines.* London: Queen Mary University London, http://www.languageandlearning.qmul.ac.uk/wid/index. html

Montaigne, M. de (1958), *Essays.* London : Penguin.

Myers, G. (1992), 'Textbooks and the sociology of scientific knowledge'. *English for Specific Purposes*, 11, (1), 3–17.

National Committee of Inquiry into Higher Education (1997), *Higher Education for a Learning Society*, www.leeds.ac.uk/educol/ncihe/ (accessed 12/01/06).

O'Donovan, B., Price, M., Rust, C. (2004), 'Know what I mean? Enhancing student understanding of assessment standards and criteria'. *Teaching in Higher Education*, 9, (3), 147–62.

Ong, W. (1982), *Orality and Literacy.* London: Routledge.

Owston, R. D. and Wideman, H. H. (1997), 'Word processors and children's writing in a high-computer-access setting'. Journal of Research on Computing in Education, 30, (2), 202–20.

Parker, J. (2003), 'Reconceptualising the curriculum: from commodification to transformation'. *Teaching in Higher Education*, 8, (4), 529–43.

Polanyi, M. (1997), 'The tacit dimension', in L. Prussak (ed.), *Knowledge in Organizations*. London: Butterworth-Heinnemann.

Pomorska, K. (1978), 'Russian formalism in perspective', in L. Matejka and K. Pomorska (eds), *Readings in Russian Poetics: Formalist and Structuralist Views*. Massachusetts: Michigan Slavic Publications/MIT Press, pp. 273–80.

Prior, P. (1998), *Writing/Disciplinarity: A Sociohistoric Account of Literate Activity in the Academy*. Mahwah, NJ: Erlbaum.

Propp, V. (1978) (1928), 'Fairytale Transformations', in L. Matejka and K. Pomorska (eds), *Readings in Russian Poetics: Formalist and Structuralist Views*. Michigan Slavic Publications, Massachusetts: MIT Press, pp. 94–114.

Rampton, B., Harris, R. and Leung, C. (2001), 'Education in England and speakers of languages other than English'. *Working Papers in Urban Languages and Literacies*, 18, King's College London.

Read, B., Francis, B. and Robson, J. (2001), '"Playing safe": undergraduate essay writing and the presentation of the student "voice"'. *British Journal of Sociology of Education*, 22 (3), 387–99.

Russell, D. R. (1997), 'Rethinking genre in school and society: an activity theory analysis'. *Written Communication*, 14, (4), 504–54.

Russell, D. R. and Yañez, A. (2003), 'Big picture people rarely become historians': genre systems and the contradictions of general education', in C. Bazerman and D. R. Russell (eds), *Writing Selves/Writing Societies*, http://wac.colostate.edu/books/selves_societies/. pp. 331–62.

Rust, C., Price, M. and O'Donovan, B. (2003), 'Improving students' learning by developing their understanding of assessment criteria and processes'. *Assessment and Evaluation in Higher Education*, 28, (2), 147–64.

Saussure, F. de (1974), *Course in General Linguistics* (trans W. Baskin). London: Fontana.

Scott, M. (1999), 'Agency and subjectivity in student writing', in C. Jones, J. Turner and B. Street (eds), *Students Writing in Higher Education*. Amsterdam: Benjamins. pp. 172–91.

——(2005), 'Student writing, assessment, and the motivated sign: finding a theory for the times'. *Assessment and Evaluation in Higher Education*, 30, (3), 297–305.

Searle, J. R., 1969, *Speech Acts: An Essay in the Philosophy of Language*. Cambridge: Cambridge University Press.

Sharples, M. (1999), *How We Write: Writing as Creative Design*. London: Routledge.

Street, B. (1984), *Literacy in Theory and Practice*. Cambridge: Cambridge University Press.

——(2001), 'Introduction', in B. Street (ed.), *Literacy and Development*. London: Routledge. pp. 1–17.

Swales, J. (1990), *Genre Analysis*. Cambridge: Cambridge University Press.

Thesen, L. (2001), 'Modes, literacies and powers: a university case study'. *Language and Education*, 15, (2/3), 132–45.

Thesen, L. and van Pletzen, E. (eds) (2006), *Academic Literacy and the Languages of Change*. London: Continuum.

Thornton, G. (1987), *Language Testing 1979–1983: An Independent Appraisal of the Findings*. London: HMSO, Department of Education and Science.

Titunik, I. R. (1986), 'The formal method and the sociological method' in V. N. Volosinov, *Marxism and the Philosphy of Language* (trans L. Matejka and I. R. Titunik). Cambridge, MA: Harvard Press. pp. 175–200.

Tobin, M. (1999), 'Editorial to the How It Really Happened series'. *American Journal of Respiratory (?) Critical Care Medicine*, 160, 1801–1999 available from http:www.atsjournals.org.

Todorov, T. (1976), 'The origin of genres' (trans R. M. Berrong). *New Literary History*, 8, (1), 159–70.

Turner, J. (1999), 'Academic literacy and the discourse of transparency', in C. Jones, J. Turner and B. Street (eds), *Students Writing in Higher Education*. Amsterdam: Benjamins, pp. 149–60.

Ventola, E. (1983), 'Contrasting schematic structures in service encounters. *Applied Linguistics*, 4, (3), 242–58.

Volosinov, N. N. (1929/1986), *Marxism and the Philosphy of Language* (trans L. Matejka and I. R. Titunik). Cambridge, MA and London: Harvard University Press.

Womack, P. (1993), 'What are essays for?'. *English in Education*, 27, (2), 42–8.

Wood, J. (1999), 'The culture of academic rigour: does design really need it?' Conference paper at Design Cultures, Sheffield University, available from http://futures.gold.ac.uk/.

Index